Discordant Development

Anthropology, Culture and Society

Series Editors:
Professor Vered Amit, Concordia University
and
Dr Jon P. Mitchell, University of Sussex

Recent titles:

DISCORDANT DEVELOPMENT

Global Capitalism and the Struggle for Connection in Bangladesh

Katy Gardner

First published 2012 by Pluto Press
345 Archway Road, London N6 5AA

www.plutobooks.com

British Library Cataloguing in Publication Data
A catalogue record for this book is available from the British Library

ISBN   978 0 7453 3150 8   Hardback
ISBN   978 0 7453 3149 2   Paperback
ISBN   978 1 8496 4706 9   PDF eBook
ISBN   978 1 8496 4707 6   EPUB eBook
ISBN   978 1 8496 4708 3   Kindle eBook

Library of Congress Cataloging in Publication Data applied for

This book is printed on paper suitable for recycling and made from fully managed and sustained forest sources. Logging, pulping and manufacturing processes are expected to conform to the environmental standards of the country of origin.

10   9   8   7   6   5   4   3   2   1

Designed and produced for Pluto Press by Chase Publishing Services Ltd
Typeset from disk by Stanford DTP Services, Northampton, England

Contents

Series Preface

Anthropology is a discipline based upon in-depth ethnographic works that deal with wider theoretical issues in the context of particular, local conditions – to paraphrase an important volume from the series: *large issues* explored in *small places*. This series has a particular mission: to publish work that moves away from an old-style descriptive ethnography that is strongly area-studies oriented, and offer genuine theoretical arguments that are of interest to a much wider readership, but which are nevertheless located and grounded in solid ethnographic research. If anthropology is to argue itself a place in the contemporary intellectual world, then it must surely be through such research.

We start from the question: 'What can this ethnographic material tell us about the bigger theoretical issues that concern the social sciences?' rather than 'What can these theoretical ideas tell us about the ethnographic context?' Put this way round, such work becomes *about* large issues, *set in* a (relatively) small place, rather than detailed description of a small place for its own sake. As Clifford Geertz once said, 'Anthropologists don't study villages; they study *in* villages.'

By place, we mean not only geographical locale, but also other types of 'place' – within political, economic, religious or other social systems. We therefore publish work based on ethnography within political and religious movements, occupational or class groups, among youth, development agencies, and nationalist movements; but also work that is more thematically based – on kinship, landscape, the state, violence, corruption, the self. The series publishes four kinds of volume: ethnographic monographs; comparative texts; edited collections; and shorter, polemical essays.

We publish work from all traditions of anthropology, and all parts of the world, which combines theoretical debate with empirical evidence to demonstrate anthropology's unique position in contemporary scholarship and the contemporary world.

Professor Vered Amit
Dr Jon P. Mitchell

1
Discordant Developments:
An Introduction

A field, a few kilometres away from the Kushiara River in Habiganj District, north-east Bangladesh: a small group of foreign men stand under the hot sun taking measurements from the damp soil. They have travelled here in a gleaming four-wheel drive, bumping along the dirt track that branches from the Sylhet to Dhaka Highway, past a seemingly endless vista of electric green paddy fields and small hamlets, the mud and thatch homes occasionally interspersed by the brick houses that characterise this *Londoni* (UK migrant) area. Bundles of straw lie drying across the road; the jeep's progress has been frequently interrupted by the bleating goats and runty cows that have wandered in its path. Now that they are finally here the men work quietly, studiously ignoring the small crowd of children who have followed them from the road, and, amidst much hilarity, are calling *laal bando!* (red monkey!) from the safety of the path. It is not the first time the men have visited the area and, judging from the results of these early explorations, it will not be the last. They work for the company Occidental, and are prospecting for natural gas. It is the late 1980s.

March 2007: The rice fields have gone. In their place is a large gas plant, spread over 50 acres and connected to the newly metalled road by a grid of steep banked highways that cut across the surrounding agricultural land with industrial precision. Known as the 'South Pad' this is linked to the 'North Pad' a few miles away, as if both sites involved a mission to the moon. The North Pad was constructed by Occidental in the late 1990s at Dighalbak, close to the Kushiara River. But it is the completion of the South Pad in 2007 that heralds the opening of what becomes known as 'the Bibiyana Gas Field'. Constructed and operated by the American oil giant Chevron, this is to be the smartest and most technologically advanced gas field in Bangladesh and is inaugurated with a fanfare of publicity. By 2010, it is predicted, it will be the biggest supplier of natural gas in Bangladesh, producing energy for the next

1

twenty to thirty years. Included among the guests at the opening ceremony are government ministers, the US ambassador and the President of Chevron Bangladesh. Speeches are made, congratulations extended for the efficiency with which the project has been completed, corporate backs patted. In the national context of acute power shortages, where only a year earlier, farmers' frustrations at the irregular supply of electricity boiled over into violent protest leading to the death of six people in Shibjanj,[1] and where industrial growth is held in check by limited and faltering energy flows, the country's newly discovered natural gas reserves are the cause of significant optimism. If there have been national protests concerning the details of profit-sharing arrangements between Chevron and the government and rumours of a pipeline that will export the gas to India, not to say local agitation at the loss of land, now is not the time to mention it. In the four villages that surround the plant, glimpsed distantly across the shimmering fields, life appears to go on as normal.

Nadampur, December 2008: half a mile from the South Pad. I watch as the harvested paddy is threshed in the homestead yard. This year, for the first time, the crop is fed to a mechanical thresher rather than spread on the earth and trampled by circling bullocks, the traditional way. About half a mile away, towards Karimpur, I can make out the gas flare through the haze. At night we hear the thump of the drills; where a decade ago a car moving along the track towards Enatganj was a rare occurrence, today the traffic on the road is constant.

On the other side of the old house, built with British remittances back in the 1970s, Shuli prepares the evening meal, feeding the open flames of the earth *chula* with fuel sticks that are rolled in cattle dung, dried in the sunshine then stored in the bamboo walled kitchen. In the section of the house that is owned by her now long-departed British cousins, there is another sort of kitchen. Built only a few years earlier, it is furnished with the utensils that the British contingent is accustomed to: a stainless steel sink rather than the pond, wooden shelves rather than the floor, a gas cooker. The room has, however, never been used for its original purpose. Instead, it has become a storage area, filled with sacks of betel nut and rice. Thick dust covers the sink and the cooker. When I ask Shuli why she doesn't use the latter, she laughs. There's no gas supply, she says. The village has never been connected.

Natural gas: drawn from the depths of the earth and pumped along a network of pipelines to distant processing plants and power stations, it is both intensely localised and, in the act of its extraction, spatially dispersed, released from underneath the fields, then channelled to far-away destinations where it is converted to fuel, a commodity to be bought and sold, a prerequisite of industrialisation and modernity, a cause of celebration and of dispute. 'Under our fields is gold', Amma tells me. Savvy entrepreneurs that the locals are, everyone is aware of the economic potential of the gas that the foreigners discovered. Local people would get rich, some said; there would be industrial development around the field, a fertiliser factory or a power plant. Best of all, Chevron would offer jobs and development. Poverty would be a thing of the past.

What people hoped for in these early days of the gas field was connection, not simply to the gas supply that was now being pumped out at a rate of 250 million cubic feet a day, or even to Chevron, but more generally to the sources of global capitalism and industrial development that had the power to transform a person's situation from poverty to prosperity. This possibility, of transformation gained through links to foreign capitalism, is not new to the area, for since the 1960s men have grown rich by migrating abroad; the two- or three-storey houses of successful *Londonis*, with their TVs, fridges and spacious rooms are testimony to the power of such links, if only one could access them.

Such connections have always been inherently social. To get work, visas or airfares for travel abroad, land or business opportunities, one has to be connected to the right people: relatives, village patrons, politicians, government officials, nothing can be achieved without knowing someone (or failing that knowing someone who knows someone). Just as the gas is both located in the *desh* (homeland) and pumped to *bidesh* (foreign places: in this case, anywhere outside the immediate locality), local connections – to social networks, sources of credit and, of course, land – go hand in hand with global connections. It is migration to the UK, after all, that has enabled some families to accumulate large amounts of land and build themselves the smart brick houses. The opposite state, *disconnection*, is as disastrous as *connection* is desirable. Those disconnected, cast out from their families or severed from their land, become untethered from the *desh*, drifting from village to village in search of alms or casual work. Meanwhile in Dhaka deals are brokered, connections made between foreign multinationals and the government, money channelled and moved around, just as the pipelines connecting the gas field to the often failing, but economically vital national grid, pump the gas outwards, and away.

*   *   *

Today, the South Pad takes up an area of around 50 acres of what was once prime agricultural land situated between four villages in Habiganj, Sylhet: Kakura, Karimpur, Firizpur and Nadampur (see Figure 1.1). Joined to the North Pad by a single road, both sites, and the road that links them, involved the loss of agricultural land and are distinguished by their proximity to human habitation. At the South Pad site, for some homesteads in nearby Karimpur and Firizpur the flaring of the gas is so close that the occupants complain of the increased heat, not to mention the smell. Safety issues are foremost in everyone's mind: a 'blow-out' like those which took place at the nearby Magurcchara and Tengratila gas fields in 1997 and 2005 are a nightmarish spectre which, as we shall see in Chapter 7, provide the content for stories that have attained almost mythical

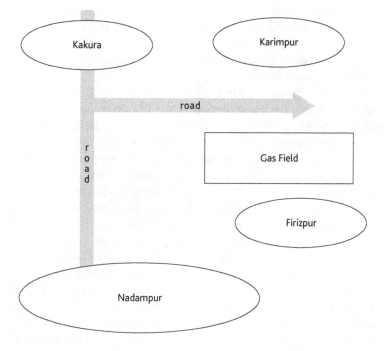

Figure 1.1   Location of villages and the Bibiyana Gas Field

status: dark allegories of violent disconnection and death that speak volumes about people's fears of the risks and ruptures of the new economic order.

A second distinguishing feature of the Bibiyana Gas Field, involving stories of a very different nature, is that, like many transnational extractive companies but unlike any other gas plant in Bangladesh, Chevron has a programme of 'community engagement' in the surrounding villages as part of its policies of corporate social responsibility (CSR). As we shall see in the chapters that follow, two forms of 'development' are therefore taking place. The one that is desired by local people is that which is most elusive: reliable infrastructure, a transparent and accountable state, and secure employment: inclusion, in other words, in the benefits of neoliberal capitalism. In contrast, the 'development' that is on offer from Chevron's CSR programme draws on the work of non-governmental organisations (NGOs) such as the Grameen Bank, much lauded in the development industry but, as we shall see, less attractive for many locals: micro-credit, income generation, training programmes.[2] 'Development' is thus a slippery and elusive character in the story, its meaning shifting according to who is using it and in what context.

What can the social relations that encircle the gas field teach us about the connections and disconnections that people in different places have with global capitalism? How might we analyse and write about them? What follows is neither a case study of CSR nor, indeed, a simplistic tirade against multinationals. Instead it is an ethnography of globalisation which interrogates the complex layers of morality and practice that surround industrial development and foreign corporations in Bangladesh, whether in the villages adjacent to the gas field, their transnational communities or the domains of global capital which are materialised at the gas field. What we see is how these different moralities are utilised in the claims that people and corporations make over material resources.

Story telling and narrative play an important role. The chapters are based around various stories, some authored by me, others by those involved in the complex contestations around what 'economic development' ought to be, and what it actually is. All are 'true', in that they narrate lived experiences and observations, yet all too often are constructions of reality drawn from particular personal and political locations (Clifford and Marcus, 1986). Central to my account is the argument that just as stories can be read as claims or political statements, so can other forms of claim-making (for example, promotional literature published by Chevron) be analysed as stories, which frame the world in a particular way, propagating various messages and moralities while editing out others. Whose stories are heard, whose believed and whose dismissed is of course crucial: story telling as social practice cannot be understood aside from its political context. This book is as implicated in these processes as slick narratives of corporate benevolence, told through artistically presented PowerPoint slides or glossy brochures, or indeed, lamentations of dispossession and loss, told by landless women. My use of fictional or 'creative' writing styles at points in the narrative deliberately reveals my authorial presence and power: this is my version of events, edited, stylised and shaped according to my own beliefs and claims. I make no pretence at 'giving voice to the poor', though it is my intention that some of their experiences and preoccupations will be revealed.

Naming is an important element of story telling, especially when these stories are linked to political and economic claims. While the names of actual villages and towns in this book remain unchanged, rather than referring to the area that surrounds the South Pad as 'Bibiyana', I refer to it by the fictionalised name of Duniyapur ('World village'). My reasons are political. While the Bibiyana Gas Field is indeed a gas extraction plant operated by Chevron, naming the geographical space that extends beyond the perimeters of the plant's high wire fence as 'Bibiyana' is more problematic. Based on the name of a small river that runs past Nadampur, Firizpur and Karimpur, 'Bibiyana' is used by Chevron to refer not only to the gas field, but also what officials are apt to refer to as 'our communities'. The name thus creates a territorial field as well as a site for gas extraction, an area in which the company's discursive practices produce particular relationships and moral orders. The name is also contested. Indeed, since the inauguration of the Bibiyana Gas Field at the South Pad in 2007, residents at the overlooked North Pad have claimed that the site should be known as the 'Dighalbak Gas Field'. Their story, which took place in the days of Occidental rather than Chevron, is significantly different from those of the villages surrounding the South Pad and is not detailed in the pages of this book. In order to protect the identity of our informants I have also changed the names of everyone we spoke to, scrambling some personal characteristic to further disguise their identities. For a few well-known public figures who would be instantly recognisable, I have not done this.

In writing the book, my motivations are both professional and personal. Since my doctoral work I have been interested in the engagements that Bangladeshis have with globalisation and neoliberal capitalism, whether manifested as industrialisation, migration abroad or 'development'. My first book, based on fieldwork in the late 1980s, examined the transformations associated with prolonged migration from Sylhet to the UK (Gardner, 1995). Subsequent work has traced the ongoing role of place, movement and connections in shaping economic hierarchy, poverty and transnational 'habitus' (Gardner, 1993, 2006; Gardner and Ahmed, 2009). Fieldwork among elders and children in London has led to perspectives on the relationship between the life course, gender and place (Gardner, 2002; Gardner and Mand, 2012). Moreover, an early postdoctoral stint as a junior social development adviser at the Overseas Development Agency (now Department for International Development, DFID) led me to reflect upon the ambivalent and morally charged relationship between anthropology and the development industry (Gardner and Lewis, 1996, 2000). In a context where the mantras and practices of development are increasingly being taken up by multinational corporations in the name of corporate social responsibility Chevron's 'community engagement' programmes are a prime example of what some might hail as ethical business conduct, offering developmental rewards in return for their use of local resources, and others, more cynically, might label 'greenwash'.

More importantly, the gas field in particular, and the presence of Chevron and other multinationals in Bangladesh in general, have much to teach us about the workings of global capitalism via the endless seeking out of new territories and profits by energy companies, their ambivalent relationship with the states and populations of the places where they work, and their peculiarly twenty-first-century requirement for good publicity, or 'reputation'. The book is not, however, an institutional ethnography, though the enterprise of 'studying up' is vital (Guterson, 1997; Marcus and Fisher, 1986; Nader, 1974), as is the attempt to 'see it like an oil company' (Ferguson, 2005).[3]

Instead, the chapters that follow are largely based on the perspectives of people who either live in the vicinity of the gas field or in the area's transnational communities in the UK. By listening to them, one gains insight into 'the grips of worldly encounters' which Anna Tsing calls 'friction': 'the awkward, unequal, unstable and creative qualities of interconnection across difference' (2005:

4). It is these worldly encounters, not so much between the binaries of 'local' and 'global', or 'the villagers' and 'the corporation', but between a range of actors who are both localised and global yet who have vastly different types of connections and entitlements, which are my primary focus. To this extent, what follows is an ethnography of twenty-first-century capitalism, or, as the Comaroffs would have it, 'Millennium capitalism', which: 'appears to both include and to marginalise in unanticipated ways: to produce desire and expectation on a global scale' (2000: 298). How some people are included and others marginalised, and the desires and expectations that they have, lie at the heart of the book.

Since anthropological methodology is largely based upon experiences during fieldwork, the distinction between the personal and professional is somewhat fuzzy. Having said this, I *do* have more of a personal interest in the Bibiyana Gas Field than if it were elsewhere in South Asia, for it is adjacent to Nadampur, the village where I carried out my doctoral fieldwork in 1987–8, which I have been visiting on a regular basis ever since. It was on such a visit in 2005 that I first saw the Chevron traffic safety billboards that line the road from Syedpur. There was a new road too, cutting across the fields just outside Nadampur. As we approached the village we passed trucks filled either with mud, or with labourers sporting yellow safety helmets of the type common to British or North American building sites, but not Bangladeshi ones. As the road broke away from Kakura, a village a mile or so to the north of Nadampur, I saw where the trucks had originated: a vast industrial site, spread over what had previously been an uninterrupted vista of rice lands. I was accustomed to changes taking place in the area; every time I returned there were new or rebuilt houses, and over the twenty or so years since my doctoral fieldwork the small area of tea stalls that had somewhat optimistically been referred to as 'the bazaar' had grown so much in size and variety of shops that it was virtually a mall. But this was different: not caused by the individualised wealth of *Londoni* migrants, who for generations had used their remittances to build smart houses, mosques and roads, but a huge multinational, whose logo was emblazoned on billboards, the health clinic we had just passed and the t-shirts of the children who lingered by the road. Something exceptional was happening.

Friends in Nadampur soon filled me in. Foreigners had discovered gas, they said. The District Commissioner had informed them that they would have to give up their homes and fields; the 'Chairman' (of the local *union*, like a local council) had been negotiating with the company to make sure that they were paid compensation; no-one knew what was going to happen, or where, if they were to lose their homestead land, they would go. There was a resistance campaign, I was told; people from Dhaka had come to assist in the fight.

My visit that time was a short one. A week later I was back in Britain, trying to find out more. From what I could gather from the web and from friends in Dhaka, the situation was not quite as alarming as I'd originally supposed. Negotiations over land compensation were taking place; no-one would lose their homes, for the gas plant was to be built on a relatively small area of agricultural land. This was not to be the same situation as in the Vendata Mine at Nyamgiri, Orissa, for which thousands were to be evicted from their sacred lands in the forests.[4] Indeed, some local people supported the development, hoping it might lead to jobs and improved infrastructure.

What actually happened to my friends in Nadampur is, in part, documented in the chapters that follow, though as it turned out it was three other villages, Kakura, Karimpur and Firizpur that were more directly affected by the gas and '*Sevron*' (local rendering of Chevron). What happened to me is that I received a grant to study the relationship between the gas extraction, local livelihoods and social networks in the area.[5] While the research has encompassed the four villages that surrounded the South Pad and included their transnational communities in the UK (the area that, for the purposes of this book, I call Duniyapur), our fieldwork focused in particular upon Karimpur and Kakura, each of which have distinctive histories and socio-economic characteristics, which I shall outline in more detail in Chapter 3.

The research was necessarily transnational, and would not have been possible without both my own connections in Nadampur and Jahangirnagar University in Dhaka. In Nadampur, introductions to leaders and gatekeepers in the research villages were eased by the unlimited generosity of Shuli's family, who provided me and my colleagues from Jahangirnagar with food, accommodation and advice. Since 1987 this family has treated me as an adopted daughter, opening their house and lives to me with the affection, patience and resourcefulness that characterise many of the local people. For their love and care, I am forever in their debt.

From the outset the political situation in the area was so fraught that I doubt the research would have been possible had I not already been known to many people, including the director of the NGO working with Chevron on their 'Alternative Livelihoods Programme', Friends in Village Development, Bangladesh (FIVDB). Crucially, I would never have been able to gather the detailed 'micro data' of household livelihoods, coping strategies and so on, which involved intense fieldwork conducted over twelve months in Kakura and Karimpur, without the assistance of Professor Zahir Ahmed, who led two accomplished young researchers (Fatema Bashir and Masud Rana) in the field.

Our methodological strategy was various and multi-sited. Fatema and Masud worked in Kakura and Karimpur, focusing largely upon landless or land-poor households (of which, as we shall see in Chapter 3, there are many). Meanwhile Zahir spent time talking to, and interviewing, many of the key players: local politicians, village bigwigs, the higher-status and wealthier patrons who invariably have strong connections to the UK. Over a series of shorter visits, I talked to as many people as I could; this included meetings and interviews with Chevron officials both at the gas plant and in Dhaka, plus fieldworkers and policy makers at FIVDB. In Britain, Zahir and I travelled to Burnley, Newcastle, Ilford and Tower Hamlets to meet people with close links to the area. Many of these had lost land, and, as we shall see, were deeply upset by what had happened. We also met and interviewed a number of British-based activists and journalists, who had close links to the national campaigning organisation, the National Committee to Protect Oil, Gas, Mineral Resources, Power and Ports (referred to throughout the book as the National Committee). In Dhaka, I interviewed the leading activists Nur Mohammed and Anu Muhammed.

The worldwide web – arguably the greatest connector of all – has also played an important role in the research. Newspaper articles, blogs, interviews and corporate press releases have all been available at the click of a button. Some of these documents have not simply been secondary sources, but primary texts, with their own complex stories to tell. Chevron's *CSR Report* (2007), for example (of which we shall be hearing more in Chapter 5), features – on its front pages – a large photo of a young man I have known since he was a boy. The statements, theories and arguments of national-level activists have been easily accessed via my laptop, as have many other websites and blogs which seek to unsettle the comfortable statements of 'community partnership' made by the representations of Chevron. A comprehensive review of these sites and the contestations they reveal is simply not possible here, though the arguments and narratives contained in them provide vital context for what follows.[6] Similarly, this book is not a detailed critique or polemic regarding Chevron's role in a globally warming world, its environmental management or its relationship to dubious Third World governments. There are already plenty of anti-multinational campaigners and environmentalists happy to provide such accounts.[7]

Instead, our research followed a different remit: to investigate the faltering and uneven spread of globalising capital in one small corner of the world, attempting to appreciate the meanings this has for everyday lives, whether via neoliberal techniques of control and governance, shifts in the relative access of different groups to resources, or complex and localised power plays. The wider context: of national contestations over natural resources, the shape of economic development and the relationship between Bangladesh and foreign interests is ever present.

Research of this sort is inevitably entangled with local politics and relationships. The project was positioned in a particular way from the outset, and appeared in different guises according to who was involved and in what context. The result is that while we gained access to some people and some domains, we were denied access to others. Associated with a white English woman, who some people knew well and others had only heard rumours of, the research was both compromised and enabled in complex ways. The rumours and theories concerning what we were up to were significantly different from those I had encountered as a doctoral student in the 1980s. Then, I was thought to be a spy for the British High Commission, come to check up on immigration cases. In 2007–9, many people assumed that since we were outsiders and I was foreign, we must be employed by Chevron. As I describe in Chapter 6, others came to the opposite conclusion: we were activists, seeking to undermine the good works of the CSR programme.

Anthropological research, and the core method of participant observation, is by definition a messy affair. Unlike structured questionnaires, baseline surveys or satisfactorily completed PRA (Participatory Rural Assessment) sessions,[8] sitting around and chatting to people, or watching events take place over a series of months or years, rarely feels like 'proper' research and certainly doesn't cut the mustard within a development discourse that relies upon supposedly 'objective' statistics and surveys.[9] Participant observation is, however, the only way that the detailed contexts of peoples' lives and the ways that these unfold can be understood. While much of this book is based upon more formal research methods, a great deal is also rooted in my personal, long-standing knowledge of the area and some of the people who live in it, built up over twenty years. Hedged in and shaped by particular relationships, political contexts and predispositions, it is unavoidably and unapologetically subjective. While I present and analyse much of what follows in terms of narrative, the primary narrative – this book – is mine.

The remainder of this introduction is divided into two parts. In the first, I outline some of the background debates surrounding global capital and industrialisation in South Asia, natural resources and 'the resource curse' and corporate social responsibility. In the second, I outline the ideas and arguments that frame the book.

'ACCUMULATION BY DISPOSSESSION': INDUSTRIALISATION AND CONFLICT IN BENGAL IN THE 2000s

The events and contestations that surround the Bibiyana Gas Field are illustrative of a much broader story currently playing out across large parts of South Asia. Or rather, it is one story among many of the same genre. The loss of land and livelihoods to the encroaching needs of industrial capitalism is a central plot-line, but so too are the contradictory demands of twenty-first-century 'development': the need for adequate infrastructure (roads, bridges, reliable sources of energy) to enable a higher standard of living as well as economic growth and employment, versus the rights of individuals, communities and the general population to have a say in the form that these changes take, and, indeed, to reap at least some of the benefits. In Bangladesh political instability and state corruption have played a key role in the twists and turns of the narrative, as has the long-standing history of colonial and neocolonial capitalism. The denouement depends, in part, upon one's political propensity. Some stories:

January 2006, north-west Bangladesh: thousands of farmers are protesting against the constant interruptions to their power supply. It's the dry season and their fields need water yet the pumps that are used for irrigation don't work because of the unreliable electricity; what is euphemistically referred to as 'power shedding' means that factories and farms are unable to dependably produce the food and goods upon which individual livelihoods and the national economy depends. The demonstration, involving a reported 10,000 people, centres on the local electricity board office at Shipganj. An earlier protest had resulted in the arrest of several men. Now, tempers fraying, the mood turns violent. Police vehicles are set on fire, and in turn, the police turn their guns on the crowd: six are killed and hundreds injured.[10]

The incident is not a one-off. Whereas people once rioted over food, increasingly civil disturbance in Bangladesh is caused by power shedding, with anger focused on electricity boards and their officials, who are accused of only providing regular electricity to those who can afford generous *baksheesh* (bribes). Later the same year, over 200 are reported injured by riots over electrical supply in Mirpur, Dhaka,[11] a scene that is repeated many times in other parts of the country over this and subsequent years.

A few months after the deaths at Shipganj, north-west Bangladesh is the scene of more riots and more police shootings. This time the disturbances are reported across the globe. The cause is a proposed open cast mine to be operated by the multinational Asia Energy at Phulbari in Dinajpur district, displacing 40,000–50,000 people, many of them members of 'tribal' groups from their homes and causing many more to lose their livelihoods. As news stories go, the protest is perhaps more easily digested by the Western media than farmers rioting over electricity supplies. Vast multinationals planning environmentally damaging mines which will dispossess 'indigenous peoples', photographed brandishing bamboo sticks,[12] make a good story, slotting into the conventional trope of the 'indigenous' resistor protesting against a faceless, exploitative multinational. The disturbance is widely reported across global media.

The success of the Phulbari campaign is not so much about its international coverage but, more importantly, the pressure that this and the national agitation place on the government. Let us not assume that multinationals, donors or governments always get their way. After mass protests which spread to Dhaka, the Bangladesh Nationalist Party (BNP) government and the Asian Development Bank, which has been pushing the project, are forced to back down. The project is thrown out, at least for the time being.

Not far away, in Singur, West Bengal, another protest is gathering momentum, again attracting international attention and forcing the (Indian) government to change direction. The issues are similar: local farmers are threatened with large-scale loss of land and livelihoods in order to make way for industrial development. This time it is Tata, the vast Indian car manufacturer that is at the centre of the storm. The company plans a huge complex in order to produce the much-heralded Nano, the 'cheapest car in the world'. The proximity to Kolkata makes the site desirable, but Tata has not taken account of the scale of local anger at the forcible loss of land, or indeed the Stalinist state government's inability to control the swelling opposition movement. By 2008 the government has forcibly acquired 997 acres, forcing 13,000 farmers off the land, but the backlash has attracted the attentions and energies of urban intellectuals, opposition parties and the world's media. In August 2008, road blocks, threats to Tata employees and widespread demonstrations close the plant down, forcing the government to consider returning 300 acres to the farmers. By October, Tata has pulled out in despair, cutting their losses (the £350 million factory is nearly complete) and moving their operations to Gujarat.[13]

While the Singur and Phulbari protests have attracted considerable commentary, there are countless more examples of the conflicts unleashed by what might loosely be glossed as 'industrialisation' in the Bengal region. All involve struggles over resources in which ordinary people are either denied a public good (electricity, for example), supposedly a generalised benefit of economic development, or in which they lose access to the land on which their livelihoods depend.

On the one hand the story seems to be that of the avaricious reach of corporate finance, seeking expansion in ever more peripheral or problematic territories, or what Harvey has described as 'spatio-temporal fixes', in which the continual crises of over-accumulation facing capitalism are solved by territorial expansion and delayed profits (Harvey, 2003: 115; see also Arrighi, 2006: 202; Neilson, 2010: 3). When capital moves out of established territories it often leaves a trail of devastation in its wake; one need only think of the ex-mining villages of north-east England. When it moves into new territories, what Harvey refers to as 'switching crises' ensue, as the area moves from one system of accumulation (for example farming) to another (car factories or mining) and resistance occurs. One solution is what Harvey calls 'accumulation by dispossession', when the state releases assets (for example land) at low cost to get the process of accumulation going (Harvey, 2003). Another is the use of state-sponsored, or -tolerated, physical force:

> An unholy alliance between state powers and the predatory aspects of finance capital forms the cutting edge of a 'vulture capitalism' that is as much about cannibalistic practices and forced devaluations as it is about achieving harmonious global development. (Harvey, 2003: 136; cited in Arrighi, 2006: 2004)

Within this analysis states play an enabling role in the movement of capital across territories, promoting policies such as Free Economic Zones, in which foreign corporations avoid taxes or other forms of regulation. As we shall see later in the book, in Bangladesh the state's role as enabler of the spatio-temporal fixes of capital is contradicted and undermined by other concerns, be these its inability to control dissent, ambiguity towards foreign multinationals or the actions of self seeking individuals within government who use Machiavellian strategies to direct profits their own way.

Yet, as the news stories cited above indicate, there is a further complication in the tale of avaricious capital expanding into new territories. While the actions of Chevron, Asia Energy and Tata provide excellent examples of Harvey's 'accumulation by dispossession', we must not collapse analysis of the predatory nature of capitalism into a simplistic tale of exploited peasants resisting development. In Bangladesh, everyone bar the most idealistic of NGO workers or elite intellectuals desires development, if what this means is functional infrastructure, regular employment, higher standards of living and modern (i.e. transparent, democratic and trustworthy) government. The accounts of resistance to land loss and multinational capital at Singur and Phulbari must therefore be juxtaposed with the accounts of riots at electricity board offices. To put it bluntly: people need electricity, and unless 'alternative' sources such as solar energy become cheap and accessible on a very large scale, in order to have electricity the country needs to exploit its natural resources. Whether or not Asia Energy or Chevron, or Petrobangla (the government-owned company) extract the coal or gas, the same land loss and dispossession result. Let us not romanticise rural life in the southern hemisphere: working the land by hand is gruelling and unpleasant, as is living through a summer without a fan or a fridge. Crucially, too, the industry which has driven the Bangladesh's growth rate of 6.6 percent (in the first part of 2010) is dependent upon a regular power supply. As a recent report by the Asian Development Bank states: 'acute power and energy shortages (in 2010) have reduced Bangladesh's short term growth prospects'.[14]

While Bangladesh's industrial and manufacturing sectors are almost completely dependent upon natural gas to produce electricity, agricultural production is largely dependent upon urea, a fertiliser produced from natural gas. Yet despite the recent developments of sites such as the Bibiyana Gas Field, with news from Chevron in 2010 that the reserves are possibly double what was originally believed, and frantic bids to develop offshore reserves in the Bay of Bengal, the country is far from achieving energy security. At the time of writing, proposals to build two nuclear reactors with Russian assistance were being debated, as were the actual extent of known gas reserves, with some predicting they might run out by 2013.[15]

What this means is that, as new gas and coal reserves are discovered, the pressure to extract as much as quickly as possible is immense. How this is done, and by whom, is ferociously contested both nationally and transnationally, but while the environmental and human costs of Phulbari may have proven too great,[16] and doubts have been raised about the environmental effects of seismic surveys carried out in delicate forested areas (Khan, 2009), few would seriously suggest that gas reserves found under ordinary fields should be left unexploited.

I shall return to the broader national political and economic context in the next chapter, where we shall see how Bangladesh has long been subjected to the exploitative presence of colonial and neocolonial capitalism. This history has contributed to the development of a weak and corrupt state, which in turn has necessitated various forms of patronage at all levels of social and economic life. The need for connection with more powerful others lies at the heart of many of the stories that Duniyapur has to tell.

More generally, Bangladesh is often presented in news stories as 'on the brink', whether in terms of political meltdown/civil war,[17] catastrophic, globally warmed flooding[18] or indeed economic lift-off, slowly transforming from an agriculturally based economy into one which is reliant upon 'hands not land' via industrialisation and manufacturing, encouraged by neoliberal economic policies of tax-free Special Economic Zones for multinational companies wishing to capitalise on the abundant supplies of cheap labour (Toufique and Turton, 2002). While donors such as DFID, the World Bank and the Asian Development Bank are keen to push such policies, the state remains ambivalent about holding out an open-door policy to multinationals. In 2006, for example, Tata suspended what was to be a $3 billion investment in Bangladesh, in despair at government delays and red tape. Those with knowledge of Bangladesh may well shrug their shoulders and mutter 'typical'.

Economically, the country is growing steadily, albeit not as fast as India, its neighbour to the west, or Thailand, its more distant neighbour to the east. Indicators of 'human development' are also encouraging. The 2010 Human Development Report (United Nations, 2010) places Bangladesh third among countries showing the most improvement in human development indicators since 1981; since 1970, life expectancy has surged by 23 points. The garment industry and remittances from overseas migration have considerably boosted gross domestic product (amounting to over 25 percent of GDP) yet 45 percent of the population is primarily employed in agriculture and the economic growth rate of around 5–6 percent per year since 1996 is, in comparison with other Asian success stories, modest.[19] Overall, the US intelligence agency ranks the country as 200th in the world in terms of GDP.[20]

The question of whether 'economic growth' brings benefits to all is pertinent to the whole of this book. Yet let those of us sitting in comfortable post-industrial societies in the West not be taken in by essentialised and ignorant images of 'sustainable rural life': there are few if any agrarian contexts where economic growth has not been matched by an overall improvement in living standards. How often do small children die? Is medicine and care available for the sick? Do children go to school? Is there enough to eat? In countries such as Bangladesh, these are the 'bottom line' questions. As Amartya Sen (1999) has argued, 'development' is not just about economic growth, but freedom.

The story of Bangladesh is thus filled with contradiction. Political stagnation and deadlock, interrupted by periodic crises which lead to everyday disruption but no real change exists alongside entrepreneurship and innovation; wealth is increasing and standards of living gradually rising for some, but within a context of extreme inequality; the country's NGOs are lauded for pioneering work on micro-credit, but approximately 36 percent of the population still live below the poverty line.[21] Meanwhile, the population of this small country continues to rise: 160 million in 2008; 220 million expected by 2050.

For those with an interest in the relationship between natural resources, multinationals and 'development' (by which I refer in general terms to increases in the well-being of the population), Duniyapur clearly raises important questions. While this book is primarily focused on connection and disconnection, knowing and silencing, power and repression, questions concerning the relationship between economic change and poverty, generally addressed by development experts, have underlain the research. Will Bangladesh's natural gas and coal reserves add to the prosperity of its population? More specifically, can multinationals such as Chevron contribute positively to the communities in which they work, or will they always 'accumulate through dispossession'? At the heart of the story of Duniyapur and the Bibiyana Gas Field are various virulently contested beliefs and passionately defended positions concerning the relationship between Chevron and the Bangladeshi government in particular, and the role of foreign multinationals in assisting or preventing economic development in Bangladesh in general. The chapters that follow will go some way in addressing these issues, albeit by focusing not on macro economics but on relationships at the fraying and sometimes fractured edges of globalisation, detailing just some of the 'friction' caused by life on the borderlands of capitalist transformation. For now, let us step back from Duniyapur for some background to the debates.

THE 'CURSE' OF NATURAL RESOURCES?

While some people in Duniyapur originally believed that the discovery of natural gas under their fields would lead to wealth, jobs and improved infrastructure, the experience of communities living close to or on the sites of natural resources elsewhere in the world might have given them pause for thought. As has been widely documented, abundant natural resources, especially in the shape of oil or minerals, can lead to increased problems in the places where they are found. What has been dubbed the 'resource curse' is associated with economic stagnation, corruption and political instability, including an increased risk of civil war.[22] Combined with the macro-economic and political effects of the resource curse, we also have localised dispossession and large-scale environmental destruction, processes documented by anthropologists Stuart Kirsch (2006) in Papua New Guinea and Suzana Sawyer (2004) in Ecuador.[23] I shall return to these and other ethnographic accounts of the encounters between local people and mining companies in a short while. For now, let us consider the 'resource curse' in more detail. Much of the following is based on observations of mineral- and oil-rich countries, but may contain lessons for Bangladesh, whose natural gas and coal reserves are still being explored and have attracted substantial attention from energy multinationals keen to expand their territories.

One might assume that an abundance of natural resources would lead to economic prosperity. Yet while there are noteworthy exceptions[24] there are also many countries where this abundance has had the opposite effect. According to Paul Collier, for example, 29 percent of the 'bottom billion' countries live in resource-rich economies (2007: 39). Indeed, World Bank economists have come to the startling conclusion that the greater the extent to which a poorer country depends upon natural resources for its export sector, the greater the *decrease* in GDP. A study published by the World Bank in 2002 shows that if natural resources constitute 6–15 percent of exports, then GDP falls by 0.7 percent per year; if they constitute 15–50 percent of the sector, then GDP falls by 1.1 percent; and if they constitute over 50 percent, GDP falls by 2.3 percent (Weber-Fahr, 2002). Why should this be so?

In his analysis of 'the bottom billion', Collier (2007) argues that 'the natural resource trap' is one of the main traps that poor countries fall into. A major reason is that when large revenues are gained from natural resources, people stop earning money from normal productive activities, relying instead upon the revenue derived from resource extraction. This can lead to economic stagnation for middle-income countries such as Russia and the Middle East, which rely on oil revenue for a large proportion of their GDP, and worse for much poorer countries, who never reach the 'lift off' of an established manufacturing or industrial base when their natural resources are abundant.

A second cause of the trap is what is referred to as 'Dutch Disease'. This phrase refers to a process whereby the income earned by exporting natural resources is so high that the country's currency rises too quickly, making its exports uncompetitive. While revenue from oil, minerals or, indeed, natural gas, may be pouring in, it isn't worth developing the production of other goods for export. During the early days of the Nigerian oil boom in the 1970s, for example, the country's traditional exports of cocoa and peanuts fell into abeyance (Collier, 2007). We shall be returning to Nigeria shortly.

Another reason why natural resources – in particular oil, gas and minerals – often don't lead to economic growth is that the productive techniques involved are capital intensive: the plants which extract the resources don't employ many local people. Nor do they lead to a growth of nearby factories or service industries, since the extracted materials are taken away from the sites for sale elsewhere (Auty, 1993). In poorer countries a large capital input from foreign companies is also usually required. This leads to 'enclave tendencies' (Auty, 1993: 3), with only very modest local production and low revenue retention, since a large proportion of profits go abroad to service the foreign capital investment. This is the situation in Duniyapur, where the gas field has not, as was hoped, led either to the creation of local jobs, substantial infrastructure (besides the enclave of the plant, and the roads which link it to Sherpur), or the growth of service or manufacturing industries in the area.

Finally, revenues from natural resources can lead governments to overspend and over-borrow in the first flush of wealth. Since the global prices for oil, minerals and gas are highly volatile this can spell financial disaster if and when prices drop and revenue suddenly decreases. Again, oil- and mineral-rich countries are particularly vulnerable, but natural gas, timber (and even drugs) are similarly susceptible to market volatility. In Nigeria, the oil boom of the 1970s led to massive overspending by the government and the rapid enrichment of elites. When oil prices collapsed in the 1980s, living standards halved (Collier, 2007). When viewed in terms of their political rationale, however, these 'mistakes' in economic policy can seem quite rational since politicians seek short-term goals in their efforts to be re-elected (Robinson et al., 2006).

Such economic effects go some way in explaining why oil is often associated with corruption and escalating violence. In Nigeria, where corruption is endemic, kidnappings of oil workers commonplace, and mafia control of resources routine, the state-sanctioned murder of troublesome opponents such as Ken Saro-Wiwa, an activist who called Shell to account for environmental damage and was executed by the military government in 1995, is, one suspects, merely the tip of the iceberg. In his vivid exploration of the effect of oil wealth on the country, Michael Peel writes:

> As the venality and corruption that envelop the industry come clear for all of us to see, it is hardly surprising that the local battles for Nigerian crude have become increasingly gangsterish. It is, after all, the tried and trusted method to get rich off the country's main resource. (2009: xvii)

Why is there such a strong relationship between resource abundance and 'venality and corruption'? Collier argues that the high revenues gleaned from resources such as oil can, in particular contexts, *cause* political corruption. As he puts it: 'The heart of the resource curse is that resource rents make democracy malfunction' (2007: 42). This effect has been noted by a range of commentators (see, for example, Bannon and Collier, 2003; Robinson et al., 2006; Ross, 1999). According to Collier (2007) the main reason is that when governments receive abundant revenue from natural resources they use it for short-term gains, for in democracies politicians focus first and foremost on their future electoral chances. Rather than gaining revenue from taxes and investing in long-term public projects which will benefit the general population – health or education, for example – politicians take the easy option, buying the support of opinion formers and local leaders. Once the tendency to use bribes has started it becomes hard for others to buck the trend since an expectation develops that political support will only be given in return for material benefits. An abundance of resource rents thus 'lets in the politics of patronage' (Collier, 2007:44). Collier concludes that 'oil democracy' is virtually an oxymoron.

Do natural resources cause corruption, letting the rot into well-established and functioning democracies or is the see-saw of cause and effect more complex? In their analysis, based on a wide range of case studies, Robinson et al. (2006) conclude that 'the resource curse' is predicated on pre-existing state and civil institutions. If these are accountable and transparent, and the state competent (as, for example, in Norway or the US), then countries tend to benefit from resource booms. If, however, they are none of the above, then the effects will be negative, because in already corrupt political systems revenues are used by politicians to garner favour in elections via bribery. One solution is that revenues gained and contracts held with transnational mining companies should be made transparent (Ross, 2003), an idea which has taken form in the guise of the Extractive Industries Transparency Initiative.[25] As we shall see in Chapter 6, the transparency of government deals with multinationals is a major demand of activists in Bangladesh.

The news gets worse. Not only does the 'resource curse' create/ exacerbate escalating levels of corruption, it is also associated with violent conflict and civil war, 'bitter struggles over oil and blood stained land' as Suzana Sawyer puts it (2004: 17). This is partly because the poverty and decreasing GDP associated with the export of natural resources are often underlying causes of civil war. As Ross writes: 'Resource-rich governments do an unusually poor job of providing education and health care for their citizens' (2003: 20). Indeed, twelve out of twenty mineral-/oil-dependent states were recently classified by the World Bank as 'highly indebted poor countries' (Ross, 2003). Sudden increases in poverty, alongside the political corruption and weakening of democratic institutions noted by Collier, are all underlying causes of civil unrest, insurgency movements and civil war. The inequalities caused by the new-found wealth of those controlling resource revenues is another.

A pertinent example of the relationship between resources and conflict is provided by Acche, in Indonesia. Here, the opening of a large gas plant in the 1970s was linked to the development of an ethnically based separatist movement which has led to conflict in the region that continues today. The gas plant displaced thousands of people, causing an 'anti-immigration' backlash which the separatist movement capitalised upon. Health problems caused by gas and chemical leaks exacerbated the social unrest, as did the large police and military presence brought into the area. The main source of discontent, however, was that revenue from the plant was not being shared with local people and few jobs were created (Ross, 2003). In his discussion of the conflict, Ross argues that the movement capitalised on these discontents, exaggerating the extent of wealth that the plant might create and comparing Acche to oil-rich Brunei. As we shall see later in this book, though there have been no calls for Sylhet to become a separate state, similar themes have been played out in Duniyapur. Ross (2003) suggests that a number of things can be done to reduce the potential for conflict, including the use of CSR programmes in the area by the multinationals involved and 'community consultation'. Making information publicly available on revenues gained from gas or oil production would, he argues, undermine the claims of resistance movements. These recommendations of 'what can be done' seem geared more to helping multinational energy companies do their work than assisting the communities affected, and can hardly be applied to the worst cases of resource extraction, when large-scale mining projects lead to the forced removal of people from their land and what amounts to environmental Armageddon. Indeed, in these cases 'community consultation' is a Band-Aid that fails to stick, for good reason.

This leads me to a central cause of conflict in contexts of resource abundance, one which those writing within mainstream development discourse such as Paul Collier and Michael Ross are oddly quiet about. This is quite simply that mining operations usually take place without the permission of local people. Land is forcibly taken and no compensation offered for the destruction of collective assets (such as forests, common grazing land or water resources). Mining has a tendency to cause untold damage, pollution and destruction to the environment. When sanctioned by a distant government more concerned with economic growth and foreign revenue than the distant and 'undeveloped' wilderness where extraction takes place, it is hardly surprising that violent conflicts flare.

The case of Bougainville in the Solomons Archipelago is among the most well-known example of war resulting from the attempts to extract resources by a distant state: in the first instance, the colonial Australian administration and, later, the in-coming Papua New Guinean (PNG) government. Not only were Bougainvillians offered desultory levels of compensation for the loss of their assets, but the livelihoods of many were destroyed by the pollution to rivers and land caused by mining in the region. Protests and negotiations for compensation had been taking place since the first development of the mine in the late 1950s. When it finally became clear that neither the PNG government nor Rio Tinto would acknowledge the scale of destruction, the people of Bougainville mobilised. That was in 1989. Since then the civil war has cost thousands of lives (Havini and Johns, 2002). While Bougainville is an extreme example, there are few cases where the large-scale extraction of resources by multinationals in poor countries has not led to local protest and mobilisation. In Duniyapur, experiences of dispossession and feelings of powerlessness and fear concerning the environmental, and health and safety consequences of the gas field are shared by many people.

In sum, the prospects for Bangladesh, were it to be rich in natural gas and coal, are somewhat worrying. Here we have a country with a government that is already noted for its corruption and lack of transparency,[26] plus high levels of poverty and a fragile state which, as we shall see in the next chapter, is already mired in the politics of patronage. Could a gas-rich Bangladesh take a similar path to Nigeria?

At this stage, I think it unlikely, though there are some interesting parallels. For a start, it is gas and coal, not oil, that have been discovered in Bangladesh, and as yet the reserves are hardly abundant. Indeed, one of the main issues debated by those who support and those who oppose their extraction by multinationals is just how large these reserves actually are, with some commentators declaring that they're more limited than originally thought. For example, while in September 2010 the discovery of new reserves in Sunamganj, in the western part of the Surma Basin, was being hailed as the biggest find yet, at the same time contracts were being signed with India for the import of gas.[27] Indeed, gas and coal do not make a significant contribution to GDP, half of which is made up of the service sector; in 2009 garments and remittances contributed to around 25 percent of the GDP. As these figures indicate, Bangladesh already has an established manufacturing base, with an economy that is slowly growing rather than one that is shrinking. Most importantly, gas is not yet being exported. 'Dutch disease' is therefore unlikely, at least so long as the government continues to use the reserves for the domestic market.

Yet the dangers remain. Indeed, some of the effects of the 'resource curse' are already discernible in Duniyapur: increased unease about corruption and the need for transparency are central plot-lines in many of the stories that follow, as are heightened local conflict and increased levels of struggle over resources. The environmental effects of the gas field pale in comparison with the horror stories cited in the next section, but changes to the fragile eco-system, with its dependence upon seasonal inundation of water from the Kushiara River, are central to many people's accounts of changes to their livelihood. The role of the transnational mining company is also vital. As Auty (1993) suggests, an important aspect of the resource curse is that, because large capital investments are necessary, the lion's share of profits goes to the multinationals who are able to make the investment rather than national governments.

That foreign companies profit from natural resources at the expense of national interests is the central concern of those who oppose the presence of companies such as Chevron in Bangladesh. Meanwhile others argue that the country needs foreign investment and that, with their vast financial and technological clout, Chevron and others are best placed to drill for and extract the gas. In addition, their supporters argue, Chevron operates according to international standards, following ethical codes of corporate social responsibility. Corporate documents such as 'The Chevron way'[28] suggest that local communities are supported by Chevron, that their environmental practices are beyond criticism, and their employees offered fair and equitable contracts. Others go further, hailing CSR as playing a potentially progressive role in combating poverty and supporting human rights and good governance in the developing countries where transnational corporations work.[29]

Can transnational mining companies contribute in positive ways to the places where they operate? The tension between those who believe this is possible and those who are convinced that their activities are inherently exploitative is a central aspect of the story of Duniyapur.

TRANSNATIONAL EXTRACTIVE CORPORATIONS: FROM DISPOSSESSION AND DESTRUCTION TO 'CORPORATE SOCIAL RESPONSIBILITY'?

To say that transnational mining companies have a reputation for global misdemeanours is an understatement, to say the least. The BP oil spill at Deepwater in the Gulf of Mexico in 2010, possibly the biggest environmental disaster of our time and certainly that which has attracted the most publicity, reveals the momentous environmental risks taken in the name of profit. From April to July in 2010, 185 million gallons of crude oil gushed into the sea, destroying the fragile marine environment for hundreds of miles as well as the fishing and tourist industry in the Gulf. Despite efforts over recent decades to brand themselves as 'green' and 'sustainable', BP was now a corporate pariah, its global reputation in tatters. Once again it seemed that transnational mining companies were in the spotlight, accused of 'crimes against nature and humanity'.[30]

Deepwater is of course not the first such disaster or scandal associated with a transnational mining corporation and doubtless it will not be the last. Two of the most notorious examples, taken from a long and horrendous list,[31] are, first, the actions of Royal Dutch Shell in the Niger Delta, where, as well as widespread environmental damage, the company has been accused of complicity in the human rights abuses of the military government, and, second, the alleged dumping of around 180 billion gallons of toxic waste water into the Amazon by Texaco (now Chevron) in Ecuador from 1964 to 1990, causing profound damage to the forest eco-system and serious health problems for the local people (see Donzinger, 2009).[32] As Stuart Kirsch has eloquently argued, the phrase 'sustainable mining', increasingly beloved of corporations such as BP that present themselves as 'green' and ethical, is an oxymoron (Kirsch, 2010a). Since mining involves the extraction of natural resources which cannot be replaced, it can never be 'sustainable'.

Environmental devastation usually means that those close to the sites of resource extraction lose their homes and livelihoods. Dispossession of people from their traditional lands, their forced resettlement and/or destruction of their livelihoods is a depressingly regular occurrence in the history of mining corporations, from their colonial antecedents to the present day (Korten, 2002). Presided over by distant and authoritarian states, often with the assistance of the army, with profits siphoned into the pockets of politicians before the lion's share goes abroad, and leaving nothing but a trail of destruction, it is hardly surprising that mining has become known as a dirty business. The following excerpts, taken from articles on Boungainville and the Freeport Copper and Gold mine in West Papua, illustrate what, tragically, has become an 'archetype' of devastation. In Bougainville, the story goes like this:

Over a billion tonnes of poisonous tailings from the mine were dumped straight into the Kawerong and Jaba Rivers.... The tailings contained heavy metals such as copper, zinc, cadmium, mercury and molybdenum – these washes are also high in sulphur, arsenic and mercury. The systemic effects of cadmium include fatal illnesses, severe breathlessness, lung and kidney damage, anaemia and adverse reproductive effects. The early symptoms of mercury poisoning include psychological and emotional disturbances, tremors, kidney disease, nerve degeneration and also adverse reproductive effects. Before the mine even started, hundreds of hectares of forest were poisoned then chopped down and burnt. Whole forests died. Birds, flying foxes and possums disappeared. The Panguna Valley was turned into a huge crater. By mid 1971 the naturally clear rivers were already silted, had increased in size and intensity and widened, causing blocked stream flows in many places, causing flooding and new swampland. The toxic wastes were carried down the Jaba River to the coast, leaving a trail of death 35 kilometres long. (Havini and Johns, 2002: 140)

Accounts of the Freeport Copper and Gold mine in West Papua are depressingly similar:

When Freeport arrived in the late 1960s, the Amumgme and Kamoro were living subsistence lifestyles in a spiritually significant landscape. They now live amidst a sea of industrial technology that has transformed their homelands into a heavily populated, militarised metropolis, mining pits, hazardous waste dumps and flooded coastal plains where tropical rain forest once stood. The pace and scale of change are hard to imagine. A deluge of economic migrants to their homelands, and daily deposits into their rivers of more than 200 000 tonnes of mine tailings have destroyed the life they knew. (Kennedy and Abrash, 2002)

My point is not simply that mining is dirty (in the most literal meaning of the word) or that it has long been associated with human rights abuses, colonial exploitation and horrific environmental damage.[33] It is also that transnational mining companies have acquired an extremely bad reputation on the global stage.

To say that the practices and rhetoric of 'corporate social responsibility' have arisen solely as a reaction to this reputation is overly simplistic, but the 'sins of the fathers' may go some way in explaining why CEOs (chief executive officers) today are so keen to stress their ethical credentials. Over the last decade there are few, if any, transnational extractive corporations that do not participate in the discourse of CSR, whether through signing up to global codes of ethical business practice such as the Global Compact,[34] funding community development at or close to the sites where they operate, or presenting themselves as 'ethical' employers in their corporate literature. All major transnational mining companies today publish annual CSR reports. As we will see in Chapter 5, phrases such as 'partnership' and 'sustainable' abound.

Corporate philanthropy is not of course new. Industrialists have been providing social welfare for their employees since the nineteenth century, when companies such as Cadbury's provided education, housing and other benefits for their workers (Rajak, 2008: 6). Indeed, few CEOs would admit that their businesses were ever 'unethical'. As Rio Tinto's CEO Robert Wilson put it in a speech in 2001:

> Debate about Corporate Social Responsibility may be of recent origin but caring, responsible management is certainly not. Few, if any, large companies have ever pursued profit at the expense of all other values. In many companies there has long been recognition that there is more to business than simply short-term profit. Indeed, in complex and sensitive businesses, such as those in the extractive industries, the creation of long-term shareholder wealth is incompatible with a purely near-term profit focus.[35]

While some observers might be rather less congratulatory about the ethical provenance of companies such as Rio Tinto, it is correct to state that *all* economic practices are embedded in particular moral orders; this, after all, is the premise of economic anthropology, from Mauss onwards. Perhaps one of the distinguishing characteristics of the contemporary period is not so much that morality exists but that the discourse of CSR makes it explicit and attempts to turn it into (economic) value. Combined with this, CSR is significantly different from the philanthropy and paternalism of previous epochs of 'caring capitalism', underscored by different ethical imperatives such as 'sustainability' and 'partnership'. Over recent years it has mushroomed from being something special associated with a few 'ethical' companies (for example, the Body Shop or fair-trade coffee) to a range of practices and codes that most large companies in need of the approbation of shareholders and consumers are almost duty bound to engage with. Presented as 'the friendly face of capitalism',

CSR involves an attempt to 'balance the needs of stakeholders with the need to make a profit' (Doane, 2005: 3).

Viewed in utilitarian terms, CSR is justified and expounded for two reasons. The first is that it is good for business. The second is that it is good for development. In the statements of CEOs and donors alike, CSR thus produces a 'win win' situation: capitalism extends the hand of friendship to the Third World, partnerships are forged, the lot of the poor is improved and – best of all – neoliberal values extended, new markets created and profits made. As we shall see, there are many reasons why this scenario is an unlikely outcome. The main one is that the need to make a profit and the work of development are in many ways contradictory, although this obviously depends upon what one believes 'development' to be. I shall return to the CSR = good development paradigm shortly. First, let's consider the first proposition: that CSR = good business.

CSR = 'Good' Business

Can business be 'good'? If by 'good' one means 'thriving and profitable', the answer is obviously 'yes'. But if by 'good' one means 'morally upstanding', the answer is highly complex. What makes CSR such a slippery concept is that those who support it claim that it is 'good' in both senses and, indeed, that bringing morality into business not only makes sense in utilitarian terms, adding to profits and reducing operational risks, but somehow – in ways that are submerged and reach deeply into the moral orders underlying early twenty-first-century neoliberal capitalism – economic growth, the extension of particular forms of economic and political organisation and the creation of certain kinds of consumers/producers are themselves morally worthy activities.

The growth of CSR – as a discourse and as a set of activities – is due in part to growing awareness of, and international outcry against practices deemed unpalatable by First World consumers: child or bonded labour, exploitative terms of trade and actions that are environmentally damaging are high on the list, plus a growing awareness of the interconnectedness of global economies: that cheap clothes in high street stores mean cheap and thus exploited labour somewhere else is generally accepted by most morally concerned shoppers. This shift in thinking is exemplified by Naomi Klein's book, *No Logo* (2002), which linked exploitative labour relations and other misdeeds to major brands such as Nike, McDonald's and the Gap, as well as the wider anti-globalisation movement. Today, as never before, *exposés* of child labour in Mumbai can be circulated globally by journalists working alongside NGOs and civil society organisations, the images ricocheting across the world in YouTube footage and Facebook activism so that, within only a few hours, consumers reaching for their bargain-basement garments in Brighton, Stockholm or Boston may have second thoughts.

Debates concerning the morality, or immorality, of 'bad' business are not new; what has changed is the way they are carried out and the impact they have. The role of the East India Company in causing the Bengal Famine of 1770, for example, caused outrage in Britain, with Horace Walpole declaring that: 'we have murdered, deposed, plundered, usurped, – nay what think you of the famine of Bengal in which three millions perished, being caused by a monopoly of provisions of the servants of the East Indies?' (cited in Robins, 2006: 95). Yet, as Nick Robins documents, despite such attacks, the company shrugged off the criticism and continued to go about its business in the same way as before. Similar moral qualms were also expressed over slavery, so key to the growth of nineteenth-century capitalism (Blowfield and Frynas, 2005: 500).

What *is* different in the current period is that ethical concerns, or at the very least, international exposure of unethical conduct, matters so much more. One reason for this, which Dinah Rajak explores in her ethnography of the CSR practices of Anglo American in South Africa, is that the employees and directors of transnational companies themselves subscribe to the moralities and values submerged in CSR and present deeply personal reasons for engaging in it, with romanticised views of participation, empowerment and so on (Rajak, 2011).

Crucially, too, global reputation affects stock price (the value of BP shares plummeted over the summer of 2010), for, as Rajak (2011) argues, morality has entered the market as never before. Indeed, rather than simply aiming at profit, nowadays business is *expected* to carry out its affairs in an ethically acceptable manner. If it doesn't, it is in danger of global *exposés* and the loss of consumer confidence: moral panics surrounding particular goods and companies are commonplace, creating arenas where ethics can be negotiated and tested. The recent panic surrounding exploitative labour practices in India to produce cheap clothes for Primark is an example *par excellence*.[36]

A major reason for these moral panics, which are invariably followed by changes in practice and the hasty uptake or reinforcement of codes of conduct by companies accused of ethical breaches, is the linking of morality with consumption. The individualism and privatisation of societies in the post-industrial West mean that morality is expressed as lifestyle choice and these 'lifestyles' invariably involve consumerism. Discourses of human rights, democracy and justice, core to such moral orders, are thus extended to the market as well as the state and other spheres of public life. Indeed, within twenty-first-century neoliberalism the market, in the guise of 'consumerism', is perhaps the 'natural' place for them to end up. The fair-trade movement, and 'bench marks' such as the Soil Association for organic produce or Rugmark for carpets made without exploitative labour relations, are pertinent examples.[37] As Stuart Kirsch argues with reference to the BP oil spill:

> the neo-liberal response to environmental disaster is to transfer responsibility from corporations to consumers. The philosophy of green consumerism asserts that consumer preference will be more effective in changing corporate behaviour than government regulation.... In this formulation political agency is equated with purchasing power; one must literally buy into the system to express one's point of view. Green consumerism also offers a striking example of how political sentiments are converted into non-political modes of action: the transformation of the environmental movement into green consumerism makes the world safe for shopping as usual. (2010a: 298–9)

Yet while shoppers and stockholders can exercise their moral judgement by refusing to buy particular types of clothing, coffee or shares in companies with morally dubious provenance, and processes of globalisation – in particular the internet – mean that bad reputation can be easily acquired, for transnational extractive corporations the 'risk to reputation' is not confined to consumerism. Indeed, for corporations involved in the extraction of oil, coal or gas, appeasing the moral qualms of high street shoppers is not really an issue: we might be aware that the oil on which we depend is linked to environmental destruction, human rights abuses and war but, as consumers, only a handful of highly 'alternative' individuals can seriously attempt to live without it.[38]

Shareholders may of course put pressure on companies such as BP, Shell or Chevron to conduct their business in a more ethically correct way. The AGMs (annual general meetings) of transnational mining companies are often targeted by activists hoping to undermine the corporate image of global do-gooder. In May 2010, for example, five activists were arrested after they interrupted Chevron's annual shareholders' meeting in Houston.[39] The importance of reputation means that claims of corporate morality are often foregrounded in advertising campaigns, a strategy which leaves companies vulnerable to their critics and can create fertile ground for satire. Corporate narratives of morality thus slug it out with activist accusations of hypocrisy, often via the internet. In October 2010, for example, in response to the launch of Chevron's 'We Agree' campaign,[40] the arts activist group the Yes Men in conjunction with the Rainforest Action Network and Amazon Watch released their own spoof website, satirising Chevron's claims.[41]

One way for companies to deal with criticism is to co-opt their fiercest critics. In his article 'When corporations want to cuddle', Burton (2002) explores this process, describing how in the 1990s PR consultants advised corporations such as Rio Tinto that the best way to deal with critics was not to deny accusations of malpractice, but admit to mistakes, even letting the critics 'win' and offering to collaborate in future endeavours. Partnership with human rights groups, NGOs and even some (former) activists has thus become a key element in CSR, a process accelerated by the United Nations (UN) Global Compact in 1999, in which 'partnership' between UN agencies and corporations was key (Burton, 2002). What Doane (2005) calls 'partnering with the enemy' has become an important corporate strategy in fighting off attacks to reputation and 'looking good', though the relationships can be perilous for NGOs which also have good reputations to maintain.

Writing of Rio Tinto's CSR programmes, Paul Kapelus argues that partnership with local NGOs 'provides them with a cloak of legitimacy that serves to protect them from charges by other groups ... and enables them to continue with their activities with a minimum of disruption and cost' (2002: 280). Centrally, too, dialogue with critics helps produce the self-justifying narratives of corporate executives and CSR practitioners, affecting future tactics and discursive representations (Welker, 2009: 147). By using the language of NGOs and environmental activists, CSR managers become experts in 'talking the talk', disguising the fact that they rarely 'walk the walk'.

If 'partnering with the enemy' might be described as 'greenwash', so might the volunteerism that ethical codes such as the Global Compact involve. This does not mean that either are cynical fakery; there can be little doubt that the majority of CSR practitioners and corporate executives genuinely believe that such strategies are morally good. Seen more cynically, signing up to international codes of conduct is hardly difficult, especially when corporate compliance to these codes cannot be enforced and there are few mechanisms to demonstrate real accountability. Indeed, as Kirsch (2006: 128) argues, neoliberal policy reforms transfer responsibility for monitoring impacts from states to corporations. One effect of this is that people have to make their compensation claims to companies and not states or international bodies. The long-running case against Chevron by communities in Amazonian Ecuador, where, it is claimed, oil extraction has led to pollution on a horrific scale, is a case in point.[42]

As Jenkins (2005: 528) notes, it is significant that the Global Compact does not refer to equity or poverty reduction. Given claims that CSR is 'good for development', this seems an odd omission, but perhaps it depends on what is meant by 'development'. While Chevron executives in Bangladesh were not aware of the Global Compact, the company is introducing its own environmental and social auditing, which, I was assured, would be 'rolled out' over 2010. Such procedures mean that companies give the impression of being motivated by ethics rather than being forced to comply with international regulations. It also means that external auditing procedures pass them by: projects are evaluated by hired consultants rather than disinterested outsiders, and the results of their auditing not made publicly available. It is perhaps no coincidence that, despite efforts put into auditing, social and environmental risk assessments and so on (which I was not allowed to see) during the period of our research, Chevron Bangladesh had no grievance procedures in place for people in the communities that are their 'partners'. Chevron's statement of ethical principles, 'The Chevron Way' is given in Appendix 1 (see also Global Compact Principles, page 246, note 34).

While much CSR and the PR that it involves is aimed at global reputation, there are other, more utilitarian reasons why 'good' business equals good business. The first is that for companies seeking to expand their territories or to 'accumulate by dispossession' (Harvey, 2003), CSR is conscious strategy to gain the permission of local people to carry out operations or a 'social license to mine' (Rajak, 2011). In some contexts this may appear to be little more than 'bribery'.[43] In others, notions of compensation or 'giving back to the community' are elided in the moral justification for CSR programmes made by executives. In Duniyapur, the rationale for the 'Alternative Livelihood' programme, which was key to Chevron's 'community engagement' strategy, was explained to me as being motivated by the desire to support local people who had lost their livelihoods but had not been able to claim financial compensation as they were sharecroppers and not owners of the land.

In local contexts, 'Reputation' is vital because if this is 'bad' the company will have to deal not only with activists at shareholders' meetings, but also localised opposition, which may physically prevent the mining from taking place. Phulbari was a corporate nightmare: not only did the opposition campaign against Asia Energy's attempts to develop the coal mine attract international media attention, but it also actively prevented the Bangladeshi government from issuing a contract to the company, closing Asia Energy's offices in Phulbari Town and making it impossible for local people to work for the company (Nuremowla, 2012).

Security issues are thus closely aligned to CSR. To this extent it can be understood as the friendly face of Dispossession Capital, the hand-shaking, appeasing technocrats who promise 'development' and 'partnership' stepping in smilingly after the gun-wielding security forces have departed. The complex relationship between Soft-spoken CSR and Hard-faced, even Violent, Security is described with great effect by Marina Welker, who shows how local elites, already organised into NGOs and civil society organisations, were co-opted by the Newmont mining development in Batu Hijau, Indonesia. Since these groups gained control of the community development benefits being offered by Newmont, it was in their interest to violently repress anti-mining protests by environmental activists. While Newmont is a signatory to the Global Compact and mine guards have been given human rights training, Welker argues that the CSR programme has 'produced fresh zones of struggle and new forces of violence' in the area (2009: 146). Rather than being the work of mine guards, the violence was carried out by the elite groups against environmental protesters, who, by attacking the mine, were attacking the source of benefits and 'development' on which the elite's interests were staked. By eliding themselves with the environmental movement, CSR managers were able to undermine the claims of the protesters, using the discourse of criticism to counter-attack the protesters (Welker, 2009).

In Chapter 6 we see how, in Duniyapur, local protest against the development of the gas field was halted in part by Chevron's offers of community development. According to the accounts of some people in 2005–6, a section of the protest movement's most vociferous leaders were effectively co-opted into the CSR programme, a move which carried risks as well as rewards for these individuals. To this extent, CSR acts as an 'anti-politics machine', the neoliberal language of participation and partnership erasing histories of opposition and dispossession (Sawyer, 2004: 19; Zalik, 2004).

If CSR programmes are linked to security concerns at the local level, aiming at community compliance (or 'partnership'), they may also be analysed as a form of governance, extending the control of the company over its territories. Such governance is not confined to road safety awareness campaigns or the health and safety of employees, even if these are the most visually explicit signs. Instead, anthropologists have argued that CSR involves the implicit transmission of neoliberal values via programmes that stress income generation, micro-credit and particular styles of work. Geert De Neve's research in the garment factories of Tripura, for example, shows how ethical codes of conduct are insisted upon by multinational buyers, but sometimes impose conditions of employment that local workers find inflexible and inappropriate (2009). As Dinah Rajak writes: 'The moral economy of CSR represents not an opposition to the contemporary world of corporate capitalism but the very mechanism through which corporate power is authenticated, extended and endowed with moral authority' (2007: 282). In Chapter 5 I shall be extending this perspective to Duniyapur, where we see how the narratives and performances of successful 'community engagement' produced by Chevron's executives not only bring moral value of a certain kind to the company, but attempt to override alternative narratives, of conflict, rupture and loss.

Is CSR good for business? The answer is that in today's globalised moral economy, big business runs considerable risk to reputation without it. In a recent editorial in *The Economist* (January 2008), Daniel Franklin suggests that CSR has become so ubiquitous and diverse that it is almost impossible to evaluate. Categorising CSR practices into three levels (old style philanthropy, damage limitation and, finally, 'doing well by doing good'), Franklin argues that very few companies engage in the third form of CSR, raising various complex questions. Is 'being green' really good for business? Should companies work with their competitors in developing their CSR strategies? How can success be measured?[44]

CSR = Good Development

While the public face of global corporations means that representations of ethically correct practice are now mandatory, there is little evidence to suggest that CSR programmes necessarily lead to 'good' development, despite the claims made for it. Again, it depends what is meant by 'development'. As Jenkins (2005) points out, definitions have shifted over recent decades from being based around state-led economic growth to the UN Millennium Goals, which are more focused upon human indicators of well-being such as health, education and so on. In this context, the employment and income generated by multinational industries alone are not enough to promote the right kind of 'development'.

One of the problems of trying to assess whether or not CSR 'works' for development is that the term covers a huge range of practices, from the 'add-ons' of community-based projects surrounding a mining site, to the insistence of global brands that their suppliers follow particular ethical codes of employment. In an Issues Paper on CSR (2001) DFID states that the development potential of CSR is not the programmes or initiatives it might fund, which are little different from conventional corporate philanthropy, but the influence that corporations can put on governments and other stakeholders to uphold ethical codes concerning employment, transparency, anti-corruption drives and human rights.[45] Overall, international business is good for development, the paper argues, and can produce positive changes via 'multi-stakeholder partnerships' as well as their core operations, which produce knowledge, income and employment.[46] The real challenge, however, is for international business to engage in public policy, influencing governmental processes of transparency and so on.[47]

To this end, schemes such as the Extractive Industries Transparency Initiative (EITI) have been set up, encouraging mining companies to support transparency and accountability in the countries where they work, setting a standard for them to publish what they pay and governments to disclose what they receive from natural resource revenues.[48] Chevron is a signatory to the EITI but since the government of Bangladesh is not, the company does not have to reveal details of its contracts there. Meanwhile, American legislation which will force companies registered on the US stock market to reveal information about all their global projects has not yet come into force.[49] And while movements are afoot in the UK to support European legislation that forces mining companies to reveal the financial details of their deals with governments (in this case in Africa),[50] to date the pressure is moral rather than legal and left to lobbying groups such as Publish What You Pay to enforce. As I shall argue at the end of the book, transparency of this sort is crucial if multinationals extracting natural resources are to have a positive impact in countries such as Bangladesh.

While for some the development potential of CSR involves the pressure that multinational corporations might potentially put on governments and other institutions and 'multi-stakeholder partnerships', the question of whether big business can lead to the alleviation of poverty is slightly different, especially in the case of the extractive industries. Indeed, as Jenkins aptly states: 'Almost by definition, the poor are those who do not have a stake' (2005: 540).

If the aim of greater state transparency concerning business deals or the establishment of ethical codes of employment and so on don't directly benefit the poorest, who are unlikely to gain employment in the plants of extractive multinationals or ever become stakeholders, there are other ways in which the 'community development' add-ons of what DFID terms 'corporate philanthropy' are limited in their effectiveness. As we shall see in Chapter 5, these programmes, and the CSR managers who run them, often have contradictory aims. Instituted as part of a policy to promote global reputation, the long-term, frustrating and tricky business of 'community development' is often sacrificed for short-term glory. Buzz words and glossy publicity photos rule the roost, while difficult questions concerning who actually has benefited and what 'participation' and 'empowerment' really mean are dodged. In Duniyapur the 'development' aspired to by CSR executives is of a globally 'saleable' kind: rural peasants 'empowered' to have sustainable livelihoods. What people want, however, is a more old-fashioned 'development': infrastructure and basic services, jobs and political security.

More generally, whether or not the presence of extractive multinationals in countries such as Bangladesh leads to a lessening of poverty depends upon one's ideological stance. While DFID and the World Bank clearly believe that the exploitation of the country's gas and coal reserves by multinationals will lead to growth, and hence contribute to a reduction in poverty, others argue that a positive link between the presence of multinationals, natural resource extraction and poverty is far from guaranteed, for resource extraction invariably involves dispossessing large numbers of people from the land and profits are accumulated by the elite. Indeed, there is ample evidence that global capitalism has a habit of increasing inequality and hence *exacerbating* poverty, especially at its territorial fringes. As Li argues: 'interventions that set the conditions for growth simultaneously set the conditions for some sections of the population to be dispossessed. Winners and losers do not emerge naturally through the magic of the market; they are selected' (2007: 20).

While multilateral and bilateral donors such as the World Bank and DFID are largely positive about CSR, international NGOs tend to be more critical, possibly because they have a more poverty-focused approach to development and do not see economic growth as an end in itself. A report by Christian Aid in 2004, for example, argues that: 'CSR is a completely inadequate response to the sometimes devastating impact that multinational companies have' (Christian Aid, 2004; 2, cited in Jenkins, 2005: 526). The literature on the developmental potential of CSR is therefore divided between what Kirsch calls the 'light greens', who believe that the market is the solution to the problem and are willing to collaborate with corporations, and the 'dark greens', who view the market as part of the problem and remain sceptical about corporate claims to self-improvement (Kirsch, 2010a: 2).

In concluding this section, let us ponder the words of Rio Tinto's Robert Wilson:

This brings to mind a little story told to me by Rio Tinto's senior anthropologist.

'Over a hundred years ago', he said, 'anthropologists wrote books about savages on the basis of armchair reflection. Instead of visiting savages, the authors designed questionnaires in their studies and sent them to reliable travellers and others in the field in the hope that, once completed, they would confirm what the armchair anthropologists had thought in the first place. Since it was commonly believed that savages were promiscuous, any salacious details about savages tended to be believed and repeated without any of the armchair anthropologists bothering to test the quality of the information.'

In much the same way, I would suggest, tales that conform to the popular stereotype of the wicked global corporation tend to be believed today. None of the eminent armchair anthropologists thought it was necessary to go and live with savages in order to understand them. When asked if he had ever met any of the savages he so convincingly described, Sir James Frazier, the early Cambridge anthropologist replied:

'Good Heavens, no!'

How many latter-day James Fraziers are there out there in the new social science of 'Socially Responsible Investment?'[51]

The answer to Sir Wilson's question is: 'You won't catch many anthropologists of CSR sitting in their armchairs. They're too busy probing questions of power and inequality, whether this takes them to the air-conditioned offices of mining companies or the mud and straw huts of those at the receiving end of those companies' "socially responsible investments". Very few, if any, come up with conclusions that you would feel comfortable with.' Indeed, rather than simply asking whether or not CSR 'works' or is good for business/development, anthropologists such as Catherine Dolan, Dinah Rajak and Geert De Neve are analysing CSR as discourse and, as such, an exercise in power, focusing on the nuances of how such power is exercised and what it does, whether intenionally or not (De Neve, 2009; Dolan, 2007; Rajak, 2011). Throughout this book, I will take a similar approach, neither aiming to give Chevron's programmes a stamp of approval, nor dismiss them simply as 'greenwash', but asking throughout what forms of power are legitimated or changed by the community engagement programmes in Duniyapur, what realities they shape, and the ensuing struggles within which they are implicated.

In the final part of this introduction, let us move from the more pragmatic and immediately political questions of the role of multinationals and CSR and their intended or unintended consequences, and turn directly to the arguments and theoretical perspectives which underpin the book.

IDEAS AND ARGUMENTS

Entitlements and Claims

In the chapters that follow we see how the lives of people in the villages that surround the gas field are largely dominated by constant and often bitter struggles over scarce resources: food, land and employment. Within national and global as well as local domains, gas reserves are another site of struggle, in which the attempt to establish extractive rights over the reserves by multinational energy companies is fiercely contested by a range of actors. The context is one of vast disparities of wealth and power which exist at every level. Unlike the struggles against mining companies described by Suzana Sawyer (2004) in Ecuador or Stuart Kirsch (2006) in Papua New Guinea, where the companies are opposed by indigenous groups that appear to be largely united and undifferentiated by class, in Duniyapur inequalities are firmly entrenched, not just between Chevron and its 'partners in the community' but also within those communities, between landowners and labourers, transnational migrants and 'their own poor', and 'village leaders' and those they are imagined (in the romanticised anti-politics of neoliberal development discourse) to be leading.

The extent of poverty and degree of inequality cannot be overstated. While smart cars whisk executives and highly trained foreign staff along the purpose-built roads and into the gas field, some of the people they have passed along the way are profoundly malnourished, missing meals in lean periods, living in darkness after sunset, without electricity and unable to afford much in the way of medicine or education. How can this be so?

One way to theorise these struggles for resources and the inequalities in which they are embedded is via Amartya Sen's theory of *entitlement* (1982, 1999). In his analysis of famine Sen writes that:

> Starvation is the characteristic of some people not HAVING enough food to eat. It is not the characteristic of there not BEING enough food to eat ... food supply statements say something about a commodity (or a group of commodities) on its own. Starvation statements are about a relationship of persons to that commodity ... [these] translate readily into statements of ownership of food by persons. In order to understand starvation it is therefore necessary to go into the structure of ownership. Ownership relations are one kind of entitlement relations. It is necessary to understand the entitlement systems within which the problem of starvation is to be analysed ... (1982: 1)

For Sen the entitlement that people enjoy over food depends upon their *endowment* (what they own and their labour power), their productive possibilities and the conditions of exchange that prevail (1999: 162–3). In Duniyapur, these endowments are formalised in terms of property ownership and the markets where food, commodities and labour are exchanged. Yet while these formal economic conditions and relationships are vitally important in determining who is entitled to what, people's endowments also involve informal social relationships through which other claims over resources can be made. For example, in addition to selling her labour, a landless woman might need to gain 'help' from local patrons or relatives, who because of their social connection to her and the claims she is making on them, will loan or donate rice or cash in times of need. In the labour market, too, people are often hired because of pre-existing social relationships, usually in the form of long established patron–client relationships. People who rely on selling their labour as their *endowment* often only do so as the result of claims made on their patrons, just as those seeking land as sharecroppers may make claims on landowners based on kinship and/or patronage.

While Sen is writing of famine and extreme deprivation, in the chapters that follow I expand on his ideas to consider how, within the systems of entitlement that structure access to resources in Duniyapur and its transnational sites, different types of claim are made. Financial compensation for forcibly acquired land involves a legal and bureaucratic claim made by landowners, just as Chevron's claim to be in Duniyapur and extract gas from under its fields is based on a legal contract between the company and the government of Bangladesh. Yet surrounding these formalised claims and systems are others, based on various moral orders and epistemologies. For example, in their CSR programmes in Duniyapur, Chevron are making a claim based around the ethics and moralities of global neoliberal capital: they have the moral right to be doing their work, since they are contributing to community development and other good works. Similarly, claims for compensation in the form of employment at the gas field by local landless people are based on moralities of justice and analyses of global exploitation, while claims for *shahajo* (help) made to local and transnational patrons are based on moralities of kinship and Islamic charity.

I shall return to these various forms of claim making in a short while. For now, let us consider more closely the importance of connection in the entitlement systems of Duniyapur.

Getting a Connection: Power and Connectivity in Duniyapur

Connectivity is vital in Duniyapur. In order to do or get hold of almost anything, one has first to be connected to other people, whether they are located within the area, in state bureaucracies, or across transnational space. The very poor access extra cash or rice for their evening meal via their social connections to neighbours or patrons to whom they may or may not be related; the less poor migrate via connections to *Londoni* relatives who are already securely connected to the UK. These relatives either help arrange marriages in Britain or provide the capital for labour migration to the Middle East (Gardner, 2008; Gardner and Ahmed, 2009). Meanwhile farmers requiring fertilisers or land to cultivate need connections either to the government bureaucrats who control the supply of fertilisers and seeds, or landlords who own the land.[52]

Within this context Bourdieu's notion of social capital is useful. Bourdieu defined social capital as:

> the aggregate of the actual or potential resources which are linked to possession of a durable network of more or less institutionalized relationships of mutual acquaintance and recognition. (1983: 249)

While Bourdieu was largely focused on how links in social networks help maintain privileges among elites (via knowing the right people), by recognising how social networks are themselves resources, one moves away from a reductive analysis of power and class which focuses solely upon material capital: land, say, or money. For the poor in Duniyapur, social resources are vital. Indeed, it is the poor who are most dependent upon social connections; those with formal connections to material resources may rely upon knowing the right people in arranging marriages with *Londonis*, making business deals or getting things done within state bureaucracy, but they are not dependent upon them for their everyday survival.

This observation, which has also been noted by Geof Wood (2005) runs counter to Bourdieu's perspective of social capital as working to the advantage of the elite, but chimes directly with an analysis of patron–client relations, in which one's links to relatively wealthy patrons (one's social capital) are key to economic and political survival. While for the privileged their social capital helps maintain their positions at the top of the pile for the poor it can mean that they can *only* get and do things via their connections to more powerful patrons.

Patronage thrives in places where the state fails to deliver basic services and social protection such as health care, pensions, social welfare and so on and where formal economic institutions such as banks, insurance companies or pension schemes have a limited reach. While *connectivity* is a key plot line in Duniyapur, almost every story that follows can be traced to the ongoing inability of the Bangladeshi state to provide for its population. Inefficiency, corruption and political instability are recurrent tropes, as is global inequality – Bangladesh is still one of the poorest countries in the world.[53] Underlying this state of affairs is a long and unhappy history, in which the conditions for a weak and corrupt state, and the poverty over which it presides were put in place by British colonialism, the division of East from West Bengal and the subsequent divisions with, and independence from, Pakistan – a history which I shall briefly cover in the next chapter.

Bourdieu was mostly interested in the maintenance of class position among elite groups in France, and the implication of his theory of various sorts of capital is one of stasis: a person's relative levels of social capital keeps them in their place. In Duniyapur however, connectivity can lead to the transformation of one's social and economic standing, for it is via social connections that one can access particular places, in particular the UK, and these places, as centres of global capitalism, can bring transformation (Gardner, 1995). As we shall see in Chapter 2, once these geographical connections have been secured via residency visas or citizenship, the opportunities for radical economic change are considerable, and the need for social connections to the *desh* (homeland) becomes more emotional than economic. In this sense, the potential of connectivity is contextual: it can keep some people in their place while offering others the chance of transformation.

While in Bourdieu's analysis social capital is related to the functioning of class hierarchy, in other contexts the term is used to denote a range of positive characteristics. Putnam's work, for example, has informed the World Bank's approach to social capital, in which it has been detached from social theory and turned into a developmental good, for which a range of policies can be instituted. As Putman puts it:

> Whereas physical capital refers to physical objects and human capital refers to the properties of individuals, social capital refers to connections among individuals – social networks and the norms of reciprocity and trustworthiness that arise from them. In that sense social capital is closely related to what some have called 'civic virtue.' The difference is that 'social capital' calls attention to the fact that civic virtue is most powerful when embedded in a sense network of reciprocal social relations. (2000: 19)

What Putman describes is not far removed from David Cameron's 'Big Society' – a Tory utopia where the state has withdrawn from the provision of basic services, allowing reciprocal civic virtue to arise in its wake. In Bangladesh, the micro-credit movement, pioneered by, among others, Muhamad Yunus of the Grameen Bank, builds upon similar ideals: developing lending schemes within the context of firmly established cultures of reciprocity, individual duty to the collectivity (*samaj*, or society). This is what we might think of as 'nice' social capital, in which social networks provide informal support and resources in place of a state that is either retreating or has never performed such a role. The 'nasty' side is a patron–client system in which the elite maintain their position, the poor remain dependent and the state has few if any responsibilities.[54]

Although in their analyses of social capital Putman and Bourdieu take different theoretical and political positions, in Duniyapur both perspectives are useful, for connectivity – the need to know the right people – has both nice and nasty sides. The stories that follow arise in part from these contradictions. What in one context appear to be laudable responsibilities of care to relatives or 'one's own poor', or 'informal social protection', in other contexts manifests as corruption, patronage and the maintenance of the social and economic hierarchy. Unravelling the different moral orders that are linked to the nice and nasty sides of social capital is a core aim of this book.

While localised and transnational 'social capital' is a vital factor in determining who does and who doesn't gain access to particular resources, in what follows I wish to widen my use of the term *connectivity* to encompass broader forms of connection to places, institutions and structures of entitlement. People need social relationships in order to survive, but if they are lucky these social relationships enable them to get hold of something more tangible and secure. What everyone aspires to, for example, is connectivity to the UK, in the form of British citizenship. Nowadays this is largely only possible via the marriage migration of sons and daughters (Gardner, 2006; Gardner and Ahmed, 2009). Social connections are vital for arranging these marriages, which are often between cousins. Yet while reaffirming and extending family relationships, plus the security that marriage with relatives hopefully brings is an important aspect of transnational marriages,[55] from the perspectives of families in Bangladesh a second aim is secure legal connection to Britain, with its formalised systems of social protection, economic opportunities and prosperity.

If connection to Britain or the US is not possible there are other destinations that attract migrants from Duniyapur. As described elsewhere (Gardner and Ahmed, 2009), within the culture of migration that has developed in the area, places are arranged hierarchically, with the old and established centres of capital accumulation at the top: the UK, the US and occasionally destinations in Europe, and other destinations in the Middle East or

South East Asia beneath. The possibilities for long-term settlement and the degree of economic opportunity are the main factors which make different destinations more or less attractive. While it is relatively easy to gain an employment contract for the Middle East, settlement is out of the question, and, however hard one might work, the economic opportunities are limited (with restrictions upon foreigners owning businesses or property, for example). For others, illegal migration is the only possibility: either to the Middle East, or taking one's chance and facing the huge risks of arduous and dangerous journeys West or East.

Whether boarding a plane to Heathrow to start a new life as the husband of a British-born cousin, or trekking across treacherous South East Asian jungle in the hope of earning a decent wage in Malaysia, all journeys to *bidesh* (foreign places) result from people's pressing need for connection to sources of global capital. In Duniyapur people's aspirations and imaginings of a better future largely centre on foreign countries, *bidesh*, a term resonant with implications of progress and prosperity, as well as rupture and danger for, in order to gain connections with these foreign centres of capital accumulation, people are prepared to take huge risks, physically, economically and emotionally.

Bidesh is more than simply an economic project. The construction of strong and successful manhood in Duniyapur is linked to overseas migration; for the younger generation, whose cousins or uncles are settled in the UK and for whom employment opportunities at home are limited, it sometimes seems as if they can think of nothing else but finding a way to join their extended families in an idealised *London* (Gardner and Ahmed, 2009). Similarly, the pull of modernity, whether towards the democratic, free and secular West or the wealthy Islamic modernity of the Middle East plays an important role. Yet primarily it is the need to earn a living, to extend life's chances beyond the everyday struggles for basic resources which motivate overseas migration. To this extent, what people want is not necessarily connection to *bidesh per se*, but to the sources of capitalism that provide such opportunities.

Corporations such as Chevron appear to offer just this. In the early days of the gas field, when land compensation was being negotiated and the construction of the plant was still under way many people hoped that the gas field would bring jobs, industrialisation in the form of a power plant and factories, services in the form of a hospital and school, and infrastructure in the form of good roads and a connection to the gas supply. Within this context, global capitalism, with its apparent promise of employment, business and modern services, is not located abroad but has arrived in the *desh*. Materialised by the industrial plant that rises from the rice fields and embodied by the foreigners who are driven in and out of the high-security site, here again access is only possible via social connection. While in the early days Unocal's people visited the surrounding villages, holding 'community consultation' meetings and distributing their business cards, today even the community engagement staff have largely retreated behind the high-security perimeter fence.[56] To speak to these officials one needs to know the right people.

The possibilities are tangible, almost within grasp. The roadside billboards with their explicit messages of road safety and implicit signals of corporate governance say it all: this is Chevron Country, a place where the standards of the modern world are adhered to. Salaried employment, satellite industry, roads, maybe even a hospital: all seemed possible with the arrival of the corporation. As in the Zambian Copperbelt, though on a far smaller scale, the people of Duniyapur glimpsed in the gas field the possibility of meaningful connection to something we might gloss as 'modernity'. As James Ferguson describes in Zambia, copper mining led to high expectations of economic development and modernity; indeed, in the 1950s and 1960s Zambia was to be the great African success story. Yet by the time of Ferguson's fieldwork in the 1990s, the global price of copper had plummeted and the Zambian economy had gone into sharp decline; disconnection, impoverishment and crushing disappointment were the result (Ferguson, 1999).

Ferguson's more recent work on oil companies in Africa is telling in a different way. Here, rather than a 'rolling out' of global capitalism and the resulting cultural homogenisation which James Scott (1998) suggests, Ferguson argues that while capital is 'global' it doesn't cover contiguous space. In sub-Saharan Africa, where most capital investment takes place in order to extract natural resources, capital doesn't flow, but 'hops' to specific sites, where enclaves of security, managed and governed by the oil companies, are created (Ferguson, 2005). The gas field is a similar site, an enclave of modernity, economic progress and corporate governance yet situated in rural Bangladesh rather than Angola or Nigeria. While it is by no means the only form of connectivity to modernity that can take place, for the history of transnational migration in the area has had a far more profound impact, it is tantalising in its material reality: located so close to the villages, spread across the land of the *desh*, yet for the vast majority who lack the connections that are necessary to get the contracts or the jobs, impossibly distant.

This detachment from local realities was bought home to me one night as I lay awake in the late spring heat. Nights in Duniyapur are rarely quiet: barking dogs compete with cicadas and the howl of jackals, while the distant chanting of *milad* prayer or the beat of Hindu *puja* drums frequently drift across the fields. Tonight, though, what I could hear was the unmistakeable boom of Western rock music. *Sevron* was having a party, I was told the next day, to celebrate the first year of the operation of the plant. Did people from the surrounding villages attend? I asked anxiously, berating myself for missing what might have been an interesting event. The answer was categorical: no, the party wasn't for local people, only Chevron's salaried employees.

The way in which the gas field simultaneously signals modernity and progress while excluding the local population is encapsulated in an anecdote recounted by a town councillor I met in Burnley in north-west England. The man was not from Duniyapur, but an area 20 or so miles away. He'd been living in the UK all his adult life, but, like many of his generation, liked to visit the *desh* on a regular basis. He spoke eloquently of his ambivalence towards Bangladesh, a deep emotional attachment mixed with frustration at the country's ongoing problems. He had heard about the gas field, he said, and he and a group of other *Londonis* on a visit home decided to hire a minibus to visit it, proud of the role that the *desh* and its gas reserves were to play in national development. The trip ended in disappointment however, for the men were turned away at the gates, and no amount of pleading would persuade the security guards to let them through.

The irony is striking: while local people are physically, culturally and economically disconnected from the gas field, Chevron must claim connection with them in order to promote its global reputation for 'partnership' is core to the corporation's much touted 'community engagement programme'. Here, an imagined connection with 'the community', constructed as homogeneous and united in its partnership with *Sevron*, is turned to economic value by a multinational which needs to show connectivity with the locals in order to look good. In Chapter 5 I shall discuss the community engagement programme and its construction of 'development success' (cf. Mosse, 2005) in more detail. As we shall see, these claims of connection draw on very different ideologies and types of knowledge than those of the landless inhabitants of the villages that surround the gas field.

In the chapters that follow we see various ways in which people are both connected and disconnected, from each other but also from resources, security and modernity in Duniyapur. As I shall argue, secure connection to resources and services is one form of 'development'; a state of entitlement that brings freedom from the everyday struggles of ordinary people in rural Bangladesh, in which very little is certain and one has to rely upon the goodwill of other, more powerful people, to survive. This is not the 'development' conjured up by CSR programmes stressing the virtue of 'nice' social capital (and its twin, self-reliance), participation and partnership and organised around micro-credit, training in crafts, animal husbandry and so on, but the 'development' that people actually want: jobs, formalised social security, and access to basic resources and services provided by an accountable state, a state of progress that most people in Bangladesh hope desperately will one day come.

Making Claims and Being Moral

While the struggles that people in Duniyapur are engaged with largely concern their relative access to basic resources, their entitlements mediated via the degree of connection that they have to other people or places, the arenas in which such struggles take place are underlain by cross-cutting and sometimes ambiguous moral orders. At times these seem to elide, sliding into each other without apparent contradiction. Everyone subscribes to moralities of 'helping', and few would contest the idea that democracy and transparency are 'good'. Yet at other times different moralities and the wider discourses to which they are attached become clunky and non-commensurate, and the hierarchies and power struggles which they underlie are revealed.

While I am not suggesting that each social or political group has an exclusive and bounded moral order, in the chapters that follow we see how different people make claims and strategies which draw on particular moral orders. By 'moral' I refer to the ideas and practices surrounding what it is to live as a good person. As Joel Robbins shows in his work on cultural change and Christianity in Papua New Guinea, the moral domain is one in which actors make conscious ethical choices; the struggles involved are therefore deeply felt (Robbins, 2004: 315–16). This is somewhat different from Foucauldian *discourse*, in which norms, knowledge and ways of seeing are taken for granted, unconscious and unquestioned.

In Duniyapur, claims to food or credit are made by the very poor via their insistence on social connections to the better-off and draw upon the moral imperative for wealthier individuals to 'look after their own'. Similar moral injunctions underlie attempts to get jobs at the gas plant via social connections to officials or leaders with strong links to Chevron. As Chapter 4 describes, patronage in Duniyapur is underscored by Islamic moralities concerning alms giving and social care, and has long been a means by which the poorest get by. Their reliance upon the morality of personal connection, 'helping' and charity, and the types of narrative and ways of knowing that it involves, is thus central to their survival. Appeals to kinship, whether real or fictional, or their counterpart in angry accusations that the rich and globally connected (whether transnational villagers or multinational corporations) are not doing their duty to their 'own' poor and are thus morally deficient, can be read as narrative acts, used politically to make claims over others.

Yet while the discourse of 'nice' social capital is used with effect in these contexts, in others the moralities of modernity dominate and social capital (aka patronage/corruption) turns 'nasty'. Again, what is contested is relative access to resources but here the scale has shifted from interpersonal relationships embedded in local and transglobal kinship, to domains where the state should be functioning in a 'modern' way. In contexts where people should, within the discourse of modernity, have formal entitlements, the moralities of modernity are drawn upon, and the ideals of democracy, equality, accountability and transparency contrasted against accusations of corruption and immorality (cf. West and Sanders, 2003).

The ways in which these different moralities and the practices which accompany them coalesce, contradict and countervail each other is highly contextual. This echoes Daniel Jordan-Smith's account of Nigeria, where, he argues, corruption is 'the ultimate symbol of modernity and its malcontents' (2007: 27). While in both Nigeria and Bangladesh, corruption-talk is a way of imagining and appealing for modernity, at other times and in other contexts patronage and nepotism are appealed to and celebrated in the name of 'tradition'. As we shall see, imaginings of modernity and what it should involve are used by a variety of claimants and at a variety of 'scales', be these individuals in Duniyapur drawing upon notions of transparency and compensation in their attempt to make claims on Chevron, or nationalist activists contesting the presence of multinationals in Bangladesh and insisting that global standards of transparency and accountability be maintained.

There are other claims to be made, by even more powerful actors. These also draw upon specific moral orders. Claims of entitlement to extract the country's natural resources made by multinationals such as Chevron, are, as I have already intimated, underscored by virulently asserted moralities of global citizenship and ethical business practice, involving the will to do philanthropic good in the contexts where they work, a corporate belief in 'partnership' and their contribution to the holy grail of 'development'. Like those who seek to oppose them, Chevron's executives and their global publications constantly have recourse to the moralities and languages of citizenship, rights, environmentalism and even 'empowerment'.

The making of claims and the narrative forms and moralities involved are thus constantly shifting and elusive. They are also context specific: the same person might call upon quite different formulations of what is right or proper, according to where and with whom she or he is. Rather than being subject to 'double-consciousness' (Robbins, 2004: xxvi), or the arrival of Occidental's prospectors leading to a negotiation between tradition and modernity, or 'indigenous knowledge' versus 'technocratic knowledge' such shifting of positions and negotiations between different claims, aspirations and identities has long been a feature of life in Duniyapur as it has for much of the world. The discovery of gas has, however, raised the stakes: there are higher expectations, more claims to be made and greater losses to be borne. Contestation, opposition, denial and accusation are thus drawn into narratives which, just as they make claims to some connections and resources, nullify others.

Telling and Knowing

As one observes the passionate contestations surrounding energy resources and the role of multinationals in Bangladesh, it sometimes seems as if the opposing groups are speaking different languages. In some ways this is actually the case: the offices of Chevron in Dhaka, staffed at the most senior levels by expatriate Britons and Americans, use English as their lingua franca. So too do nationalist activists, who write newspapers articles, academic papers and blogs in English as well as the *shudu Bangla* (correct Bengali) of the intellectual elite. Meanwhile in Duniyapur the largely illiterate rural poor speak Sylheti, a dialect which some argue is a separate language, impossible to understand by middle class, Dhaka-based Bengali-speakers.[57]

These linguistic differences are matched by the ways in which different actors draw upon particular forms of knowledge in the making of their claims. As Foucault (1972) has shown, governance and power are exercised by discourses that are underlain by 'architectures of knowledge', which rely upon specific epistemologies that order the world in particular ways, structuring a range of practices which, while appearing as 'natural' or 'obvious', involve the exercise of control. 'Development' is a prime example of a discourse, much explored by anthropologists (see Gardner and Lewis, 1996). As we shall see in the chapters that follow, the moral injunctions, aspirations and ideologies, as well as the practices and power play that the term involves, are intrinsic to many of the struggles that are taking place in Duniyapur.

For those seeking to make their claims via narratives of 'development', or 'empowerment', a very particular sort of knowledge is drawn upon. Like all epistemologies, development knowledge involves specific methods and techniques. For example, the 'community development' of Chevron's CSR programmes is associated with 'problems' that can be measured via surveys and PRA exercises, and achievements that can be quantified via consultancy reports and auditing procedures. As Li (2007) has argued with reference to similar 'programmes of improvement' in Indonesia, the moral injunctions of neoliberalism are key. These narratives of change and improvement are compelling and difficult to counter: drawing upon data gathered by their consultants, community engagement staff meet any questioning of the reach of their programmes with quantitative data, questioning the validity of qualitative methods which they label 'hearsay'.

'Development' is not the only way that seeing and knowing square up for the fight over Bangladesh's natural resources. The activism of anti-multinational intellectuals draws upon a different sort of knowledge: neo-Marxist structural analysis and regional or global history, underscored by the moralities of Bangladeshi nationalism. Nationalist activists forming the Committee for the Protection of Oil, Gas, Mineral Resources, Power and Ports (the 'National Committee') are led by a group of left-leaning intellectuals, some with professorships in economics. Their interest is in numbers of a different sort: the content of the deals made between multinationals and the government, rather than the numbers of 'beneficiaries' of Chevron's CSR programmes. Meaningful dialogue between advocates of Chevron's 'community engagement' and those opposing the activities of Chevron is thus tricky, for each group is drawing upon a different type of knowledge and narrative form in making their claims. This was brought home to me at a dissemination event run in Dhaka towards the end of the research, to which members of both groups were invited. While the intellectuals sought to question Chevron's role in Bangladesh *per se*, Chevron's representatives, and the NGOs involved in their CSR programmes in Duniyapur gave a PowerPoint presentation concerning the programmes they were running and numbers of people benefiting from their projects.

In Duniyapur people tend to draw upon narrative styles of a different order, which draw upon other forms of analysis and ways of knowing. Story telling, and complaint, rumour and lament feature largely, especially among the poor. Excluded from the development-knowledge gathered by consultants (who, we were told, rarely if ever returned to share their 'findings' with the local population), those with the least power in Duniyapur are excluded from debates concerning international economic history and not given the chance to contest the number crunching of CSR managers since these narrations take place in domains that are largely inaccessible to them: the internet, for example, or newspapers that those who haven't had the privilege of formal schooling are unable to read. The landless and land-poor people of the villages surrounding the gas field do of course have their own, firmly rooted knowledge of the impact of the gas field, as well as strong views on the global economy (and their role in it), national politics and the role of multinationals in bringing or preventing 'development' from taking place in Bangladesh. Within their narratives and claims, however, it is knowledge of interpersonal relationships, regional, village and family history that is mobilised, drawing upon the moral orders of ethical personal conduct, charity and *shahajo* (helping).

People in Duniyapur also have an extensive knowledge of the environment and agriculture which is based on their long-term observation and use of the land and encompasses a holistic understanding of social relationships involved. For farmers in Duniyapur and their transnational outposts, land involves a tight web of relations, practices and moralities. Like the environmental knowledge of the Yonggom at the site of the Ok Tedi mine in Papua New Guinea, this contrasts with the scientifically based 'findings' of environmental impact assessments carried out by mining companies (Kirsch, 2006). In Duniyapur these assessments are made internally by Chevron, which are based on scientific assumptions and not made available to the public. Meanwhile local farmers' knowledge of environmental changes is either ignored or disputed by Chevron. I am not suggesting that a discrete body of 'indigenous knowledge' exists in Duniyapur which can be contrasted with the 'scientific' knowledge of the corporation or the developers. Rather, in Duniyapur, people tend to use particular narrative forms and types of knowledge in making their claims for connection and hence their entitlement to resources. These contrast with the narratives of others, who seek to assert their claims in what are often incommensurate ways.

Who Speaks? Who Is Heard?

In his fascinating ethnography of lament in Bangladesh, James Wilce (2003) shows how the complaints of particular people (often young women) are either ignored or violently suppressed, using a justification of *pagholi* (mad woman) to silence them. As Wilce argues, the tradition of lament in Bangladesh is used by those with the least power, a way of addressing passionately felt injustice and inequality. Yet while laments are condemned as 'mad talk', their content ignored, the speech acts or narratives of the powerful are listened to and accorded respect.

Recognising that the narratives of different people are accorded varying weight is central to my analysis of the contestations surrounding the gas field. Just as they order the world, construct and reveal identities and are used as political tools, narratives are also accorded differential value by their audiences. Indeed, people's relative ability to control the discourse is central to the struggles over resources that the book documents (see also Kirsch, 2006: 4). As ever, power relations dominate. Who speaks, and who listens? Who persuades others that particular actions are right or wrong, and who is never heard? While a boardroom in Dhaka is filled with Chevron executives anxious to hear (and contest) the opinions of a foreign anthropologist, in the villages surrounding the gas field, people tell how there is no-one to hear their grievances concerning the installation. Meanwhile, as Chevron recites fine tales of partnership and community support to an audience of millions via internet reports and global advertising campaigns, the narratives of dispossession and suffering of the people in Kakura, with their subtext of compensation and justice, are dismissed by NGO workers and wealthier neighbours as evidence that, once again, they are being 'too demanding'.

Listening to someone is not the same as being persuaded by them. As far as I know, none of the 'recommendations' that I made in my representations to Chevron were acted upon by the company. And while family women may gather around a dispossessed widow to listen to her lament, they are unlikely to give her much more than a handful of rice for her troubles, though narratives of suffering can lead to greater support if the audience is socially connected to the narrator. Audiences may also contest, disagree with or undermine the narrative, even when made by the powerful. As we see in Chapters 6 and 7, rumours are a powerful way of unsettling the narratives of success and ethical conduct propagated by Chevron, as are the counter-campaigns of activists who seek to ridicule their claims of globally ethical conduct.[58] Locally, humorous stories of the 'reality' behind Chevron's show-casing and self-congratulatory prize-giving ceremonies do the same job, yet for a smaller (though equally gleeful) audience.

But while no-one successfully dominates the discourse, for there is no single discourse, those who seek to narrate Chevron's story on national and international stages, as well as within the communities of Duniyapur, have infinitely more reach than those who seek to narrate the individual stories of dispossession and poverty that I attempt to describe here. Drawing attention to how some versions of reality are silenced and edited out, while others powerfully propagated to global shareholders and consumers, is one of the main aims of this book.

STRUCTURE OF THE BOOK

In Chapter 2 I set the scene for the contestations and claims that surround the gas field by recounting some of the most salient aspects of Bangladesh's recent and colonial history. While much of the present political and economic structure has been shaped by imperialism and exploitative global capital, we also see how many people in Sylhet have been active and enthusiastic participants in these processes via transnational labour migration, which has enabled them to establish secure connections with foreign sources of capital, especially Britain. This in turn has helped transform social and economic relations in the *desh* (homeland), leading to the domination of a new, geographically created class of people: *Londonis*, who, while they are rarely physically present, own nearly all the land in the villages that surround the gas field.

In Chapter 3 I examine structures of entitlement within the area in more detail, showing how land remains a key economic and social resource, even for those who do not own it. As in much of Bangladesh, the agrarian economy is changing, relying less on traditional informal relations of labour and sharecropping, and more on financially based arrangements. Like the environmental changes associated with, though not confined to the gas field, these have tended to have a bigger impact on the land-poor and landless (of whom there are a great many), who are increasingly being squeezed off the land and struggle to find a livelihood. Whereas they once hoped that the gas field might provide regular and secure work, they have been disappointed, for not only does the field require little manual labour, Chevron also only hires labourers via contractors, many of whom come from distant parts of Bangladesh. These contractors control their employees via their geographical and social connection to them, rather than via formal contracts. To this extent, by removing land from agriculture the gas field has led to a reduction in the productive resources in the area yet has not provided new connections in the form of formal employment.

In Chapter 4 I turn to the informal connections that provide the poor with economic support in times of crisis, showing how this informal system of entitlement is underlain by particular forms of morality, involving charity and kinship. Similar ideas and relationships are involved in people's attempts to access foreign countries: *Londonis* are expected to 'help' their relatives back in the *desh* to gain footholds in the UK via the arrangement of marriages and financial support. The claims of both would-be migrants and the very poor draw upon these moralities, as well as reckonings of kinship, in which those most closely related are entitled to most support. As I suggest at the end of the chapter, stories of loss and pain can partly be understood within this context; while story telling helps connect people to each other and frame their experiences, it is also a way in which claims to support can be made.

In Chapter 5 we turn to a different sort of story telling: corporate tales of successful community engagement, which provide Chevron with a good reputation and involve claims of ethical business practice, thus asserting their entitlement to extract natural gas at Bibiyana. While the stories and claims of Chapter 4 were all about social connections, Chevron's community engagement programmes involve claims of 'partnership with the community', yet the moralities involved are of global development, not localised cultures of giving. These moralities of global development stress neoliberal ideals of 'self-help' and sustainability involving not connection to donors but disconnection. What we also see is how very different versions of 'development' are utilised in these programmes than those desired by local people: rather than industrialisation, employment and an accountable state, which provides services such as health care, education and energy to its population, the programmes of community engagement involve 'helping people to help themselves' via micro-credit and small-scale income-generation activities.

Chapter 6 describes how corporate stories of successful community engagement are radically undermined by contrasting accounts of protest and activism. By tracing the history of opposition that surrounded the early days of the gas field, we see how local politics has been altered by the presence of Unocal and Chevron, exploding the image of a homogeneous and content 'community'. Complaints of oppression and rumours of corruption are central to the stories told by local leaders about the history of the gas field, often centred around their analysis of village politics and framed as attacks on particular individuals. Indeed, rumours of corruption can be analysed both as critiques of wider conditions of exploitation and powerlessness, as well as attacks aimed at one's enemies. The narratives of nationalist activists draw upon different types of knowledge and ways of telling, yet also elicit the theme of corruption and inequality, though at a national and global rather than a local level. In Bangladesh, struggles over natural resources are also struggles over the role of the state and the direction of the country in the global economy: transparency and accountability are posited as being central to the modern democracy that people desire.

In Chapter 7 we turn to the stories of violent rupture and loss told by people in Duniyapur. These are organised around two themes: the dread of a 'blow-out' at the gas field, and narratives of environmental change and destruction. I suggest that while these accounts reflect empirical conditions, including the flaring that takes place at the gas field, the stories can also be analysed as metaphors for disconnection – from the land, and also from sources of support – the ultimate disaster for people who rely upon connections for their survival. As I argue in the concluding sections of the book, if poverty can be understood as a state of disconnection, then 'development' might be thought of as a process whereby connections are strengthened, not via policies which promote 'self-help' or 'social capital', which can only strengthen the informal and inherently risky connections of the rural poor, but involving a process whereby people obtain formal connections and entitlements, via properly contracted employment and the provision of services by an accountable state. Making the details of contracts with governments available, and supporting them to become more accountable, is, I argue, the main way that multinationals such as

Chevron can truly claim to be 'socially responsible', for in doing this they will be supporting formalised connections, or 'rights', rather than following 'the ethics of detachment' (Cross, 2011) via discourses of 'helping people to help themselves.'

2
Histories of Connection: Colonialism, Migration and Multinationals

Foreigners aren't welcome inside Finlay's Tea Estate. It's probably because in the late 1980s there was a damaging *exposé* of labour conditions in the Scottish-owned tea gardens,[1] published in the Scottish newspaper, the *Daily Record*. Today, security guards are instructed to prevent unknown visitors from crossing into the estate, situated in an area of gentle hills and forest a few miles north of Sylhet Town. Luckily I have contacts. My companion, an employee of one of the NGOs funded by Chevron as part of their community engagement programme, grew up on the estate; the families of many Hindus living around the towns of Sylhet and Sri Mongal are employed in the tea sector and his father worked in a white-collar job in Finlays. After a bit of haggling, our car is waved through.

Our destination is the British graveyard, which we find half a mile or so inside the sprawling plantation. It has been well maintained: the Victorian gravestones are free of weeds, the grassy paths carefully tended. There they lie, distant echoes of another age: the Scottish names and cherubic statues incongruous in this quintessentially Sylheti scene: the manicured terraces of tea, the women labourers moving quietly among the rows of plants, baskets balanced on their heads, the distant beats of Bollywood drifting from a tea stall opposite the labourers' dwellings. *Alexander Macintosh, born in Dundee, died in Kherghat, Southern Sylhet, 1889, by drowning; Elizabeth James, born 1874 and survived but a few hours; William MacBride: he died on his way home and was buried at sea, 1883.*

Today, the British have gone: the estate passed into Bangladeshi hands in 2004, almost a decade after the British Overseas Development Administration withdrew support for the tea industry (see Gardner, 1997), its consultants and advisers moving out of their Sri Mongal compound, with its neat lawns and swimming pool, in the mid 1990s. The graveyard, however, remains a fitting monument to the colonial history of the region, a history which continues to inform events and attitudes today, from the first incursions of the East India Company in the seventeenth century, to the rule of the British, the Partition of India, when the territory became East Pakistan, and finally the War of Liberation and the birth of Bangladesh in 1971. This particular history, however, is only one of various stories that could be told, for the global connections of Duniyapur and beyond stretch in many directions which are marked by various monuments.

Take, for example, the shrine of Shah Jalal, the Muslim missionary who is said to have brought Islam to Eastern India from the Yemen at the beginning of the fourteenth century. Stories tell how, after taking advice from the mystic Nizam Uddin Awlia in Delhi, Shah Jalal set off to rescue Sheikh Burhan Uddin, who was held captive by the Hindu ruler, Gaur Gavinda. Rather than using more conventional methods, he crossed the River Surma (which runs through Sylhet Town) on a prayer mat. After eventually defeating Gaur Gavinda, Shah Jalal settled in Sylhet, where he preached Islam until his death in approximately 1347. With him came 360 disciples, whose shrines are scattered over the region, embodying a localised Islam with Sufi leanings that has characterised Bengali Islam for hundreds of years yet has recently come under increasing criticism from reformist Muslims, both within Bangladesh and in the wider Bengali diaspora (see, for example, Glynn, 2002; Hussain, 2006; Ul-Hoque, 2011).

This growing intolerance towards Sufism was probably the reason for a bomb attack on the shrine in 2004 which killed two people and injured around thirty during a festival that hard-liners would have judged un-Islamic. No-one has ever claimed responsibility, but Islamic extremists, known to abhor the dancing, music and Sufi practices of Sylheti *pir* (saints), are the likely culprits. The bomb was followed by another a few months later, during a visit by the British High Commissioner Anwar Chowdhury, who was injured in the attack.[2] It was the first time Chowdhury had visited the region, for, like many British Bengalis, he was brought up in the UK. Shifting religious sensibilities, political violence and modernity vie for starring roles in this story: we learn not only of Sufi legends, but also of the degree of ideological change and contestation that has come to Sylhet and the tensions involved. True, the British High Commissioner was Bengali, but he was British, not Bangladeshi. And while Bangladesh has a long way to go before it becomes the 'second Afghanistan', as predicted by alarmist reports in the mid 2000s (Riaz, 2004), the bombs were not isolated events in a country where political antagonism is routinely accompanied by violence.

A third burial site with stories to tell is closer to home, located in the midst of fields which spread between Nadampur and Karimpur. Less than half a mile away, the gas plant shimmers in the hot sun, the horizon dissected by the arrow-straight road that links the site to Kakura and beyond. Here, in the shade of an ancient banyan tree, is a small *koverstan* (graveyard) where a returned *Londoni* is buried. One of the original *lascars* (ship workers), the old adventurer's body was returned to the *desh* (homeland), where he was buried in his family's land, imbued as it is with the spiritual genealogy of this, the land of *pirs* (saints).[3] As for other men of his generation, employment on British ships that left from Calcutta to destinations around the world led eventually to a life in London, where Indian sailors often 'jumped ship' in the first half of the twentieth century, making the first tentative steps in creating a large and established population of Bengalis in Britain.

The linking of the *desh* with foreign countries, in particular the UK, is another crucial element of Duniyapur's history, for transnational connections with Britain have been of major importance to the area and have in turn informed people's relationships with the gas field. The grave under the banyan tree tells us of local attitudes to land, the *shonar zommeen* (golden fields) of poetry and national sentiment. Buried in the soil, yet after a lifetime of travel, the ancestral *lascar* embodies one of the central themes of this book: the relationship between embeddedness and movement, the shaping of local lives by global capitalism, connection and disconnection, disjunction and flow.

In what follows, I sketch out some of the most salient histories of Bangladesh and Duniyapur, providing a background for the rest of the book. As we shall see, these are histories of connection, as well as exploitation and inequality. Colonialism in its various forms has been central, not only as the precursor for the country's current economic situation but also in shaping the Bangladeshi state, labelled variously as 'failed' (Lewis, 2011: 317), the result of 'illiberal democracy' (BRAC, 2008) and a 'rotten core' at the heart of the apparent success story of Bangladeshi development (Devine et al., 2008). Lack of trust in the state, which in 2002 appeared at the top of Transparency International's Most Corrupt Countries List (and after an improvement in the mid 2000s, appears to be slipping back once more)[4] is central to current activism against multinationals, and is both caused by and continues to cause a 'politics of patronage' (Lewis, 2011), in which access to resources and power only comes via one's links to others. To understand this, let us start with the more formal history of Bangladesh, the nation state.[5]

A COLONISED TERRITORY: THE EAST INDIA COMPANY, BRITISH RULE AND PARTITION, 1750–1947

One cannot begin to appreciate the strength of feelings against foreign companies in Bangladesh, which, according to the narratives of anti-multinational activists, 'plunder' the nation,[6] without understanding the role of the East India Company in Bengal. The British were not, however, the first occupiers of Bengal, for the region has a far longer history of colonisation, dating back to the Mughals, who gained control over an independent and plural Bengal (which included the territories of Assam, Orissa, Tripura and some of Bengal) in the middle of the sixteenth century. The occupation met with substantial resistance; in a precursor to the War of Liberation some 400 years later, for example, Isa Khan attempted to defend Bengal against Urdu-speaking outsiders and is sometimes spoken of as a Bengali hero (Lewis, 2011: 69).

Despite colonial domination, Bengal prospered under the Mughals. For a period, Dhaka was the capital, and the region increasingly opened up to traders, developing the manufacture of textiles, which found an expanding market in Britain, via traders from the East India Company. This had expanded across India over the Elizabethan period, becoming increasingly militarised and governmental by the eighteenth century. By 1750, Bengal accounted for 75 percent of the company's goods, with Dhaka at the centre, famous for its fine embroideries (Metcalf and Metcalf, 2002).

In 1756, the power of the British was challenged by the *nawab* Suraj-ud-Daula, who briefly captured Calcutta, leading to the 'Black Hole of Calcutta' incident, in which 100 British people died. Calcutta was recaptured by Clive in 1757. Subsequent skirmishes took place with a series of 'puppet' *nawabs* put in place by the British, who followed a policy of patronage and playing groups off against each other, effectively destabilising the governance of Bengal (Lewis, 2011: 73).

The economy was profoundly damaged, too. In his detailed account of the decline and fall of what became known as 'John Company', Nick Robins (2006: 61) shows how, over the eighteenth and nineteenth centuries, British interests contributed to the underdevelopment of East Bengal's economy, systematically undermining the textile industry that had once made Bengal the most wealthy region of the Mughal Empire. By gaining control of 85–90 percent of the region's textile industries, by the end of the eighteenth century the company was able to reap around 50 percent profits, via an 'unrequited trade' that brought wealth to the company but pauperisation to Bengal, when the tide turned and protectionist policies meant that it was British textiles which flooded India rather than Indian textiles dominating the British market. Robins argues that the East India Company was a prototype for contemporary multinationals and helped shape global capitalism today. As he writes:

> The company's 'great revolution' in Bengal deserves to be placed alongside other revolutions – American, French and Russian – for the way it shaped the modern world. In the space of less than a decade [at the end of the eighteenth century] the Company had rerouted the flow of wealth westwards. Yet this was a corporate revolution, designed to acquire the riches of an entire people for the benefits of a single company. (2006: 80)

The decline of the textile industry led to many former artisans returning to the land, where taxes were now being collected by the British in the newly founded *zamindari* system. Under the Permanent Settlement Act of 1793, *zamindars* (usually high-caste Hindus) were made land proprietors and the peasantry tenants without rights, who, under their wealthy new landlords, tended to remain perpetually poor, subservient and dependent. Today the term *raiyat* (tenant) still signifies low status in Duniyapur, and can be used as an insult (Gardner, 1995). Many of the Hindu *zamindars* left for West Bengal at Partition in 1947, leaving behind a Muslim majority who had never been able to invest in the land, and the pattern of low investment into agriculture and rural poverty continued. As we shall see, a similar process, of disinvestment and underdevelopment took place in the administrative and political structures of East Bengal.

Interestingly, in Sylhet, the system of land tenure was significantly different from the rest of Bengal. Governed as part of Assam from 1874 until Partition in 1947, when it was re-assimilated into Bengal, the district was included under the Assamese Revenue System, which created a large number of single tenures rather than the small number of large tenures under the *zamindari* system. Rather than having *zamindars* as middlemen, in Sylhet the British therefore dealt directly with small independent proprietors, or *taluk-dar* (Gardner, 1995: 38–9). Some commentators have speculated that this contributed to the independence of subsequent generations, who left to work on the ships in Calcutta and, a generation or so later, the factories of post-war Britain (Adams, 1987; Choudhury, 1993; Gardner, 1995). It may also have been an underlying cause of Sylhetis' distaste for agricultural labour, leading to the use of in-migrant labourers for cultivation and the increasing neglect of agriculture as an economic activity among the better off, though the riskiness of agriculture, its low profit margin and the gains to be made from other enterprises are likely to be more influential.

By the mid to late nineteenth century East Bengal was largely an underdeveloped agricultural region, with a once thriving textile industry now in pitiful decline. While in the west Calcutta was the British capital, Dhaka was no longer the vibrant manufacturing and cultural centre it had been under the Mughals. Meanwhile in the hilly north-eastern region of Sylhet British traders were making incursions into the tea industry. With a background in trading cotton and jute, for example, John Muir of Finlay, Muir and Co. moved into tea production in 1873, rapidly buying up tea plantations across the region and establishing a cadre of tea tasters and brokers.[7] During the last quarter of the nineteenth century, the tea industry grew phenomenally, with production increasing from 6 million pounds in 1872 to 75 million pounds in 1900, and the area under cultivation rising from 27,000 acres to 204,000 (Behal, 1985). Today, while the lowlands of Sylhet are predominantly agricultural, the hilly forested areas are covered in tea estates. The labourers are largely Hindu or 'tribal' and, in many respects, the estates operate as separate, enclosed worlds; workers are born on the estates and often remain there all their lives.

Towards the end of the nineteenth century challenges to British rule increased in Bengal, often spearheaded by educated Hindus. For example the Indian Congress Party was formed by two Bengalis, Surendranath Banerjea and Woomesh Chandra Bonnerjee in 1885 (Lewis, 2011: 82). In 1905 Bengal, which now incorporated Bihar and Orissa, was divided into East Bengal and Assam on the one hand, and West Bengal, Orissa and Bihar on the other, a strategy largely arising from a British policy of divide and rule, which laid the basis for the eventual partition of the territory into its Muslim and Hindu wings in 1947. After protests Bengal was joined back together in 1911, but the division marked increasing tension between Hindus, who at the time favoured a united Bengal, and Muslims, who tended not to. Increasingly, Muslims began to feel threatened by the more vociferous and politically powerful Hindu elite and there were stirrings of a plan for Muslim autonomy. Over subsequent decades the idea of separation from Hindus took shape, with considerable support for the Pakistani project among Bengali Muslims. Others supported the idea of a separate state of East Bengal, an option which was ultimately vetoed by the British.

The 1940s were traumatic for Bengal. A catastrophic cyclone was followed by the Bengal Famine of 1943–4. Caused in part by British stockpiling and the subsequent breakdown of local food distribution systems, this led to the deaths of between 1.5 to 3.5 million people (Lewis, 2011: 89). The violent rupture of Partition followed shortly after. While the Hindu majority voted for Partition in 1947, in an about-turn from 1905 most Muslims tended to prefer a unified Bengal, with only those from Sylhet opting to join Pakistan. When the hurried decision was eventually made by the British that India should be divided into two nations: a largely Hindu India and the new Muslim state of Pakistan, Bengal was divided into Hindu West Bengal, with Calcutta as its capital, and East Bengal become the eastern wing of Pakistan, East Pakistan, with Dhaka as its capital.[8]

The partition of India led to one of the greatest migrations in human history, with over 7 million people moving across the West Pakistan border, and around 5 million moving between East and West Bengal from 1947 to 1964 (Chatterjee, 1995). This mass migration was accompanied by widespread communal violence, with estimates of between hundreds of thousands to a million people killed (Metcalf and Metcalf, 2002). As Willem van Schendel writes: 'The pain of Partition fell disproportionately on the new borderlands. Here disruption was overwhelming and almost all people were directly and personally affected' (2005: 25). Significantly, East Bengal was economically and politically fractured, leaving its capital, Calcutta, its industrial base and main port in India, and bringing the 'backward' agricultural area of Bengal and tea-growing districts of Sylhet into East Pakistan (Sobhan, 1993, cited in Lewis, 2011: 91).

EAST PAKISTAN, 1947–71

From the outset the relationship between West and East Pakistan was strained. Political and economic inequality between the two sides of the country were inherent to its conception, with West Pakistan the dominant partner. It wasn't long before West Pakistan became seen in the East as overbearing at best and colonial at worst. The Eastern territory was, however, Pakistan's largest province, with forty-four parliamentary representatives as opposed to twenty-eight from the West. Despite this numerical majority, East Pakistan's material deprivation was rapidly matched by political deprivation, with the West assuming the role of extractor of raw materials such as jute for processing in the West. There were also few senior administrators in the East, for under the British the majority of white-collar workers had been Hindus, and these had now departed for West Bengal.

These problems were epitomised by the issue of language, which soon became the focus for resistance against West Pakistan. When Urdu was declared the national language of Pakistan in 1952, riots broke out in East Bengal. The protests sparked the birth of the Bengali Language Movement and were, in many ways, the beginning of the end of what had always been an unhappy forced marriage. The dismissal of Bengali as 'un-Islamic' in West Pakistan belied an underlying snobbery towards the East by some in the West, with General Ayub Khan (who after a period of martial law, had become president in 1962) speaking of Bengalis as a 'downtrodden race' (cited in Lewis, 2011: 102).

By the time Ayub was succeeded in power by General Agha Muhammed Yahya Khan in 1969, the economic growth that had come to Pakistan was unevenly divided between East and West, with the latter enjoying the growth while the East continued to stagnate. Despite, or perhaps because of this, East Pakistan's Awami League (which united both Muslims and Hindus in Bengal) won the majority of seats in the 1970 election, returning 160 out of 162 seats from East Pakistan, while Bhutto's People's Party won only 81 out of 183 seats in West Pakistan. Unable to accept a Bengali majority in the government, General Yahya Khan suspended the Assembly. In the East, dissent and political protest against the Western administration continued to swell. When negotiations finally broke down between the parties in 1971, the West Pakistanis embarked on a military crackdown and the Bengalis, led by the Awami League's Sheikh Mujibur Rahman, declared Bangladesh to be their sovereign state (Lewis 2011: 107).

The military crackdown initially targeted university intellectuals and Hindus, whose neighbourhoods in Dhaka were shelled by the Pakistanis. The violence that followed was on a massive scale: rape and chemical warfare contributed to what amounted to genocide, with some sources estimating that up to 3 million Bengalis were killed;[9] millions more fled to India. Ultimately, it was Indian assistance that ended the war: the Pakistan experiment had ended, with massive costs to the newly independent Bangladesh.

* * *

Colonial domination, shifting administrative borders (see van Schendel, 2005), rupture and the rending apart of previously interwoven economic and political structures: all are salient themes in the pre-independence history of Bangladesh. Since 1971 these issues have continued to shape the political life of the country, which has lurched from fragile democracy to military dictatorship and back again many times in its short life. Whether the government is democratically elected or not, struggles over resources and violent factionalism rather than ideology are the name of the game. Crucially, governance has been characterised by patronage and self-interest rather than accountability and transparency. It is this that lies at the heart of activism against multinationals in the country today. Structured by colonial exploitation and Partition, the Bangladesh state's inability to provide basic welfare to its citizens and its deep-rooted corruption underscore the everyday struggles that shape the lives of the people of Duniyapur.

BANGLADESH, 1971–2010

When Sheikh Mujibur Rahman was declared President of Bangladesh in 1971 the new nation was based on a secular Bengali identity; language, rather than religion formed the basis of nationalism and India was an ally rather than an enemy. The problems facing the country were vast: a fragmented political system, a decimated intellectual and political class and an economy which, over the last few centuries, had become a supplier of raw materials rather than the manufacturer of high-quality goods it had once been. Security issues were also pressing: by the end of the war law and order had largely broken down and food supplies for the traumatised population were far from guaranteed. To make matters worse, the country's infrastructure was badly damaged by a catastrophic cyclone in 1970, which killed hundreds of thousands of people.

Already the seeds for the ensuing factionalism and politics of patronage (van Schendel, 2009) that were to characterise the country were in place; the Awami League was beset with internal rivalries that quickly developed into networks of patronage. Party loyalists were rewarded with jobs running newly nationalised industries, for example, though few had any experience (Lewis, 2011: 120). The new nationalism was not conducive to foreign investment; while Pakistani businesses were taken over and often looted, other foreign ventures were only permitted if the government had a 49 percent share. Meanwhile, a precedent was set of weak accountability and low levels of governmental responsibility (2011: 122). Few plans were made for economic development, and by 1973 the economy was starting to collapse. In 1974, government corruption and mismanagement of food supplies and distribution, the smuggling of grain to India and flooding contributed to a huge hike in the price of rice. The result was a devastating famine which killed over a million people. The worst affected were those without access to land, the agricultural labourers who today continue to constitute the rural poor. As with all famines, the problem was not so much the lack of grain, but uneven entitlement to resources (Sen, 1982). In a vivid illustration of this, my friend Habib Rahman tells of helping a group of men from impoverished and landless Kakura rob a grain store in neighbouring Nadampur. The politics of aid may have also played a role: A year earlier the US had withheld 2.2 tonnes of food aid.[10]

Disaffection with Mujibur Rahman and the chaos that the country was in led to a violent military coup in 1975, in which he and members of his family were assassinated. After more chaos and more assassinations, General Ziaur Rahman (Zia) took power. In contrast to the Awami League, which now stood accused of being too pro-Indian, the basis of Zia's political support was an alliance of anti-Indian, pro-Islamic and Pakistan Muslim League supporters. This distinction, with the Awami League being generally more secular and pro-Indian and the Bangladesh National Party leaning towards Pakistan and Islamic parties, remains today.

Zia rapidly embarked on a programme of economic development. This included the rehabilitation of the private sector and a waiving of duty on imported fabrics destined for the manufacture of export-oriented garments, laying the foundations for today's vast garment sector. In a decisive move away from the Awami League's secularist stance, in 1977 the constitution was amended to include a commitment to the values of Islam (Lewis, 2011: 130). In 1978 Zia was democratically elected president, martial law lifted and the BNP created.

The popularity and promise of Zia soon waned. By 1980 there had been twenty coup attempts against him, all of which were ruthlessly put down. In 1981 he was finally assassinated and by

1982, after another coup, General H.M. Ershad had assumed power, restoring martial law and ushering in a new phase, of a bureaucratic military state governed by a mixture of army and political leaders (Lewis, 2011: 133). Ershad's regime followed a policy of economic liberalisation, in which many of the country's cotton and jute mills were denationalised, a move that led to protests from the workers' unions. A degree of faltering economic growth followed, but, like its predecessors, the regime was marked by corruption and patronage. Under Ershad's dictatorship, direct action and protest became the only vehicle for dissent, a pattern which was to become increasingly disruptive over the next twenty years, causing significant damage to the country's faltering economy. By the late 2000s the *hartarl*, a general strike, in which movement around the country is impossible and factories and offices closed, had become a regular feature of Bangladeshi life. Opposition against Ershad began to crescendo over the late 1980s, with Zia's widow, Khaleda Zia (who was now leader of the BNP) and Mujib's daughter Sheikh Hasina, (who led the Awami League) spearheading campaigns for democratic elections. By the end of 1990, mass protests led to Ershad losing the support of donors and the regime fell.

From 1991 until 2006 the country entered a period of uneasy democracy. Many hoped this would be a new beginning but the politics of the last twenty years has been characterised by political violence, a culture of intransigent confrontation rather than negotiation, tit-for-tat reprisals and factionalism. The stranglehold over political debate and vision remains to the present day, and is embodied in the form of the arch-enemies, Khaleda Zia and Sheikh Hasina. Bombs thrown at political rallies and the murder of party activists are routine, with both parties accusing the other of attack and counter-attack. For a short while after the fall of Ershad, however, it seemed that a brighter future might lie ahead. After national elections in 1991 the government was formed by the BNP, with Khaleda Zia at the helm. Shortly afterwards another major cyclone struck the coastal region, leading to the death of around 150,000 people.

The government was unable to fulfil its promise. By the mid 1990s corruption and economic stagnation were increasingly challenged by the *hartals* and violent protests of the opposition, finally leading to the collapse of the government and the eventual election of Sheikh Hasina's Awami League in 1996. In a move that looked backwards to the days of her father, Hasina instantly revoked the immunity from persecution of those involved in the 1975 coup. Parliament, meanwhile, remained boycotted by the BNP. By the end of its term, this government was also perceived as inefficient and corrupt.

In the elections of 2001 the BNP was returned to power in an alliance with various other parties, including Jamaat-i-Islam. Political gridlock continued, with the first session of the new government boycotted by the Awami League. Primarily interested in personal point-scoring and vengeance, the new government, somewhat predictably, charged Hasina and her former ministers with corruption, matching similar charges made by her against the BNP when she was in power (Lewis, 2011: 150). Somewhat more hopefully, the government also embarked on 'Operation Clean Heart', an effort to stem violent crime. Yet while donors approved of attempts to establish 'good governance', the feared Rapid Action Battalion (RAB) and Bangladeshi police came under increasing international criticism for human rights abuses such as 'death in custody', and death during 'cross fire'.[11] The period was also marked by growing political opposition, creating a highly unstable environment for business. In 2005 there was a *hartal* almost every other week. By 2007, the deteriorating law-and-order situation, plus growing political chaos, *hartals* and demonstrations culminated in the intervention of the army, which declared a state of emergency.

Once again, Bangladesh seemed on the brink of collapse.[12] Despite continued economic growth, with GDP increasing over the 1990s at a rate of 4.9 percent per year (from 2006–7 this rose to 6.2 percent, a growth caused primarily by the garment industry and migrant remittances (Home Office, 2008)) plus some encouraging upwards shifts in human development indicators (Lewis, 2011: 56), it seemed as if the country would never break free from the cycle of instability and corruption. When a caretaker government was installed by the army, many Bangladeshis breathed a sigh of relief at the immediate crackdown on corruption and the ban on political activity. Finally, it seemed, life and business could carry on without constant interruption from *hartals* and road blocks. Some people even wondered whether democracy could ever work in Bangladesh.

Initially donors such as DFID and the World Bank were supportive of the caretaker government, which seemed to offer some hope of stability, albeit temporarily. The anti-corruption drive started well, too. Over time, however, the crackdown appeared repressive rather than restorative, and concerns about human rights abuses and the lack of political freedom swelled, with increasing calls for democratic elections. Effective opposition had, however, been pretty much decimated by the 'anti-corruption drive', in which huge numbers of politicians and business people were put into prison, including both Sheikh Hasina and Khaleda Zia, and political gatherings banned. Many predicted a return to military dictatorship, but at the end of 2008 the elections were finally held, with Sheikh Hasina's Awami League winning the majority. Democracy, it seemed, had tentatively returned. It was in this period, from the beginning of the caretaker government until the new Awami League government in 2009 that the research for this book was carried out.

In his incisive and wide-ranging discussion of Bangladeshi politics and governance, David Lewis concludes that these have:

> become a 'high stakes' game in which political competition takes the form of attempts to control and manipulate the state to serve partisan interest within a 'winner takes all' system. The accountability mechanisms that could introduce checks and balances into the system have failed to operate, with the result that conflict and confrontation are seen as more effective political strategies than negotiation. What could once have been viewed as regulatory problems of governance – such as weak law and order enforcement, regular defaulting on loans, a deterioration in the quality of administration, the politicisation of the education system and pervasive corruption – have now 'hardened' into a severe structural problem. (2011: 169)

*   *   *

What does the tumultuous political history described above mean for ordinary people? While for farmers in Duniyapur the machinations of the Awami League and BNP's rival leaders may seem geographically distant, the character of national politics is matched by political struggles at more local levels. These are directly affected by the twists and turns of government since the rise and fall of MPs and *upizila* (local council) members depends to a degree on the fate of the political parties of which they are part. As in Dhaka, politics in Duniyapur is marked by factionalism and patronage. Struggles over resources that at the level of the state are played out via bribery, backhanders and nepotism are matched within villages, where, as we shall see in the next two chapters, social connections govern one's ability to access material resources. The ambivalence caused by personal reliance on informal networks and patronage on the one hand, and a belief in a transparent and non-corrupt state on the other, is an important theme in many of the contestations surrounding the Bibiyana Gas Field, an issue I explore in Chapter 6 (see Jordan Smith, 2007; Parry, 2001).

National politics is, however, more than simply a refraction of local political relations. The political crises and state corruption summarised above have had a real effect on people's ability to earn a living, travel around and get things done without paying bribes. This can affect access to vital resources. During our fieldwork in 2008–9, for example, farmers complained that they were unable to get hold of fertilisers without paying bribes to government officials. Similar complaints were made about land compensation: the land registry offices wouldn't pay owners the compensation owed on land taken by the government for the gas field without the payment of handsome bribes. *Hartals*, which can take place over a number of days, mean that businesses and factories are forced to close and travel becomes impossible. Labour unrest can also lead to significant disruption: road blockages by garment factory workers on the outskirts of Dhaka have frequently led to the closure of the S2 Highway, linking Dhaka to Habiganj and beyond. The unions have considerable power, but their tactics involve the politics of confrontation, which is often met with ruthless action by the police. At the time of writing, for example (30 June 2010), 15,000 garment factory workers were blocking roads around Dhaka in protest over pay. A month earlier 250 factories had been closed by the same dispute, the workers only returning under a heavy police presence. Photos published on the internet show pictures of police beating children involved in the protests; whether these children work in the factories seems beside the point.[13]

Political volatility is matched by a tumultuous meteorology. The rise and fall of democratic governments and military dictatorships in Bangladesh has taken place against a backdrop of catastrophic floods, land erosion and furious cyclones. It is invariably the most vulnerable who are the worst affected, for their houses are built with bamboo and straw rather than bricks and mortar, and they are more likely to be living on insecure and marginal land, such as the banks of rivers. Floods and cyclones are, in part, a natural feature of the deltaic landscape, in which some land is seasonally under water forming large *haors* (areas of inundated land) and land masses are constantly shifting and changing. While the floods are to some degree 'natural', increasing population pressure means that they can have disastrous human consequences, not to mention causing widespread damage to crops and housing. Global warming is likely to further exacerbate the ferocity of storms and flooding in the region. Indeed, within international discourses of global climate change, the fate of Bangladesh has become something of a *cause célèbre*.

BANGLADESH IN 2011: INDUSTRIALISATION, GROWTH AND 'POWER SHEDDING'

Despite the many problems facing Bangladesh in the first decades of the twenty-first century there is also cause for cautious optimism. Since independence the country has shifted from being aid dependent, unable to grow enough rice to feed its population and with a weak export sector dominated by tea and jute, to a country that is seen in some quarters as a 'development success', with significant economic growth[14] and an export sector dominated by the garment industry, migrant remittances and the shrimp industry. The garment industry alone employs several million people (the majority of whom are women) and accounts for three-quarters of Bangladesh's US \$5 billion exports, while migrant remittances in 2007 were estimated at US \$6.526 billion. The export of labour is a crucial source of foreign income, most of which directly reaches the households of the migrants rather than being retained by the elite.[15]

The country is also largely self-sufficient in rice, due to higher-yield varieties and the use of chemical fertilisers, though concerns over food security still continue, and parts of the country still experience seasons pre-harvest food shortages.[16] Growth in GDP is also not the same as a reduction in poverty *per se*. Estimates over the 1990s put the reduction in poverty at around 1 percent a year, with approximately half of the population living in poverty in 2002 (Toufique and Turton, 2002: 17). Similar figures are cited by Unicef: using data from 1994 to 2008, 50 percent of the population is calculated as below the poverty line, which is estimated as being an income of less than \$1.25 per day.[17] As the mismatch between these figures indicates, while some people are growing more wealthy, a great many more are at best not seeing the benefits of economic growth, and at worst growing poorer. The disjunction – or synergy – between neoliberal economic growth and pervasive poverty, underscores every chapter in this book.

Though far from reaching the 'take off' of parts of neighbouring India, Thailand or Vietnam, modest economic growth in Bangladesh has been matched by a decreasing dependency on foreign aid, in which the country has moved a long way from its earlier reputation as a 'bottomless basket case'.[18] Yet while aid transfers have decreased, donors such as the UK, the US and Japan continue to play an important political role, supporting certain forms of political change and encouraging economic policies of privatisation and liberalisation. The development of Export Processing Zones in the country, in which foreign countries are given a ten-year tax holiday, allowed to hire non-unionised workers and given preferential treatment in accessing utilities is strongly supported by DFID, Japan and the World Bank. By 2002, these zones were generating over US $1 billion in export revenue (see Cross, 2011).

The Bangladesh of 2011 is thus in many ways a far cry from that of the 1970s, with its privatised, export-oriented industry, mass overseas migration and vastly improved communications, including a network of good-quality roads and bridges, largely funded by the World Bank, and the widespread use of mobile phones, developed in part by the Grameen Bank. In the twenty or so years that I have been visiting the country these changes have had a radical effect on the connections between people and places; what was once a two-hour walk across the fields to the road at Sherpur, followed by a ten-hour bus journey to Dhaka, with interminable stops for ferries, has become a four- or five-hour whizz along World Bank-funded highways. During my fieldwork in the late 1980s phone calls were only possible if one knew someone in Sylhet Town who rented a land line. Today, mobile phones and cheap phone cards mean that people in Nadampur can chat for hours to their family and friends in Britain or the Middle East.

Like many roads in Bangladesh, however, the path to 'economic development' has been somewhat bumpy. Alongside nascent industrialisation, questions of energy supply and the country's natural resources, particularly coal and natural gas, have become increasingly vital. Once again, unequal entitlement to scarce resources, corruption and violent protest are the order of the day. The stories heap up, each testimony to people's need for connection and its uneven spread. In April 2010, a power engineer in Barisal was attacked in his office by a crowd accusing him of only supplying electricity to private companies able to pay bribes, while ordinary domestic users faced 13–17 hours a day of load shedding.[19] In other places power stations have been the sites of protests against load shedding, especially in the sweltering pre-monsoon months. In Sylhet in 2006 a crowd of people ransacked the offices of the Power Development Board during the night in protest against load shedding, resulting in a reported 35 people injured.[20] These incidents might be read as allegories of contemporary Bangladesh, with ordinary people struggling to connect to vital resources in the face of shortages and corruption. In lieu of legal or bureaucratic redress, violence seems the only option.

Within this context of acute and seemingly ever increasing energy shortages, the discoveries of natural gas and coal reserves in various areas of the country have provided hope in some quarters that the constant power shedding which afflicts Bangladeshi homes, workshops and factories might become a thing of the past. In the most optimistic accounts gas and coal reserves are hailed as a potential saviour for Bangladesh, a resource that could be exported, earning crucial foreign currency, as well as being used domestically.

While around 50 percent of gas fields are government-owned, the remainder are operated by multinational energy corporations, which have production share contracts with Petrobangla, the state-owned Bangladesh Oil, Gas and Mineral Corporation.[21] This movement into Bangladesh of multinationals is partly a reflection of the difficult environment that they face, in which they are forced to exploit resources in increasingly challenging contexts in order to remain in profit (Colley, 2002: 34).

In Sylhet, Occidental carried out initial explorations for gas during the early 1990s. By the 2000s, development of three gas fields at Moulavi Bazaar, Jalalbad and Bibiyana had been taken over by Unocal, which subsequently merged with Chevron in 2005. By 2010 Chevron was producing 50 percent of Bangladesh's natural gas from Bibiyana, Jalalbad and Moulavi Bazaar, most of which was used to produce electricity for the domestic market. The remaining 50 percent of gas is produced by three state-owned companies, Bangladesh Gas Fields, BAPEX and Sylhet Gas Fields.[22] Overall, gas production contributes to 80 percent of energy consumption in the country. More recently, Chevron has been seeking to expand its operations, exploring offshore reserves, indigenous forest at Lawachara and other parts of the country since the mid 2000s. Competition is fierce: recent reports are of eight multinationals vying for contracts to develop new drilling sites.[23]

The extent of Bangladesh's gas reserves is constantly debated and disputed. In 2005, for example, the *Oil and Gas Journal* estimated that the country had around 10.5 million cubic feet. This figure was to be downgraded considerably by 2006, when the estimate was for 5 million cubic feet. During the course of our research estimates of Bibiyana's reserves were constantly changing, according to political disposition as well as geological and seismic surveys. When the site was inaugurated in 2007 it was heralded as having the capacity to produce gas for the next thirty years. Two years later, Chevron was being accused of over exploiting the reserves, which, the critics argued, were smaller than had originally been predicted. In 2010, the company was announcing that, to the contrary, the reserves were more than anyone had ever hoped and Chevron would be able to increase its production by up to 25 percent.[24] As I shall argue in Chapter 6, the only thing that is certain in disputes over gas extraction in Bangladesh is that information and knowledge concerning reserves, production share contracts and compensation are never politically neutral.

Meanwhile in Phulbari in north-west Bangladesh, the discovery of significant coal reserves in the early 2000s led to an ambitious plan for an open cast mine, to be operated by Asia Energy. In the original proposal to the government, made in 2005, the company stated that it would extract 15 million tonnes a year and install a 5,000 MW power plant to generate electricity from the coal. According to information given by the network 'Mines and Communities', the production share contract would give the government only 6 percent royalties.[25] There was another major drawback. The proposed mine was to be located on agricultural land as well as Phulbari Town, necessitating the relocation of an estimated 40,000 people. The ensuring uproar culminated in protests in 2006 that left three dead and many injured after police fired into the crowd. Since then Asia Energy's offices in Phulbari Town have been closed, though the company has not stopped lobbying for a contract to develop the mine. In 2010 new proposals were put forward to the incoming Awami League government, this time offering the government a 10 percent share in profits. The plan is largely supported by donors, including the UN Development Programme (UNDP) and GTZ (now GIZ), who have financed a feasibility study of an adjacent open pit mine at Bara Pukira. Not surprisingly, critics have been quick to attack the plans.

I shall explore national and local opposition to multinational energy companies and the production share contracts that they negotiate with the government in greater detail in Chapter 6. For now, let us note how over the last decade energy has risen to the top of the political agenda in Bangladesh. On the one hand shortages and power shedding have led to direct action by ordinary people infuriated by constant cuts in their supply. On the other, more organised campaigners have focused on the exploitative terms on which multinational energy companies operate, as well as the damage caused by accidents and environmentally dubious exploration methods.[26]

Underlying these issues is the alleged corruption of the government and its officials and the ubiquitous practice of *baksheesh* (bribery), whether involving a lone engineer taking bribes to provide electricity to some but not others, or a government minister brokering deals that bring personal advantage but providing little for Bangladesh. Allegations of corruption are a constant theme in Duniyapur, expressing widespread ideas of how the public domain *should be* as well as what is wrong with it (Parry, 2001). At the heart of this is the relentless struggle over resources. In the disputes that are described in this book the rapacious need to access new territories by multinational energy companies which must make a profit to survive crashes headlong into a series of equally desperate needs: of a country slowly moving towards some form of neoliberal industrial capitalism, of the citizens of Bangladesh needing connection to the national grid, and of local people, needing land, homes and livelihoods.

There are other stories of global connection to be told. Here, though, we see how, rather than simply being 'acted upon' by geopolitics and colonial/postcolonial capitalism, people in and from the villages surrounding the Bibiyana Gas Field have shown a good deal of agency in their articulation with the global economy. Indeed, they have been active participants in many of the processes that have brought the gas field to their *desh*. Within this history we see many of the threads that link each chapter in this book: the importance of localised networks and connections yet also of their global reach, the centrality of colonial and global economies and their articulation in particular locations, relationships between places across thousands of miles and the search for resources.

PEOPLE ON THE MOVE: A SHORT HISTORY OF SYLHETI GLOBAL MIGRATION

As Tasneem Siddiqui (2003) points out, migration has been a part of life for East Bengalis for many centuries. The region has always been characterised by high degrees of fluidity, both within and across its shifting political borders. From pre-colonial times migrants from the west settled the highly fertile but often waterlogged lands of the east, while other historical evidence points to movement in the other direction, a continual flow of people, irrespective of national borders (van Schendel, 2005). These constant, cross-cutting migrations result from both the region's turbulent history and its environment, in which floods and cyclones mean that 'belonging' can never be guaranteed. Ranabir Samaddar writes movingly that the country is: 'an insecure environment, inhabited by insecure families'. Such families dream constantly of escaping insecurity. As Samaddar continues: 'This dream has made Bangladesh a land of fast footed people, people who would not accept the loss of their dream, who would move on to newer and newer lands' (1999: 83–7).

Today, these fast-footed people are moving both internally (see, for example, Afsar, 2000; Khan and Seeley, 2005; van Schendel, 2005) and overseas, predominantly to the Gulf and to South East Asia (see, for example, Abrar, 2000; Gardner 1995; Siddiqui, 2003). The scale of this movement is vast. As Siddiqui reports, from 1976 to 2002 official figures show that over 3 million Bangladeshis migrated overseas, mostly on short-term contracts.[27] Moreover, remittances have made a huge contribution to the GDP of Bangladesh (Siddiqui, 2005). While some migrants are middle-class professionals, the vast majority are unskilled wage labourers, often inhabiting the most vulnerable and lowly paid sectors of the international labour market. Many move illegally, taking huge risks in their attempts to access foreign remittances; a large number of these unlegals are caught or deported before they have a chance to earn enough to recoup the costs of the journey, or are cheated by unscrupulous brokers.

While these migrants come from many parts of Bangladesh, in Sylhet international migration has a distinct character and history, for the region has a special connection with Britain, forged on British ships and, more recently, in factories and restaurants. In Duniyapur, while many men from the district have migrated to the Middle East and South East Asia, movement to Britain has been far more influential. Indeed, approximately 95 percent of the British Bengali population is Sylheti in origin. Let's start with the first pioneers: the *lascars* (sailors).

Sylheti Lascars

Sylhet's special relationship with Britain began in the nineteenth century, when men from the district gained a reputation as '*lascars*' or sailors, working on British ships which carried goods from Calcutta to around the world. In the early part of the twentieth century, a growing number of Sylheti *lascars* 'jumped ship' in London, where they sought work as peddlers or in London's hotels and restaurants (Choudhury, 1993: 33). Although originally employment on the ships went to men from districts such as Noakhali and Chittagong, by the twentieth century Sylhetis dominated (1993: 33–5).

The reasons are complex. Possibly the *taluk dar* system contributed both to an entrepreneurial spirit as well as the capital reserves required to travel to Calcutta.[28] Another reason may be the riverine geography of the region, which produced a population experienced in boats and shipping. As Yousef Choudhury has shown, British steamer boats on their way to Assam from Calcutta passed through Sylhet District, setting up direct links between the area and Calcutta, from which British trading ships embarked. Over the nineteenth century the steamer service expanded rapidly, employing increasing numbers of Sylhetis who worked in their engine rooms (Choudhury, 1993: 29–34). The steamers took the men to Calcutta, where they found employment with the British shipping companies based there. Gradually, as growing numbers of Sylheti men arrived in search of work, a network of Sylheti boarding houses and agents (or *bariwallahs*) developed in the city. Today, many *Londoni* families in Duniyapur trace their ancestry to these original seamen; indeed, the homestead where I stay in Nadampur is still known as *sareng bari* (homestead of ship's foreman).[29]

In these early days of British–Sylheti connections the physical topography of Sylhet coincided with the labour demands of the East India Company to produce particular geographies of migration, just as today physical reserves of gas have produced particular geographies of industrialisation. Crucially too, these pioneering migrations were characterised by patronage and social connections; key individuals dominated the recruitment of labour, leading to a 'chain' effect whereby men from particular villages and lineages gained employment through the patronage of their relatives and neighbours. In Nadampur, it was the great grandfather of my closest friends, the *sareng* who helped link the village so closely to Britain by recruiting his relatives and neighbours as *lascars*. These early social connections meant that ship workers and, later, labour migrants to Britain, became concentrated in particular villages and areas within Sylhet and Habiganj.

Over the nineteenth and into the early twentieth century a small number of Sylhetis began to settle in Britain. After the First World War, when considerable numbers of East Bengalis fought for the British, this group increased, as did the numbers of young men travelling to Calcutta in search of work on the ships. Most came from villages like Nadampur, which had pre-existing connections with other *lascars* who would help the newcomers find work and initial accommodation in Calcutta. As Choudhury argues, all hoped to become English articled seamen, who enjoyed better working conditions and pay than the *lascars*. This process involved jumping ship in Britain, obtaining an identity card and making the transition to English articled seaman. Most men failed. The majority were either prevented from going ashore, deported or lived in penury in Britain, but those who did make the transition made enough money to transform their family's economic and social status back in Sylhet (Gardner, 1995: 51).

Although still tiny, in the inter-war period the Sylheti population in Britain began to slowly increase.[30] Many more Sylheti men worked on the ships and, during the Second World War, a considerable number of these were killed. Since they worked in the engine rooms, Sylhetis were particularly vulnerable when ships went down. As Choudhury describes, back in the villages people waited anxiously to hear the fate of their relatives and neighbours; because the men were employed through networks of kinship and community, a sunk ship might mean that a lineage would lose many of its men, or almost everyone in a village face bereavement (Choudhury, 1993: 59).

British Settlers

After the Second World War the Bengali population in Britain began to rise. Most were employed by restaurants or Jewish tailoring businesses. Nearly all lived in boarding houses, sometimes owned by English landladies, sometimes by other Sylhetis or South Asians. While the majority lived in London, over the 1940s some began to move north to the Midlands to find work in factories. They were still very much 'pioneers', part of a tiny minority, who believed their stay in Britain to be temporary.

Partition in 1947 was an important watershed in the history of Sylheti migration. From 1952 East Pakistanis needed visas and passports to enter West Bengal. The *bariwallas* sold their boarding houses and, like the *lascars*, returned to their villages. Over 1952–5, cut off from their source of employment, many Sylheti seamen faced destitution. Aftab Ali, the leader of the Seamen's Union and a central player in the promotion of Sylheti migration to Britain, attempted to help them by obtaining passports for work in Britain. Despite attempts by the government based in West Pakistan to block this initiative, in 1956 he succeeded by obtaining 600 international passports for the first seamen (Choudhury, 1993: 89). In the same period he set up a Seaman's Welfare Office in Sylhet Town and, next door, a travel agency, run by his family. Choudhury describes watching large crowds of men descend on the offices when they opened in 1956, clamouring for the passports. Word was beginning to spread of the profits to be made in Britain, and by now it was not just the seamen who wanted passports (Choudhury, 1993: 95–8). In 1956 1,000 passports were issued. Other men obtained 'admissions cards' from private institutions sponsoring visits to Britain,[31] or medical passports enabling their holders to travel to Britain as patients.

While many of the men taking up these passports were originally *lascars*, or had close relatives who had worked on the ships, others had no direct social connections but came from areas of Sylhet which had already established links with Britain: they had heard of the potential for making money there, and had contacts who would help them find work and accommodation. Most came from households with sufficient capital to cover the initial costs of migration. A minority were from poorer or landless households, but through local networks of patronage obtained loans which enabled them to migrate. Today, most of these families have transformed their economic and social standing. As we shall see, in Duniyapur these early patterns of migration to Britain were to have a profound effect on local socio-economic hierarchies.

The late 1950s to 1962 was perhaps the 'golden age' of migration to Britain, when entry to the country was still relatively easy and the first immigration controls had yet to be introduced. In terms of political economy, post-war Britain still needed the cheap labour supplied by its ex-colonies and the British authorities actively encouraged labour migration into the country. In 1962, work permits (known locally as 'labour vouchers') were issued directly from Sylhet Town. Sylhetis were well placed to gain maximum advantage from these permits. With a small but rapidly growing network of men already living in Britain, the chain effect continued. Such was the demand for the 'vouchers' that, as Choudhury (1993) reports, an office of the British High Commission was opened in Sylhet.

Increasingly, large numbers of young Sylheti men began to leave for Britain. Most lived and worked in northern cities, finding employment in heavy industry. Some went directly to London, working in the garment industry as pressers or tailors. Usually they stayed in lodging houses with other Sylhetis. This was a period of consistently hard graft; the men worked as many days and hours a week as was possible, remitting their wages to their families back in Sylhet. In today's terminology, the men were 'transnationals' *par excellence*: they worked and lived in Britain but returned as often as they could to Sylhet where they were still heavily involved in social networks of kinship and village community, as well as regional and national political activities.

Family Reunification

Over the 1970s and into the 1980s Britain's heavy industry was in decline and many Sylheti men moved to London to seek employment in the garment or restaurant trades. Crucially, a growing number started to bring their wives and children to the United Kingdom (Peach, 1996). There are a number of reasons why Bengalis reunited their families in Britain during this period. The first is to do with changes in immigration law, which interacted with the stages many migrant households had reached in their development cycles. Immigration controls had been gathering pace over the 1960s, and were closely connected to shifting demands for cheap labour from British industry. Rather than seeking to attract workers from the ex-colonies, the British state now sought to limit their entry and status in Britain. The legislation also reflects the intensification of popular racist attitudes to the immigration which had been taking place over the period (see Clarke, 1992: 19), as exemplified by the race riots of 1958 and Enoch Powell's infamous 'Rivers of Blood' speech. As Clarke (1992: 20) argues, the control of black Commonwealth immigration and settlement, which became a central feature of political life over the 1950s and 1970s, became almost a British national obsession during this period.

In 1962 the first Commonwealth Immigrants Bill restricted the admission of Commonwealth settlers to those who had been issued with employment vouchers. Without British citizenship, Pakistani passport holders on trips home had to return to Britain within two years. This essentially meant that the movement of certain categories of people (i.e. non-whites) between places was to be restricted; the separation of families by law had also now become possible (Fryer, 1984: 383–4). Some, but not all Bengali men acquired British citizenship at this stage.[32] Fearful of losing their rights at home, others chose not to. From this first piece of legislation, controls over immigration into Britain became increasingly stringent.[33] The Immigration Act of 1971, for example, was another important turning point. This virtually ended all primary migration. The only non-white people now permitted entry were those allowed to do a specific job for a limited period; the state also had increasing power to deport people (Fryer, 1984: 385). Increasingly Bengalis based in Britain began to fear that they would lose their rights to move between places and, in particular, that if they were not brought to the UK as dependants (i.e. children under the age of 18) their sons would not be able to work in Britain. The 1962 law had made it illegal for children under 18 to enter the country without their mothers, so this meant bringing men's wives to Britain too.

These changes in legislation did not automatically lead to family reunification. For many migrant households in the 1970s, Britain was still seen not seen as an appropriate place for women and children. *Bidesh* (foreign countries) were almost exclusively a male domain, while the *desh* was the locus of spirituality and honour, as embodied by the women who stayed there. The Islamicisation of Britain was still in its infancy and the country was seen as a hostile place to bring up one's family (Ul-Hoque, 2011). Without suitable housing and services, many families decided that cultural codes of *purdah* and female modesty could not be maintained and delayed bringing their wives to Britain for as long as possible. In other cases women refused to leave the *desh*, sometimes causing their husbands to take second wives so that their children were accompanied by substitute 'mothers' into the country (Choudhury, 1993: 141).

In the 1980s these attitudes started to shift and families were re-united. The process sometimes took many years; immigration controls increasingly involved a highly complex process of questioning and verification, made all the more difficult by the false claims that some men had initially made for tax and other purposes (Choudhury, 1993: 141). In all cases the effects of immigration controls were combined with changing notions of the suitability of Britain for family life, as well as the circumstances of individual households.

Another reason for family reunification returns us to the history of Bangladesh. Although there was huge support for the 1971 Liberation War from British Bengalis, news of the subsequent traumatic political events, cyclones and famines contributed to a growing impression that Bangladesh was a place of instability and want. Increasingly, the perception of the settlers was that their future should be in Britain, not the *desh*. The 'snowball' effect was also important: the more Bengalis settled in specific pockets of the country, the more Bengali shops and services were set up, the more comfortable people felt about their families coming to Britain.

This growing sense of 'community' was linked to another change: movement from industrial cities such as Birmingham and Oldham to London, where there were more facilities and provisions for Muslim Bengalis. The main reason was economic. Over the 1970s employment opportunities for unskilled workers in heavy industry began to drastically fall. Forced to find new economic niches, many Bengalis sought work either in the burgeoning 'Indian' restaurant trade, or the garment industry based in Tower Hamlets.

Today, the Bangladeshi population is the youngest and fastest growing in Britain. The 2001 Census enumerated a total population of 283,063 of whom 38 percent were under 16. Fifty-four percent of Bangladeshis lived in London[34] and nearly half of these are situated in Tower Hamlets where they form over a quarter of the resident population (in some areas within the borough, this figure is higher). Statistics from 2001–2 suggest that Bangladeshis had the highest unemployment rate in the UK, with over 40 percent of Bangladeshi men under the age of 25 unemployed.[35] The Bangladeshi population in Britain has also been among those hardest hit by the recent recession, and is characterised by poverty and unemployment. According to figures released by the Office for National Statistics in 2001–2, 60 percent of Bangladeshis in the UK live in low-income housing and, over these years, had an unemployment rate of 20 percent for men and 24 percent for women (Office for National Statistics, 2002). Bangladeshis currently have the highest level of Economic Inactivity (EI) of any group in the UK – 46.2 percent in 2010 – with an unemployment rate of 16.4 percent (Office for National Statistics, 2010).[36]

Many British Bangladeshis are still profoundly linked to the *desh* (homeland), retaining a keen interest in local and national politics, owning property in their villages and maintaining close relationships with relatives there. Arguably, this is particularly the case for those born in Bangladesh, though this should not be confused with the 'first generation', for transnational marriages (often between cousins) mean that young men and women are constantly arriving from Bangladesh to marry British partners.[37] In this respect, age is not necessarily an arbiter of someone's propensity to be involved in *deshi* affairs. As we shall see, transnational relationships between Duniyapur and particular parts of the UK, where networks of villagers have settled, have had a profound effect on the various stories of the gas field.

MIGRATION AND TRANSFORMATION IN DUNIYAPUR

The broader history of transnational connections is linked to dramatic changes within the villages that originally sent men to Britain. In my doctoral research in Nadampur I found that households that had gained access to Britain in the 1960s, had, by the 1980s, accumulated large amounts of land. In contrast, those who had neither the inclination nor the wherewithal to send members abroad had, from the 1960s to the late 1980s, tended to lose it, usually to their *Londoni* neighbours. There was thus a direct correlation between migration to Britain and the accumulation of wealth; the stronger a household's links with Britain the more land could be acquired, while non-migrants were pushed, through processes of land division and rural impoverishment, to sell up. This pattern of particular groups within particular lineages using British wages to buy up land and increase their resource base is echoed across Sylhet and Habinganj, where gains became clustered in areas such as Beani Bazar, Moulvi Bazaar, Biswanath and Nobiganj (Gardner, 1995). In Nadampur and its close neighbour, Karimpur, in particular, it was the Pathans, Khans and Saiyeds who profited most from migration, though some of the highest-status Saiyed families who had chosen not to migrate had by 1988 become impoverished. Today, the broken-down huts of the non-migrant Nadampur Saiyeds can be found in the same *bari* as their migrant cousins, who have recently built themselves a three-storey house, complete with smoked glass windows and fancy brickwork.

During the decades of intense migration to and settlement in Britain the transformations were more than economic. As in other *Londoni* villages in Sylhet, in Nadampur *Londoni* households were involved in intense projects of social transformation: marrying into higher-status families, building impressive houses and sometimes changing their family names from the lower status 'Ullah' or 'Ahmed' to 'Saiyed' or 'Sheikh', thereby asserting a blood link to Shah Jalal. A proportion of these upwardly mobile families also claimed to be descendants of local saints (*pir*), claims which were often strenuously contested by their sceptical neighbours (Gardner, 1993b, 1995).

The use of remittances tended to follow a particular pattern. After paying off debts that the original migration incurred and covering household subsistence, foreign earnings tended to be invested in land, the arbiter of wealth, power and security. After this, they were generally used to build new *pukka* (stone) houses, an important asset in an environment liable to cyclonic storms and flooding. Remittances were also invested in further migration, funding the movement of close kin to the Middle East, as well as business enterprises and property in Britain. It was a process in which successful *Londonis* and their immediate families were making themselves as secure as possible, both by accumulating land in the village and laying down strong connections with Britain and other sources of foreign earnings. Social resources were important too; the processes of 'Ashrafisation'[38] and other signifiers of upward mobility were not empty 'vanity projects', but part of a wider context in which one's status directly affects the claims one can make on others.

Although the majority of villagers have never moved beyond Bangladesh's state boundaries, the net effect of thirty or forty years of connectedness to Britain has created what Steve Vertovec has dubbed a 'transnational habitus', in which geographical movement and economic success are inextricably linked in the minds of migrants and non-migrants alike (2010: 66–9). This need for connectedness is not simply 'imagined'. Local economies have become largely dependent upon remittances from foreign countries. These tangible economic changes have contributed to local imaginings of different places which, in turn, structure people's aspirations and dreams. For non-migrants 'London' is constructed as a place of economic opportunity and security. The highly visible achievements of *Londoni* households are testimony to the wealth that can be made in the UK. Exchange rates mean that even a modest wage in Britain is a fortune in Bangladesh. For example, a labourer's wages average 150 *taka* a day (about £1.50).[39] Crucially, competition over land and property between *Londoni* families has pushed local prices up so high that one needs a British income to afford it. In research in Biswanath (another *Londoni* area of Sylhet) we found that a third of an acre of land (one *kiare*) near the centre of the village costs up to 1 *crore* (1 million) *taka*: around £8,264. In other areas of Bangladesh, one might pay around £600 to £700 for an acre (Gardner and Ahmed, 2009).

Yet while overseas migration is associated with upward mobility there is also a clear hierarchy of places within local imaginings. Although in the late 1980s in Nadampur many young men were migrating to the Middle East for temporary employment, in the late 2000s the Middle East was no longer seen as a particularly desirable destination among the more prosperous households. This is because the wages to be earned there are not high enough to enable one to invest in property or businesses at home. In addition, the Middle East is perceived as a risky destination in which would-be migrants are cheated by agents, or go as insecure 'unlegals'. Migrants to the Middle East are thus from the more vulnerable lower-income households, who lack the social links to get to the UK yet are prepared take the gamble of investing savings or credit on temporary labour migration, often to lose everything to a fraudulent agent (Gardner and Ahmed, 2009).

* * *

If the economies and inequalities of Duniyapur have been shaped by global hierarchies of place, the broader history of Bangladesh tells us that these thick tangles of connectedness between people and places have been flourishing for many hundreds of years. To an extent, transnational links between Firizpur and Burnley, or Nadampur and Newcastle, are only one version of a story that characterises much of the world, in which people's search for survival and security pulls them towards centres of accumulation and wealth. Some of those who have put down roots in Britain have rarely, if ever, returned. The majority, however, remain connected to the *desh*, where other roots go deep. Meanwhile those who remain seek out the UK or, failing that, those based there. Like creepers struggling to gain traction on securely nourished plants, their grip can be tenacious.

While the relationship between places and people is far from equal, the global search for connection is not unilinear. In their need for new sources of profit – be these natural resources or raw materials, hubs of capitalistic accumulation – trading companies, colonial states or multinational oil companies seek out new places in which to embed their operations. This was why, back in the 1980s, oil (or rather, *gas*) men were frequently seen on the Dhaka to Sylhet Biman flight. They were obviously Western but, in their jeans and baseball caps, didn't look like NGO volunteers or High Commission officials. That Sylhet had reserves of gas was well known; what was changing was the need for the multinationals to explore new territories, plus the political willingness of the government to court foreign investment. A new thicket of relationships, desires and interests was about to spring up. For some, it would bring new opportunities for connection. For others it would lead to rupture.

THE GAS COMPANY ARRIVES: A SHORT HISTORY OF THE BIBIYANA GAS FIELD

By the mid 2000s, nearly twenty years after my original fieldwork in Nadampur, the villages that surrounded the land which was shortly to become the Bibiyana Gas Field had changed dramatically. The dirt track that linked Kakura to Nadampur was now metalled, there was a new high school in Nadampur, a new mosque and a host of large *pukka* houses. The bazaar, which in 1987 had sported only a few tea stalls, was now a thriving market place, filled with travel agents, electronic shops and mobile phone suppliers. Many of the more wealthy houses had indoor kitchens; nearly all had indoor toilets and bathrooms. Fridges and televisions were no longer remarkable. Indeed, the area now had electricity, though its supply was far from regular and the line bypassed impoverished Kakura, which, for reasons I describe later has a different history from the other villages surrounding the gas field, and has an extremely high rate of landlessness.

More profoundly, perhaps, many families had completely relocated to the UK, leaving their houses empty or occupied by relatives. Others had moved in: outsiders who had bought up property or land with *Londoni* money and now had a large house on the road, or situated on the outskirts of Kakura. At the other end of the economic hierarchy, in-coming migrants from poorer areas of Bangladesh lived in '*colonies*' (cheap barrack style housing) by the school and on the other side of the river, providing a supply of cheap labour and rental income for village landowners.

Yet while materially the area had clearly become more 'developed', the hierarchies and divisions that I had observed in 1987–8 remained. Indeed, they seemed more engrained than ever. The poorest villagers who had never migrated had not much improved their lot; they still lived in mud and straw huts and still struggled with precarious livelihoods and periodic crises. Some households had managed to grasp hold of a connection with *bidesh*, perhaps via the marriage of a son or daughter, though these opportunities tended to be confined to more prosperous families who already had good contacts. More usually, a son had been sent to the Middle East as a labour migrant. For a minority, this had paid off, especially if they already had connections with wealthier relatives or patrons. Abdus Khan, for example, who in 1988 was a newly wed Saudi migrant, living in a mud house with a thatched roof with his sister, wife and mother, had by 2010 built himself a large house and a 'colony', which he rented to landless in-migrants.

For the majority of the landless poor, however, there seemed to be little improvement or hope of change. This was especially the case in Kakura, where no-one was related to the locally powerful lineages, few people owned land and even fewer had contacts abroad. It was into this context that the gas men, arrived, with their four-wheel drives, their technical equipment, their plans and their promises.

The arrival of the foreigners was not so surprising. By the 1990s several gas fields were operating in the Sylhet region; these were run by foreign multinationals as well as the government-owned Bangladesh Gas Fields Ltd, a subsidiary of the government-owned Petrobangla. The earlier explorations for gas in the area were carried out by Occidental during the 1990s. In 1997 a small field was developed in Dighalbak next to the Kushiara River, a kilometre or so north of Nadampur. This was now known as 'North Pad'. A few years later Occidental had been taken over by Unocal (UBL) which discovered two new gas fields, one at Moulavi Bazaar and one situated between the villages of Kakura, Karimpur, Nadampur and Firizpur. The latter was said to be of 'world-class' quality, with the potential to become one of the largest fields in Bangladesh. By 2004, UBL (which in 2005 would be merged with Chevron) had submitted a development plan to Petrobangla to develop the field, which was termed 'South Pad' in the technical reports. It was during these early developments that the area was named 'Bibiyana'. Like so much else, the name was contested: people from Dighalbak, who had lost land to the North Pad a decade earlier, protested that the development was not to be known as the Dighalbak Gas Field, and it was named instead after a small river running through Nadampur.[40] As I shall argue later in the book, processes of naming and identification are important techniques of governance, in which, within the discourses of Chevron officials, local areas became 'our communities'.

Whatever it was to be called, news of the development was passed to local people by the District Commissioner, who informed them that 50 acres of prime agricultural land lying between Nadampur, Firizpur and Karimpur, plus more land for the new roads, would be acquired and that landowners should claim compensation from the government. A report on community engagement commissioned by Unocal in 2005 describes subsequent events under the gloss of 'why things went wrong' (Reyes and Begum, 2005). Initially the main issue, at least for landowners, was the compensation price set by the government, which originally was 84,000 *taka* per acre; a consultancy on land values at the time suggested that this was possibly as low as one-tenth of the actual market value. In what reads like a case study of 'how not to carry out community relations', the report continues to describe how the company held no consultation meetings with 'stakeholders' (i.e. local people), but deferred to the District Commissioner, having been warned not to get involved in the acquisition process (Reyes and Begum, 2005). According to the report, the Minister of Energy assured Unocal that force would not be used. Later in the same report, however, security measures such as armed police escorts, and an agreement by Unocal to provide barracks for a special police contingent comprised of reserve police – who were described as 'young, inexperienced, courageous and the least restrained' (Reyes and Begum, 2005: 23) – are mentioned, leading to questions over the extent to which Unocal was or was not complicit in the threatened use of state violence. As the report continues: 'There is some cause to doubt that the D.C. ever considered the government's price to be reasonable, however, since he saw fit to take a "truckload" of police to inform the community about payment and compensation' (2005: 26).

As the well-protected DC anticipated, the news was not well received. Under a united leadership, local people quickly mobilised to block the road and stop construction of the plant.

> Attendees forcefully made it clear that the price was unacceptable. He [i.e. the DC] returned 4 or 5 days later with a number of senior UBL staff to inform people that the law allowed no further discussion on price and to ask that work be allowed to proceed … [this] second meeting was described … as a 'farce', as 'hasty' and as 'one sided'. According to one UBL staff member there was no prior announcement, nor would the DC allow his presence to be announced by loudspeaker. (Reyes and Begum, 2005: 26)

During this meeting, the DC reminded people that similar issues in Bangladesh were often resolved by troops.

After this, work was stopped for another week. According to the Reyes and Begum report, building contractors received threats and equipment was damaged. Now the UBL president became directly involved, negotiating with the government and 'community leaders' until a price of 500,000 *taka* per acre was eventually agreed. It was at this stage that local leaders began to be identified by Unocal/Chevron, and that their 'demands' were put forward: a hospital, a school, a fertiliser factory and connection to the gas supply were included in the lists made by the newly instituted 'Demand Realisation Committees'. For local people this was a time of great anxiety. When I visited Nadampur in 2005 I heard rumours that a vast site was to be built and the whole village to be relocated.

Compounding these fears was huge concern about the safety of the operation. In 1997 there had been a 'blow-out' at Magurchhara, a forested region close to Sylhet Town, when Occidental was drilling for gas. In 2005 a series of accidents occurred at the Tengratila gas field, operated by the Canadian company Niko in Surnamganj, Sylhet. In the second blow-out within six months at Tengratila, flames leapt up to a height of 150 feet after a loud explosion, leading to widespread panic in surrounding villages. Luckily no-one was injured in these incidents, though the environmental damage was considerable. As we shall see in Chapter 7, the spectre of 'blow-out' looms large in Duniyapur, an understandable preoccupation, given the proximity of many homes to the plant.

Meanwhile it was increasingly clear that, whether landowners liked it or not, they would lose their land. After the offer of 500,000 *taka*, the protests stopped. Another reason for the cessation of direct opposition against the plant was that political pressure from the highest levels was put on local leaders to capitulate. Significantly too, promises were made. According to the accounts we were given, locals were told that the area would become industrialised, there would be plentiful employment and new business opportunities as well as investment into schools and medical facilities. As one man put it:

> We were given good hopes, dreams for the future. They promised us: 'if the road goes past your village you will get transport facilities, industries will be built, you will get jobs ...'

Later, the same man, a landowner, concludes:

> Chevron came to see me several times, requesting that they could take my land. Now all that is over. They don't come to see me. They have my land so they don't need to come. Whenever we want to say something against them they file cases against us. That's why no-one says a word against them.[41]

Today, Chevron officials claim that 97 percent of land has been compensated. While our research did not collate firm figures, some of our informants had ongoing disputes with the company or were still awaiting settlement. As we shall see in the next chapter, this was particularly the case in Karimpur, where much land was informally acquired from Hindus in the 1960s and 1970s. According to the accounts of landowners we met in Duniyapur and the UK, the bribery of land registry officials was the only solution: a 25 percent 'commission', taken by the land office in order to register the land and produce the requisite documentation so that it could then be compensated. As one landowner put it:

In fact the government of Bangladesh is not good. It was the government who prevented us from receiving the actual price of our land. Chevron wanted to pay proper compensation but the government stopped us.[42]

Whether they received full compensation or not, we did not meet anyone who was happy that their land had been (forcibly) acquired by the government for the construction of the gas field. The following quote, from an interview with one of the largest land losers, poignantly sums up the feelings of many, for whom their land was emotionally meaningful and irreplaceable:

I got my compensation money but that's not the point. I lost my land. Money runs out, but land always remains. I can see that land from my house; it always gives me such pain to see it, as a landowner I can't bear it. From my house I used to see the land, but now all I see is the flare of the gas. Just as fire rises from the fields, fire is in my heart. (Interview notes, 2008)

By 2006, the plant was under construction. Initially hundreds of local people were employed as labourers, hired via contractors rather than directly by Chevron. Many were from Kakura. Trained in safety procedures and given identity cards and documentation, most believed that the gas field would be a permanent source of employment. This was not, however, to be. By the time it was opened in 2007 only a handful of security guards and a small number of road construction workers were from Duniyapur for gas production is not labour intensive; those who are employed tend to be highly skilled. In total, around ten households in Karimpur had lost significant amounts of land to the plant; others in Firizipur also lost large holdings; many more lost smaller plots due to the building of the roads. Some of the owners were located in the UK, and had to give power of attorney to their relatives to act on their behalf to receive their compensation. Hundreds more people, who had worked the land as sharecroppers or agricultural labourers, or used the land to graze their cattle, would also be affected by the loss of land, as would an even larger group by wider environmental changes linked to the high banked roads and changes to the Kushiara River that local stories now blame on the gas field. It is to the struggles and stories of these people that I shall turn in the next chapter.

Like that of the broader national context, the history of Duniyapur is thus one of connections: to colonial powers and systems of extraction, to global centres of capital accumulation via labour migration, and to multinational companies via the natural gas that had been discovered under the fields. In the chapters that follow we see how these connections bring deep ambivalence and contradiction. Connection to sources of global capital are necessary if one is to prosper, yet global capitalism bring connection's antonym: disconnection and rupture. Seeking employment and modernity from the gas field, the majority of people in the area have found that there are no jobs, and precious little in the way of economic development. Instead they are increasingly disconnected from the land on which their livelihoods have depended. And while transnational villagers living in the UK seek to connect with their homeland, the loss of land has further removed them from their villages, for they no longer have that vital social and political resource: fields which enable them to 'look after their own'. If the naming of the field, carried out by Dhaka-based officials, disconnects some sections of the population from what they had hoped would be 'their' 'Dighalbak Gas Field', the most tangible sign of connection – to the supply of gas – has never come to the area, despite the early promises of Unocal officials.[43]

At the heart of all this is the struggle over resources which characterises so much of Bangladesh's history. In the next chapter we turn to the material nature of these resources. As we shall see, land remains central to the lives and livelihoods of most people living in the area, yet particular systems of entitlement mean that while some remain connected to this vital resource, the majority are increasingly dispossessed and disconnected.

3

Material Connections:
Resources and Livelihoods in Duniyapur

Spring 2008: San Mahmud[1] squats patiently before the fence, staring through the barbed wire into the orderly space of the gas plant. It's another world inside: a place where uniforms are donned, workers' attendances carefully clocked, and health and safety regulations strictly upheld. A placard near the entrance declares the number of days since the plant was inaugurated. Underneath this, another sign shows the number of safety breaches which have occurred since then (nil). A short distance across the gravel a row of gleaming four-wheel drives are neatly parked next to a manicured square of grass; on the other side rest the bicycles issued to those locals lucky enough to have gained permanent employment with the company. The contrast with the world beyond could not be more extreme: where the plant exemplifies industrial order and modernity, the scattered tea stalls and muddy paths that lead past it into Karimpur, with their rickshaws, tethered goats and wandering, undernourished cows, seem to exemplify rural Bangladesh.

It is because of this contrast that San Mahmud is here. Or rather, it's because of the opportunities that the plant appears to offer: of regular employment, decent wages and security, versus the continual, exhausting uncertainty of eking a living from the local economy. Around his neck hangs the identity card that Chevron provided him with three years ago. They trained him too, in basic safety procedures, and issued him with a number. He's unable to make much sense of his temporary contract for it is written in English, but he has it stored in the bamboo rafters of his small hut. Both the contract and the identity card are evidence of his connection to Chevron and he'll brandish them at anyone who'll look. He can't stop talking about Chevron, or shouting, for that matter, about how badly done by he is, for San Mahmud is a '*paghol*' (mad man), a local figure of fun, hanging around the gas plant with his matted hair and lunatic eyes. Once, he rants, the company was employing hundreds of local men; the wages brought regular meals and more. But now 'they give nothing'. The building of the plant was completed and the labourers turned away, their work over. So here he is: half mad and dirty, lamenting his fate outside the gates.

*   *   *

September 2009: Mohammed Samsun Khan is standing beside the same fence, squinting politely at my camera. We have walked the short distance here from his large village house, with its dark rooms and muddy courtyard, where we were entertained with biscuits and lemonade, and now are on our way to the main road. The house belongs to him, but Samsun Khan doesn't live there any more, not since Chevron took his land. Indeed, this morning he has travelled from Sylhet Town to discuss our research with us. The interview over, he is returning immediately to the city. He is no longer comfortable here, he says: seeing the plant spread over his ancestral land brings indescribable pain. Besides, Chevron have a 'case' against him,[2] for he led the original protests against the gas field back in the days when stopping the plant from being built seemed possible. Now he no longer feels comfortable in the village where he was born.

Yet here he is, smiling and posing for the camera by the fence like a tourist in front of the Eiffel Tower. As we part, Samsun Khan heading back to Sylhet and Zahir, Masud, Fatema and I going in the opposite direction towards Nadampur, he takes my hand and requests that when I meet with Chevron officials in Dhaka I should enquire why they continue to pursue the case against a poor village man such as him. Later, as I inspect the business card he's given me, I see that it reads: 'Mohammed Samsun Khan Contractor for Chevron, Bibyana'.

*   *   *

Petrobangla Allows Chevron to Over-extract Gas from Bibiyana
Staff Correspondent
Petrobangla has continued to allow the US company, Chevron to extract more than 450 million cubic feet of gas per day from the Bibiyana gas field ignoring the warning of its expert committee that the gas reservoir will be damaged if production exceeds 450mmcfd. Sources in Petrobangla said that the officials of the state-run Oil, Gas and Mineral Corporation had virtually taken no steps to implement the recommendations which the expert committee, headed by the then director Maqbul-E-Elahi, had

submitted in the second week of November. Petrobangla also did not forward the report to the energy and mineral resources division, sources in the division said.

The committee, formed by Petrobangla to review the reserve of Bibiyana gas field, operated by Chevron, said that with the proved gas reserve of 2.51 trillion cubic feet the daily gas production from the field should not exceed 450mmcfd.

But Chevron is extracting between 450mmcfd and 500mmcfd currently 'posing a threat of early damage' to the reservoir.

'Over extraction from the field will bring serious consequences. The offshore Sangu gas field and the Bakhrabad gas field are two prime examples of how the gas fields are damaged because of over extraction,' said an expert from the Bangladesh University of Engineering and Technology. (*The New Age* [Dhaka] 14 January 2009)

* * *

Three stories: the last authored by a Bangladeshi journalist, the first and second by me. While apparently disparate, each is connected to an issue central to the lives of us all: access to resources. While in the stories material resources (land, natural gas, food) figure large, so do power relations. San Mahmud, with his crazy lamentations, has only complaint and the possibility of physical violence at his disposal. Neither will get him very far, for even were he to lash out at a passing Chevron executive, he'd probably end up with a beating from the police or local vigilantes. Samsun Khan has rather more influence over his situation. In the past he has mobilised sufficient support against Chevron for the company to initiate legal proceedings against him; despite his move to Sylhet, he still wields considerable power in his village as an elder and patron. His family are wealthy too: his brothers in the UK own several restaurants, a house in Duniyapur and Sylhet Town and more land scattered around the locality.

Yet, as we will see as his story unfolds over this and subsequent chapters, ultimately Samsun Khan has had very little influence over events. As the newspaper extract shows, those with the greatest power are the national and global players: the government, via the national energy company, Petrobangla. It was the government that forcibly acquired the land and who decide which companies to issue with contracts and what the production-sharing contract will entail. Alongside the government are the multinational energy companies – Chevron, Occidental, Asia Energy and Unocal being the main players in Bangladesh in 2009–10 – who circle natural resources, sizing them up, negotiating contracts and, if they are successful, turning them to profit.

In this chapter I examine the processes surrounding the types and degrees of access that people have to material resources in Duniyapur and beyond. While physical *things* – rice, firewood, land, units of gas – are central to survival for both individuals and multinational corporations, people's access to them is far from equal. In lieu of a fully functioning 'modern' state which allows for a socially just distribution of resources and welfare, in Duniyapur access to some of the most basic necessities is largely mediated by different forms of *claim*. As we shall see in this and the next chapter, these claims often revolve around a person's relative *connection* to others, for reliance upon informal social connectedness rather than secure systems of entitlement thrives in Bangladesh, where an ineffective state gives few guarantees that basic needs will be provided for and industrialisation – supposedly the deliverer of more formalised employment relations, regular wages, urbanisation and the 'break-down' of patron–client relations – is uneven.

The patchy and at times non-existent nature of state services plays a central role in all of the stories in this book. The poor, who cannot afford to pay for medicines, hospitals or secondary schools, are left with the patchy coverage and services of NGOs and private agencies.[3] Cash and credit are continually sought; there is never enough money, and what there is tends to be engulfed by everyday needs and upsets: a sick child, the cost of a school uniform or the bus fare to Sylhet Town can rapidly exhaust a poorer household's tenuous funds, sending them to their neighbours, relatives or other patrons for 'help' in the form of small loans that keep life ticking over.

Social connections, through which claims for resources can be made, are thus vital for the many households that hover around the poverty line,[4] for they can literally dictate one's life chances. Indeed, the case studies discussed later in the chapter show how during 2008 some of the poorest households were dipping below the survival threshold: they were simply not getting enough to eat. The 'price hike'[5] of 2008, a situation in which the price of basic foods rapidly escalated due to a vicious combination of the global recession, a dramatic reduction in the supply of imported rice and the caretaker government's anti-corruption drive which, according to many Bangladeshis, disrupted basic marketing systems,[6] meant that these households were unable to nourish themselves adequately, eating only a bowl of plain rice twice a day.

Earlier, I briefly outlined Amartya Sen's notion of entitlement, which he used to analyse the nature of famine and severe deprivation. Rather than being caused by a shortage of food *per se*, Sen argued, famines take place when large numbers of people are unable to establish their entitlements over an adequate amount of food. These entitlements depend upon a person's endowment (their ownership of productive resources and wealth, which for most people in rural economies involve land and labour) and the production possibilities which surround them. Exchange conditions, dictating the costs of labour and commodities, determine how much one gets for one's produce or labour, thus affecting one's ability to access food. Dramatic changes in these conditions can lead rapidly to famine, even if the amount of food in circulation has remained the same. In the Bangladesh famine of 1974, for example, there was greater availability of food than in any other year between 1971 and 1976. What caused the famine was floods, which, though not affecting food supply during the famine, for the spoilt crops would have been harvested later in the year, meant that large numbers of labourers lost their jobs (Sen, 1999: 162–5).

While Sen's focus on formal endowments and markets is appropriate, in understanding material deprivation in Duniyapur we also need to appreciate informal systems of entitlement for people's ability to access food, land and work is partly structured by the social connections they have to others, and the claims they can make on them. Both formal and informal systems are underscored by particular moral orders, and both are associated with certain types of claim: on the one hand, claims to legal and bureaucratic systems of redress and compensation for the loss of endowments, underlain by moralities of modernity, social justice and so on, and on the other, claims to informal support, underlain by moralities of charity and 'helping our own', the subject of Chapter 4.

Power relations are deeply implicated in both systems. These dictate not only who gets to eat what (and how much) food, but also lie at the heart of disputes concerning the access of multinationals to national energy reserves. Here, the population's deep mistrust of the state and its lack of transparency structures how negotiations concerning the contracts granted to global mining companies are perceived. Rather than acting for national interests, the story goes, government officials negotiate production-sharing contracts that give the lion's share of profits to the foreigners, an arrangement resulting from the 'backhanders', perks and opportunities offered to the officials. In some of the more complex versions of the story, donors such as the World Bank and the Asian Development Bank help to push these deals in the favour of the multinationals, a version which places government corruption in a wider context of global economic inequalities and postcolonial interests.

I shall examine these narratives of corruption and the rumour and mistrust which accompany them in more detail in Chapter 6. For now, the pertinent point is that in Duniyapur the entitlements that people have over material resources largely depends upon the types of claims they are able to make. These claims tend to revolve informally around social connections to more powerful others as well as formal claims based around legal ownership of resources and the wages people can command by selling their labour. Yet while within these formal domains people believe that their entitlements should be systematised in a transparent and fair way, what they say happens is that here, too, entitlements to resources (the money offered by multinationals or the gas supplies offered by the government) also depend upon informal social connections. In the public domain 'good' social capital therefore turns nasty and is spoken of as corruption and narrated as a critique of the failure of the state and the global economic order.

Similar accusations are made with regard to formal employment by Chevron, seen by many as the rightful compensation for the loss of land and attendant squeeze upon agrarian livelihoods. In contrast to the increasingly precarious rural livelihoods through which the majority eke out a living, regular, formalised employment in a multinational corporation which has high ethical standards and procedures, involving formal contracts, sick leave, pensions and so on, is not only highly desirable, it is viewed by some as their *right*. As one man put it: 'This company has been looting our land while paying nothing to us villagers' (Fieldnotes, July 2008). The initial employment of hundreds of local people in constructing the gas field has exacerbated this impression: Chevron *should* provide employment. It did once, but now it doesn't.

Yet while local people seek to connect to global capitalism as employees, the work is not available, for the gas field requires highly skilled labour, drawn from outside the locality and, at the most skilled levels, from abroad. To compound matters, what work is available is largely distributed informally, via labour contractors. As Sen (1999: 163) cautions, given the centrality of labour for most of the world's poor, it is crucial to pay attention to labour markets.

Yet while it was hoped that Chevron's presence might lead to a securing of work, once again local people's access to employment is largely distributed via informal social connections.

At the end of the chapter I shall return to the question of employment at the gas field. Let us start, however, with the most precious and symbolically resonant resource of all: the land on which rice is grown and gas extracted.

LAND, LAND, LAND ...

While it is gas that is sought by multinational energy companies and formal employment that people desire, land remains a significant material resource for the people in the villages surrounding the gas field. Indeed, despite a shift towards more mixed livelihood strategies our data indicates that farming remains central to the livelihoods of most local households. As much research in Bangladesh shows, landlessness is directly linked to poverty: put simply, the landless are nearly always chronically poor (Rahman and Manprasert, 2006: 2). Overall, rates of landlessness are rising in Bangladesh; as fast as – or faster than – the population rate (2006: 1). The discovery of gas under the fields and loss of land to the gas field and its connecting roads has therefore had major implications for the local population.

For transnational villagers who no longer rely materially on their fields, land is significant in a different way; it is a socio-political as well as physical resource which keeps them connected to the *desh* (homeland) and to the relatives and neighbours who use it. In the stories of dispossession told by British transnationals the ambivalence and sense of rupture that accompanies settlement in the UK has, it seems, been made even more painful by the loss of their fields. As their narratives show, land is filled with emotional significance not only for transnationals and non-migrants but also for intellectual activists in Dhaka and London, for whom it symbolises nationalist pride and notions of belonging. It is therefore with an account of the significance of land and land-based livelihoods that the story of the impact of the gas field in Duniyapur must start.

Since the villages that surround the gas plant were first settled, land has been key to local livelihood, it is the fundamental resource that people have fought over, invested with emotion, poetry and spirituality and survived from. It has also been the prime signifier of rural class. As many commentators have noted in Bangladesh and elsewhere in South Asia, though the relationship between economic class and social status is complex, social hierarchy has traditionally been correlated with landownership, at least until the 1990s (cf. Jahangir, 1982; Jansen, 1982; van Schendel, 1981). When I lived in Nadampur in the late 1980s, overseas migration and the remittances earned abroad had started to influence the local economic hierarchy, but despite this new and increasingly vital source of capital, land remained central to the day-to-day livelihoods of every household in the village and was key to the status-building projects of upwardly mobile migrant households (Gardner, 1995). Those who didn't own land sharecropped it; those who were unable to negotiate sharecropping arrangements worked as agricultural labourers. Payment for the labour of men and women was often partly or wholly in *chaal* (unhusked rice) or *dhan* (the cut crop), and beggars were given handfuls of rice rather than *taka*. After the harvest, the poorest people would forage the fields for grains of rice. Fuel was also available from the fields in the form of straw; this could also be used for thatched roofs or added to mud to construct the walls and floors of houses. Centrally too, land was used to graze livestock. As we shall see, much of this remains the same, though as has been observed elsewhere in South Asia, increasingly people of all classes are adopting non-agricultural activities in their array of livelihood strategies (see Breman, 1996, 2007; Khan and Seeley, 2005; Toufique and Turton, 2002).

Landownership in Duniyapur: The Role of Migration to the UK

Before the rush of movement to the UK in the 1960s, high-status lineages such as the Saiyeds and Pathans owned most of the local fields. Not all the families from these higher-status lineages capitalised on the opportunities to be gained abroad; some of the highest-status and highest-educated households opted to stay at home. By the late 1980s these households had lost much of their land to neighbours and relatives who had benefited from British remittances and were rapidly buying up as much of it as possible. The period from 1970 to 1988 thus involved a significant shift in landownership in the village, with some households that had previously been low status becoming wealthy landowners, who, after buying up as many fields as possible and building themselves *pukka* (stone) houses, embarked upon projects of social transformation which included changing their names, marrying into higher-status families and reinventing themselves as the descendants of holy men (Gardner, 1993b, 1995).

There is not space here to repeat my more detailed observations of these processes. Suffice to say that by the early 1990s, the households of successful UK migrants had become the largest landowners in the area, while those who had not migrated to the UK had tended to slide down the hierarchy, often becoming landless (Gardner, 1995). As Table 1 shows, while out of 26 households in Nadampur in 1987 which had no experience of migration overseas, only one owned more than 2 *Hal* of land (1 *Hal* is approximately 4 acres); out of 29 households with experience of migration to the UK, 21 had over 2 *Hal*. In a similar study in Sylhet, only 1 percent of migrant households were landless; 52.73 percent had over 5 acres (i.e. between 1 and 2 *Hal*) (Islam, 1987: 58–9).

Table 1 Landowning and migration in Nadampur, 1987

| | Land owned | | | |
Household type	0	Under 1 Hal	1 to 2 Hal	Over 2 Hal
No migration	17	6	2	1
Middle East	7	4	3	8
UK	1	5	2	21

Source: Gardner (1995: 92).

Similar processes were recorded by our work in Biswanath, another *Londoni* area in Greater Sylhet, in 2005.[7] As in Nadampur, the local economic hierarchy in Jalalgaon is directly correlated with migration to Britain. Those who originally sent members to the UK have, over the last thirty years or so, accumulated large amounts of land, as well as assets such as shops, 'colonies' (*bustee*-style dwellings where poor in-migrant labourers live)[8] and other business interests. Of the ninety seven households who have been living in the village for over a generation thirty-four are '*Londonis*' (i.e. they have members in Britain). Another seven households are, using local terminology, classified as 'Dubai', meaning that they have had experience of migration to the Gulf. Of these, three have been moderately successful and own some land. The rest are landless. The remaining fifty-seven households have no members abroad. When landholding in the village is correlated with these household types, the results speak for themselves. Of the total local agricultural land, 79 percent is owned by *Londoni* households, 6.9 percent by 'Dubai' households and 13.9 percent by non-migrants. Put another way, 100 percent (34) of *Londoni* households own land, compared to 50 percent (6) of Dubai households and 10 percent (6) of non-migrant insider households. Of the non-migrant insiders, one household owns 5 *kiare* (nearly 2 acres), and the rest 1 *kiare* or less (i.e. less than 0.3 acres).[9] Among the *Londoni* households, while 23.5 percent own up to 1 acre and 26.47 percent own between 1 and 2 acres, the rest own over 2 acres, with 23.5 owning over 5 acres (Gardner and Ahmed, 2009).

As this data indicates, before the gas field most land in Duniyapur was owned by *Londonis* or their relatives who had stayed behind in the *desh*. Accordingly, most of the land now occupied by the gas field was owned by *Londonis* or their close relatives. While we were not able to collect firm data on those who had lost land[10] we estimated that approximately ten households were major losers in Duniyapur, each losing between 2 and 10 acres. These owners, or their relatives, lived mostly in Karimpur or Firizpur, the villages closest to the gas field. To put this in perspective, the largest landowner in Nadampur in 1988 owned over 4 *Hal* (around 16 acres), with the majority owning between 1 and 4 *Hal* (between 4 and 16 acres). As this implies, some of these landowners lost most or all of their fields.

Londoni Attitudes to Land

Most *Londoni* households in Duniyapur have now settled in the UK, a process that was gathering pace in the late 1980s. The usual pattern then and into the 1990s was for a married man who had spent much of his adult life working in various industrial cities in the UK to arrange for his wife and children to join him. The household land would either continue to be farmed (or rather, *managed*) by a brother who had never migrated or be sharecropped out, usually but not always to relatives. For many decades British based *Londonis'* incomes have therefore largely been earned in the UK. Since their grandfathers' and great-grandfathers' earliest forays to Britain in the mid twentieth century, the disjunction between the British pound and the Indian rupee/Bangladeshi *taka* has been great enough to make it nonsensical not to put all of one's energies into earning money in the UK, whether in the factories of the 1950s–1970s, or the restaurants of the 1980s–2000s.

But this does not mean that land owned in the *desh* is not of symbolic and social importance to those living in Britain, for those born in Bangladesh at least. As the opening lines of Tagore's poem 'Earth' indicate, land has deeply resonant meanings within Bengali culture as the source of nurture and belonging: the 'motherland'.

> Earth take me back,
> your lap-child, back to your lap
> in the shelter of your sari's voluminous end.

> Mother, made of earth, may I
> live diffused in your soil ...
> (Tagore, 2001)

While Tagore was writing in the nineteenth century as part of the highly educated Bengali elite, similar themes are repeated in the narratives and popular culture of today. For those living in cities or abroad, nostalgia for one's ancestral homeland may be expressed via images of the 'golden land' (*sonar desh*) of fields filled with ripened rice, or the *misti batash* (sweet breezes) that blow across the countryside; both were phrases that I heard many times in my research among Bengali elders living in East London in 1997–8, as well as during my fieldwork in Nadampur in the late 1980s.

In our interviews in Britain with *Londonis* from the Duniyapur area in 2009, all of the men we met alluded to the emotional meanings that their fields had for them and the devastation they had felt that this land, whether passed down over the generations, or acquired more recently from British remittances, had been forcibly sold. 'How would *you* feel, if your government seized your house?' I was asked in response to questioning about the land compensation process. An old man interviewed in north London, who had been in Britain since 1963 and who had lost around 10 acres to the plant, sat silently through a wide-ranging discussion with a large group of fellow transnational villagers about the activities of Chevron in Duniyapur, their visions of local development and feelings towards the *desh*, only speaking up at the end of the discussion to announce that he was so upset at the loss of this land that he couldn't bear to talk about it. Another, much younger man, who had left Bangladesh when he was a toddler in the 1970s, vividly described his horror at returning on a visit to his *bari* to discover that the gas plant had been built a stone's throw away across what few fields remained of his land. The plant is now so close to his house, he says, that one can smell the gas and feel the heat of the flare. He had returned to his village expecting to find paddy fields and natural beauty, he went on, but on being confronted by the industrial site opposite his house, not to say the 'unbearable noise pollution' could now no longer think of it as 'home' (Interview notes, May 2009).

While these comments indicate the romantic yearning that urban transnationals feel for the rural idyll of the *desh*, the upset felt by *Londonis* does not simply result from diasporic nostalgia for a world that is already largely lost to them. Indeed, other men we spoke to in Britain stressed the pride they felt that the gas field was located in their *desh*, for it was a sign of much needed modernity and progress. As one man put it, in describing his visits to the *desh*: 'When we don't see development we feel disappointed ... if it's there, we feel proud and happy' (Interview notes, May 2009).

Moreover, rather than signifying transnational nostalgia for the imagined *desh,* the attachment of *Londonis* to their fields is an inherent and material aspect of their on-going relationship with their homeland. As one man put it, land is a 'bond' with the *desh*, a physical link that their British based children will inherit, ensuring their on-going relationships with the villages of their fathers. Another man told us that land is an ancestral link, which stretches back for generations and keeps him connected to the homeland. Centrally, all the British landowners (or, more accurately, land losers) stressed that their land was 'for those left behind', a resource which could sustain large number of their poorer relatives. As one of the men we spoke to in Burnley put it: 'We want to provide for them.' Another of our informants added that: 'Our land isn't for profit, but for the benefit of poor people at home, because we're Muslim, and we have to think about the needs of other people' (Interiew notes, May 2009).

From these moral and emotional perspectives, financial compensation is largely of symbolic importance, for the worth of land is so much more than its market value. The value of land cannot be quantified, a member of the north London focus group explained, because it can be used forever, whereas money quickly runs out. Crucially, land can be used by future generations. In this context land is inherently social: an investment in existing and future connections with the *desh*. Small wonder that the loss of fields, often acquired at huge emotional as well as financial cost by men who have spent most of their adult lives away from parents, wives and children in order to earn the money to buy or consolidate land holdings, has created such deep resentment and feelings of powerlessness.

Land from a *Deshi* Perspective: Livelihoods in Duniyapur

While for British settled *Londonis* land is primarily a social resource, for those left behind it is predominantly an economic one. This separation between *Londonis* and 'non-migrants' is of course somewhat artificial, for there are still many households in the area in which some members live in the UK while others remain resident in the *desh*. These include brothers in joint households. Indeed, several of our UK informants told us that the land compensation process for their jointly held land was arranged by their Bangladesh-based brothers. In these households, land may still play a role in the livelihoods of the Bangladeshi settled members, but decisions concerning where to invest significant amounts of money or energy are usually focused on the UK. In other households a younger member has migrated to the UK in the last ten years, usually by marrying a British Bangladeshi woman, leaving the parental generation, or brothers, to manage the land. In one household I know of, for example, three adult sons have settled in the UK, having married their British cousins. The small amount of land that the household owns is held jointly, and remains a significant element of the livelihood of those remaining in Bangladesh. Significantly, however, larger amounts of money are invested in the family's burgeoning restaurant business in the UK. While all three UK brothers endeavour to send money back to their widowed mother, brother and sisters in Bangladesh, the demands of their family in Britain plus the expenses of their business make regular or large remittances difficult. As these cases indicate, while some households have completely relocated, others remain spread between Britain and Bangladesh.

It is also important to separate the economic significance of land for households that own it from its economic significance for those who work on it. Whilst in our study villages' land remains key to local power relations, status and of course food production, agricultural work is distinctly low status and avoided at all costs by those higher up the socio-economic hierarchy. Indeed, work is a major signifier of status in Sylhet; manual labour (especially 'earth cutting') being at the absolute bottom of the pile (Gardner, 1995, 2008). As Breman (2007: 149–56) has also observed in rural Gujarat, the landowning elite are increasingly urban oriented. In Duniyapur, landowning households have almost totally withdrawn their labour from the fields, choosing either to hire labour for agricultural activities or to sharecrop/rent it out. While during my fieldwork in Nadampur in 1987–8 I rarely saw a landowner (or rather, a landowner with more than a few *kiare* of land) getting his feet or hands dirty in the fields, it was common to see higher-status *grihusti* (farmers) overseeing their labourers as they planted or harvested the paddy. Occasionally Shuli's father would wade into the waterlogged fields to give instructions to his labourers; he also took a hands-on approach to the day-to-day management of his cattle and other chores around the farm.

Today, my impression is that landowners are increasingly disengaged from agriculture, not just because many of them are physically in Britain or elsewhere, but also because of an increasing orientation towards other income-generation activities, such as the rearing of 'broilers' (poultry) in artificially lit and heated sheds, the use of land for 'colonies' and the various economic opportunities provided by Chevron, which I shall elaborate on later.

This was also the case in our research in Biswanath, where we observed a shift from agriculturally based livelihoods to more mixed ways of making a living in the study village, and a distinct movement away from using land for farming, towards using it for property development or simply allowing it to remain fallow. As landowners in Biswanath told us, the main reason was that in comparison with other activities such as property development, and in light of the required investments in labour, seeds and fertilisers, agriculture was simply not profitable enough to make it worthwhile (Gardner and Ahmed, 2009). This trend has been observed elsewhere in Bangladesh, and is the subject of a major policy report produced on behalf of DFID, *Hands Not Land* (Toufique and Turton, 2002), which suggests that the distinction between a rural Bangladesh, wholly oriented towards farming, and an urban Bangladesh of industry and modernity is increasingly false. Instead, the report's authors argue, improvements in infrastructure and globalisation have produced a rural landscape that is increasingly 'urban' in nature, with much of the population turning to a range of livelihood activities. For those without land, the report suggests, their labour – however used – remains key to their survival; rural Bangladesh is thus undergoing rapid transformation, with diversification being key to economic change (Toufique and Turton, 2002).[11]

In the villages surrounding the gas plant there is a discernible movement towards more varied livelihood strategies, both among landowners and non-landowners. The loss of agricultural land for the gas plant has played a part in the movement of some households away from farming, especially for households which owned or sharecropped the actual fields on which the plant was built, but it is by no means the only factor in the move towards more varied livelihoods. As in Biswanath and the villages studied by researchers for *Hands Not Land*, other factors have played a major part and were taking place long before the plant was built. The reliance on remittances from the UK, the constant quest for overseas migration, an increasing orientation towards urban styles of life and 'modernity', the development of local infrastructure, plus growing opportunities in the service sectors such as rickshaw pulling, house construction or bus/truck driving, have all played important roles.

Yet while acknowledging that the local economy is no longer so reliant on agriculture, it is also important to stress that for many of the non-*Londoni* households included in our research agriculture still played a major role in their livelihoods. In our surveys of Kakura and Karimpur, for example, approximately 50 percent of households reported that either 'farming' or working as an agricultural labourer was a major element of their livelihoods. It should be noted that this data was collected *after* land was lost to the gas field, and in the context of many of our informants complaining that there was no longer sufficient land available for sharecropping. Had the survey been done *before* the gas field, the role of agriculture in their livelihoods might well have been greater.

Before examining these livelihoods in more detail, let us consider the different forms of land use in the area, as well as the basic socio-economic data for the study villages. As this shows, while landowners are increasingly disengaged from agriculture, sharecropping and working as farm hands remain key to the livelihoods of those who don't own the land, or who own only a small fraction. At a material level, the impact of the loss of land to the gas field and the roads that surround it has thus been most keenly felt by the landless people who once used it rather than the *Londonis* who once owned it.

Owner-cultivators, Agricultural Labourers, Sharecroppers and Mortgagees

Among owner-cultivators (*grihusti*) in Nadampur in the 1980s household land was farmed by household members and/or hired farm hands. While vegetables were grown in the 'garden' area around the *bari*, fields – which may have been close to the *bari*, or some distance away, depending on when they were bought – were used predominantly for rice production. If there was a surplus of rice at the end of the harvest, this would be sold in the market; the rest was kept for household consumption. Today, while the fields in the area surrounding the study villages and gas plant are predominantly planted with rice, there has been an observable shift towards some new uses of land. A handful of lower-lying fields that can be inundated with water are now used for hatching fish, for example,[12] while others are used for growing vegetables. Increasing amounts of land are used for building: new houses, a petrol station and the Smiling Sun Clinic[13] have all appeared in the last three years.

As mentioned, during my original fieldwork in Nadampur, if they were sufficiently wealthy, the men of the house would oversee work done in the fields but not get directly involved in it. Rather, the people who worked on the land were, and largely still are, agricultural labourers or sharecroppers. The labourers (*kamla*) may either be permanent employees, paid on a monthly basis and, if they have come from some distance away, given board and lodging, or they may be employed seasonally, especially during the harvesting months. As I shall describe in more detail in the next chapter, none of these *kamla* are related to their employers. During my 1980s fieldwork, for example, there were several semi-permanent labourers (*kamla*) in my hosts' house, who were treated almost (but not quite) as one of the family, given the affectionate name *mama* (maternal uncle), paid a wage on a monthly basis, and who lived in the house (or outhouses: *bangla ghor*) all year round. These arrangements are identical to those observed by our research team in Biswanath in 2005–6 (Gardner and Ahmed, 2009).

In Nadampur in the late 1980s, most if not all *kamla* came from Kakura, which provided a steady source of labour for the wealthier villages which surrounded it. I did not conduct a survey in Kakura at the time, but my strong impression from talking with, and getting to know, various permanent *kamla* was that Kakura was largely reliant on agricultural wage labour for men, usually arranged via long-standing relationships with patrons in the wealthy *Londoni* villages nearby. Women would also be employed for household or agricultural work (such as processing the paddy), though for much lower rates of pay and on a more casual basis.[14] To this extent, Kakura can be thought of as providing a 'reserve army' of labour, to be used as and when the need arose, just like the Halpati castes described by Breman (2007) in his study villages in Gujarat. In contrast, the teams of men who appeared in the area at harvest time had often come from far away: Comilla or Mymensing, for example[15] (cf. Breman, 1996; Rogaly and Coppard, 2003).

What happens to the land of people who are no longer physically present in the area or no longer interested in farming it? The most popular arrangement in the 1980s was for land to be sharecropped out (*bhagi*). While there are various sharecropping arrangements, the most common is for the land to be given over to the sharecropper for a year. The latter covers the costs of production (seeds, fertilisers, labour, hiring of power tiller, etc.) and at harvest, the produce is shared equally between owner and sharecropper. The agreement between owner and sharecropper is invariably an informal one, and is often made between relatives, or long-standing patrons neighbours.

This more traditional arrangement, in which land is managed by its owners while being physically farmed by labourers who have a long-standing relationship with their employers/patrons, is, however, undergoing rapid changes. Not only are many landowning households now wholly absent in the UK but those who remain in Bangladesh are less and less interested in the everyday management of their fields. Our livelihood data shows a shift from sharecropping to a system known as *rongjoma* in which cash has be paid upfront for the annual use of land. As the case studies cited later in the chapter show, this squeezes those with limited capital further. One sharecropper, for example, complains of a man from outside the immediate area who gained an income from his work as a doctor. Since he had the cash, he was able to pay over the going rate in a *rongjoma* contract for a piece of land. This meant that rental prices were pushed up, further disadvantaging those without access to capital. Other sharecroppers told us how most *Londonis* nowadays preferred to rent rather than sharecrop their land: working in the restaurant business in Britain and with their families wholly reunited there, they had little use for a share of the harvest, though the rental income was useful. As one man in Kakura put it:

> People used to work as farmers before, now they're not bothered with agriculture. Most of the landowners live abroad. They're rich and don't need to get involved with farming. They prefer to rent out land as *rongjoma*. They get cash as they don't need the paddy – they can buy it any time. We people are bound to farming, we don't have any alternative. The people of Kakura are especially poor. They don't have their own land. Only two or three people farm their own land. (Interview, 2008)

The repercussions for local labourers are complex. Our data indicate a shift from long-term employer–employee relationships between landowners in Nadampur and Karimpur and the landless of Kakura towards other livelihood strategies in Kakura plus widespread and often seasonal unemployment, insecurity and destitution. Some of the population of Kakura, as in Karimpur have been directly affected by the loss of land to the gas field. As one of the *Londonis* we interviewed in the UK put it: 'all the local people who used to be employed on our farms have gone … now all they can do is cut earth' (Interview notes, May 2009).

ENVIRONMENTAL CHANGE: NARRATIVES OF DEGRADATION

According to local farmers there have been other changes to agricultural production, which they blame directly on the gas plant and which fit neatly into their narratives of 'before' and 'after'. The fragile eco-system of the area has been radically changed, people say, for before the high-banked roads that link the North and South Pads, and which connect Nadampur Bazaar with the Kushiara River at Dighalbak were constructed, the fields were seasonally inundated with water. I have observed these changes over the years that I have been visiting the area. During the wet season the Kushiara River once overflowed to form a series of *haors* (naturally formed areas of inundated land, which dries out during the dry season, characteristic of Bangladesh). Now, however, an embankment built by the Kushiara in the 1990s and the roads built by Unocal/ Chevron prevent the water from flowing naturally, leaving some land waterlogged and other fields dry and in need of mechanised irrigation systems.

The change to the eco-system is striking. When I first arrived in Nadampur in September 1987 I travelled by boat to the *bari* that was to become my home (Gardner, 1991); for the first months of my fieldwork it was only possible to visit other *baris* via the small boats that all households owned. As the winter months set in the waters receded and I was finally able to walk around Nadampur on foot. Yet in a visit to the area in September 2009 the land that twenty years earlier had been under water was dry, the boats once used for getting about discarded and rotting.

The roads are not the only cause of these changes. Natural shifts in the course and flow of the Kushiara River are also influential, as is the embankment that was built by the government in the 1990s to prevent flooding.[16] Yet while the causes may be complex and multiple, what the changes mean for the local economy is that there has been a shift in land usage, away from rice farming, which requires copious irrigation, towards vegetables and other commercial crops. Mechanised pumps and irrigation systems are also required; indeed, one of the demands made by local people to Chevron has been to provide deep tube wells for irrigation. Commercial fertiliser is also required: people say that the silt brought from the river in the wet season fed the land. Now that the waters no longer come they need to add chemicals to the soil. Combined with this, the tiny fish and prawns which were once freely available in the *haors* have disappeared from local diets. Instead, some landowners are turning to commercial fish farming: converting waterlogged fields into ponds which, via loans from the Alternative Livelihoods Programme funded by Chevron,[17] they stock with fry.

The gas field has meant there is less land on which to graze cattle and goats or to gather straw and firewood, and it is the poor who feel these changes most strongly. Once again, the pattern is clear. As land and other resources are turned over to commercial interests, be these of local landowners seeking to sell vegetables or farmed fish on the market, or multinationals seeking to profit from multi-million dollar gas extraction plants, it is the poor who lose out. For them, there is no compensation, only Chevron's programme of 'community engagement', which, as I shall argue in Chapter 5, while providing some alternative income-generation schemes and sources of credit, cannot possibly 'solve' the long-term, deeply embedded problems of poverty, land loss and unemployment.

It is within this context that the narratives of environmental change and destruction cited below must be understood. While within these narratives the blame is put squarely at the corporate feet of Chevron, the following quotes should be read partly as reflections of objectively observable changes, and partly as critiques of the wider political and economic systems of entitlement that shape the struggles over resources with which people are constantly engaged. I shall return to these narratives in Chapter 7, where they re-emerge as allegories of disruption and disconnection, or political statements which reflect deep-seated disquiet about wider relationships.

In many of the statements that people made about recent environmental changes in Duniyapur the poetic imagery of 'golden' fields, or statements such as 'under our land is gold', contrast with images of dried-up and exhausted soil, denuded fertility and the imposition of roads and embankments which 'only benefit the rich'. The following is an extract from an interview with a sharecropper from Karimpur, which encapsulates the many complaints we heard from local people about environmental changes which they claim to be caused by the gas plant. While detailing the precise nature of the problems the comments also reveal a world that has been lost: a largely sustainable local agricultural economy, which relied on seasonal inundations of water from the Kushiara River and filling of the *hoars*, providing eco-systems for fish and shrimps and a source of irrigation and fertiliser from the silt.

The gas is making the soil infertile. After the gas started, the yields have dramatically decreased and the land has lost its fertility.

There've been some big problems. They've put narrow pipes into the embankments which the water doesn't flow through and crops are destroyed because the land gets waterlogged. These narrow pipes aren't big enough to allow a large amount of water to flow from east to west; not a single culvert has been built to help the water pass:[18] one narrow pipe has made our lives miserable. It's not just the acute waterlogging. The second thing is that we can't cross the road with the paddy as the slope is so high and slippery. Third, we have big problems with our livestock. We used to graze them on the fields but with the high roads we can't cross from one piece of land to another. The fourth thing is that the soil has become sandy and less fertile. The sand comes from the roads and the gas field. Some of the fields I sharecrop have got sandy. Even if we water it, the land remains hard these days, so it's difficult to plough and the plants don't grow properly ... (Interview notes, 2009)

A local leader, whose land was acquired for the gas plant, put it like this:

You can see for yourself the condition of the land. We don't get the yields we used to. We don't get the water we need. Another problem is waterlogging, due to the road. The pipes in the embankments are too narrow and have got blocked with earth.

Originally there were two haors in this area; now they're gone. If you walk around, you'll see that the land is covered with sand because sand fell into the soil (from building the roads) and it's become harder. Before, we used to get deposits from the Kushiara River, but no more ... (Interview notes, 2008)

Most people made similar observations. Variations in rainfall and flooding were mentioned too; these have always had a major role in cultivation, leading to periodic disasters such as ruined crops or houses, but the hardness of the soil and dramatic changes to the seasonal flow of water were reported throughout our fieldwork by nearly every farmer we spoke to. Reduced amounts of straw for fuel, plus a dramatic reduction in the availability of fish from the *haors* were also constantly raised during the interviews and focus group discussions.

Before the gas field the yields were very good.... Before the gas field we used to get straw from the fields [i.e. after harvest] which we used as fuel. Now there's nothing here so we have to buy fuel. We used to have fish and the land was fertile. Now a whole month will go by and we don't eat fish. Where have the fish gone? There's no water left in the river ... (Focus group discussion, Kakura, 2008)

It should be noted that these changes have been experienced by different people in different ways. The roads, for example, are viewed positively by many. Indeed, new roads were among the original 'demands' made to Unocal. In a discussion with four men from Koshbar (near the North Pad) the following comments were made:

We've benefited from the road. We used to go by foot; not even a rickshaw could go to our village as there was no road at all. In the monsoon the path became so muddy that it was hard to even walk. Now when we have to go to the bazaar we can. The road has brought us peace.

How have these changes in agriculture and land ownership, not to say the loss of land to the gas plant, affected livelihoods in our two study villages? Kakura and Karimpur have different histories, which in turn have affected the access to land and other resources that their inhabitants have. Yet what both villages have in common are very high rates of poverty as well as gaping differences between the rich and poor.

KAKURA AND KARIMPUR: LANDOWNERSHIP, LIVELIHOODS AND POVERTY

Before embarking on a description of the entitlements to resources that different people have in Karimpur and Kakura, a word about what I mean by the term 'poverty'. In what follows I define poverty as the inability of a household to meet its basic needs in a sustainable manner. What these 'basic needs' involve is of course contextual; the proportion of income used for purchasing food is often used as a basic measurement in drawing up the 'poverty line' for different countries by development or state agencies,[19] but other indices, such as literacy, access to health care and so on may also be used.[20] The problem with the 'poverty line' approach is that it tends to involve a series of statistical calculations, relying upon quantitative rather than qualitative data. As Breman (2007) argues, this reduces poverty to economic indicators, thereby neglecting the social relationships and inequalities which underlie it. In rural Bangladesh while we might take as a rule of thumb whether or not a household is able to adequately meet its basic needs, which in this context are food, health care, education, clothing and so on, we cannot ignore Breman's reminder that: 'poverty can only be understood in the social context in which it exists' (2007: 11). This point will be illustrated in the next chapter, where I will show in more detail how social connectedness is a key determinant in access to material resources and well-being. I should add that the initial survey we carried out in Karimpur and Kakura did not set out to measure poverty levels *per se*, except by mapping levels of landholding, income, housing types and literacy. As the case studies show, those at the bottom of the pile, who have no land and only irregular sources of income, were, in 2008, unable to cover even their basic calorific needs. While access to land was not the only determinant of whether a household was in poverty, or, indeed, abject destitution, lack of access to land, either via ownership or sharecropping, plus no other regular source of employment were the two major factors affecting a household's capacity to meet its basic needs. Breman defines destitution as:

a state in which a regular lifestyle is disrupted by a cumulative shortage of elementary necessities – in the first instance food – which erodes the capacity to make optimal use of the resources available. The resulting crisis of survival is no longer temporary, but permanent. (2007: 343)

Sadly, there were many households in both Kakura and Karimpur who were in this position in 2008–9.

During our research we asked households in Kakura and Karimpur to tell us which other households they were related to, and which they gave or received 'help' or support to. The results were interesting. While in Karimpur there was a high incidence of relatedness between many of the households, with tight networks of help and support linking both households which were related by blood as well as those with which weren't (for example, many Hindu and Muslim households were linked to each other, usually with wealthier Muslim households offering 'help' to their Hindu neighbours), in Kakura the links were far looser, and often non-existent. Indeed, the research showed that in Kakura there is a very low level of kinship links between households, and the level of support between households is low.

Kakura

Local accounts of the history of Kakura describe how the village was settled during the mid twentieth century by in-coming migrant labourers who were originally employed in Nadampur.[21] Like other in-migrants in the region, it is likely that these original settlers came from many different parts of Bangladesh and were largely unrelated; patterns of relatedness in the village today show very low levels of kinship connection between households, a stark contrast to Nadampur, which is inhabited by four main lineages who are variously interrelated and can trace their ancestors back for four or five generations.

Originally the migrant labourers camped in makeshift dwellings around Nadampur or found shelter in their employer's outhouses. Eventually however, political leaders living in Nadampur arranged for them to settle an area of land a mile or so across the fields, towards Syedpur. This process had already taken place by the War of Independence in 1971. Ali Mullah, one of the few larger farmers in the village explained the history of the village in the following way:

My grandfather used to work in a ship. He bought this land, and later my uncle relocated us all here. We've been living here for 60–70 years. Before, the land was occupied by Hindus and very few people lived here. Later the Hindu *Zamindar* sold some of the land to my grandfather. So we got a proportion of that as our inheritance. We were the first Muslim settlers. But the majority of people living here are landless. They live on government-owned land (*khas*). A few others own land. The mosque you see in front of my house was built before we came here, fifty years ago. There are two mosques in the village though not many people are very involved in religious activities. Since they're poor, they're not very interested in praying. This is why the village remains so underdeveloped. An area of land by the road is *khas* land, and used as commons by the people for grazing cattle and so on …

The majority of people in Kakura have therefore always been functionally landless and, in the early days at least, dependent upon their patrons in Nadampur. Rather than these patron–client relations being between relatives, however, the people of Kakura have always been seen by the villages that surround them as *chotomanoosh* ('little people', low status; see Gardner, 1995); the support they receive is highly conditional and the access they have to social connections precarious. With the exception of Ali Mullah no-one has migrated abroad, whether to the UK or elsewhere, and no-one has been able to buy up significant amounts of land. Indeed, the only landowners in the village are in-coming *Londoni* households, outsiders from elsewhere who have acquired land in the area in the last ten years. No wonder that it is in Kakura that the most forceful complaints about Chevron are heard, for it is here that secure employment/ connectedness is most desperately required.

Our survey showed that in 2008, 83 percent of the 130 households in Kakura were landless. This is vastly greater than the national average of 56 percent landlessness in 2002, a figure which has no doubt risen since then (Toufique and Turton, 2002: 9). In Kakura 60.7 percent of households reported that they were not directly involved in cultivation (though this may include people working some of the time as agricultural labourers), with 22.3 percent reporting that they sharecropped land. Out of the 22 households that reported owning some land, 13 said that they sharecropped their fields out. Only 7 percent of households in the village therefore cultivated their own land. Of those who owned land, 63.4 percent had between 0 and 3 *kiare* (i.e. less than an acre), while only 18 percent had the largest amount of land, between 7 and 9 *kiare*. My impression is that this figure would have been roughly the same in the 1980s and 1990, long before the gas field was constructed.

The livelihood sources of the people of Kakura are diverse, but very few of these provide a sizeable or regular income. Small businesses, wage labouring either in agriculture or elsewhere, begging, pulling rickshaws, working as a mason or a driver were the predominant occupations reported in the survey, with cultivation (20.7 percent) and wage labour (17.7 percent) being the most frequently mentioned. Just over 50 percent of households reported a monthly income of less than 4500 *taka*, with 11 percent of the total of 130 households reporting that they earned less than 2,500. At the time of the research, £1 was equivalent to approximately 60 *taka*; a wage labourer would receive approx 180 *taka* for a day's work; meanwhile a household with six members calculated that they spent 100 *taka* a day on rice alone during the price hike of 2008. In contrast, 12 percent reported a monthly income of over 10,500 *taka*. During time of the research the prices of basic foodstuffs were rapidly escalating, due to the 'price hike' and economic crisis of 2008. Those on these very low incomes were therefore not eating more than two meals of plain rice a day. Not surprisingly, only seven households (5.4 percent) owned a television, and only two had a fridge (1.5 percent), both being common 'luxury' items in prosperous households in Nadampur. Similarly, only 9 (6.9 percent) of houses were made with concrete (*pukka*); and 13 percent with concrete and tin; the rest were constructed with a mixture of clay, tin and bamboo. As to education, 38.5 percent of respondents in the survey said that they were illiterate, with 40 percent having only attended primary school.

Karimpur

In Karimpur there is a larger number of successful British transnationals, several of whom remain important patrons to the poorer people in the village, but the proportion of landlessness remains high: 77 percent. One reason for this is the large number of Hindu households in the village: we counted 60 Hindu households out of a total of 112 households. None of the Hindus has ever migrated abroad. The relatively high levels of education among the Hindu population may have been influential in this. Rather than being oriented towards factory jobs in Britain, their aspirations were towards higher education and professional jobs. The lack of connectedness with local Muslim migrant networks was, however, probably the most important factor.

The history of Karimpur makes an interesting contrast to that of Kakura. Originally inhabited by Brahmin *zamindars* as well as other, lower castes, in the 1960s the village was predominantly Hindu. According to the accounts of those Hindus who remain, after the Partition many Brahmins began to move away, some to Calcutta but others to Sri Mongal, situated about 30 miles away, in the centre of Sylhet's tea industry. Today, Sri Mongal has a large Hindu population, many of whom are connected to the tea industry.

Migration to the UK by local Muslims and their new-found wealth probably accelerated a process in which Hindu landowners sold up to their Muslim neighbours in Nadampur and other nearby villages. The largest landowners in Karimpur today are all *Londonis*, either part of a joint household in which one or more brothers have settled in the UK, or largely absent in the UK. These landowning *Londoni* households have close kinship links with the major patrilineages in Nadampur, where they originally came from.

As with many land transactions in Bangladesh, the deals were generally carried out informally, by word of mouth rather than via written contracts. Hindu land was particularly liable to be unregistered, for under government law it was officially 'enemy property' belonging to the state in principle, though paid for and owned by the incoming Muslims. As land and homesteads changed hands, the village became increasingly Islamicised. A mosque was built, and Hindu relics destroyed.

Not all Hindus left the village, only the Brahmins and larger landowners. Those that remain talk of there once being eighty Hindu households, compared with sixty today, all of whom are landless or land poor. Of the eight households that lost significant amounts of land to the gas field in Karimpur, two were Hindu. Landowning in Karimpur has thus radically changed over the last fifty years, with Hindu land being transferred completely into Muslim hands. As Ronju Roy, a day-labourer, told us:

> What can we do? I'm a tailor, living in my forefathers' house. We once had lots of land but now we're landless. We Hindus have neither money nor power. All the land is taken by Muslims. I don't even have a path leading to my house.... Once Hindus dominated, but now the rich Hindus have gone to Sri Mongal or Calcutta. We poor don't have the money or power to be able to move.

It should be stressed that relationships between Muslims and Hindus are, by all accounts, good. Indeed, the main landowners in the village act as patrons to their landless Hindu neighbours, with whom they have long-lasting links via the sharecropping of land, giving of loans and other forms of 'help' (*shahajo*) in times of need.

As mentioned above, landlessness is slightly lower in Karimpur than Kakura (77 percent of a total of 112 households). Among the landless households, thirty-one sharecrop land (27.6 percent). Of these thirty-one, fifteen sharecrop plots of over 5 *kiare*. Landholdings are also more spread out in size than in Kakura, where the majority of landowners only owned a small amount (63.4 percent had less than 3 *kiare*, or 1 acre; 18 percent had over 7 *kiare*). In Karimpur, however, approximately 55 percent had less than 3 *kiare*, while 27 percent had over 7 *kiare*. It should be remembered that our survey was done *after* land was forcibly sold to the government for the gas plant; had it been done three years earlier, the levels of large landholdings would invariably have been greater.

If extreme poverty is measured by income and landlessness, it seems to be greater in Karimpur than Kakura, with 21.4 percent of households reporting a monthly income of less than 2,500 *taka* (as opposed to 11 percent of households in Kakura). Yet, as mentioned earlier, these households have greater social connectedness and access to credit and other forms of support from rich patrons than the landless in Kakura; the statistical measure of income poverty should not therefore be taken as a measure of well-being/poverty *per se*. A total of 46.4 percent reported an income of below 4,500 *taka*, as opposed to 50.7 percent in Kakura. As in Kakura, the majority of the remaining households have an income of between 4,500 and 6,500 *taka* (29 percent in Karimpur and 30 percent in Kakura). Interestingly, only 5 percent of households report an income of over 12,500 *taka*. Again, this points to very high levels of inequality in the village; the relatively low number of respondents reporting a higher income is also indicative of how many prosperous households are permanently absent in the UK, leaving an impoverished population behind. Of the eight *Londoni* households in the village, four are wholly absent abroad. In the remaining four households, a mother or brother remains alone in the *bari*. The influence of *Londoni* migration explains the higher number of *pukka* houses (26.8 percent, as opposed to 6.9 percent in Kakura). The rest of the village's inhabitants live in a mixture of clay, bamboo and tin houses. Ownership of luxury goods implies a slightly larger number of prosperous households in Karimpur than in Kakura: 19.6 percent of households had a television and 4.5 percent a fridge.

While the two villages have significantly different histories, there are therefore very high levels of income poverty and landlessness in both Kakura and Karimpur. There are also high levels of inequality in the villages, with a handful of *Londoni* households owning large *pukka* houses and enjoying incomes that are often over ten times higher those of their landless neighbours. Nothing epitomises this inequality better than the houses of the rich and poor. In Nadampur, all but the colonies and huts of in-migrant labourers are now *pukka*. Some are several storeys high; one has its own private mosque. Many now have Western-style kitchens, with stainless steel sinks and gas cookers that either run on cylinders or are waiting to be connected to the supply. Most have several bathrooms with showers and WCs. In contrast, the houses of Kakura are usually small clay or clay and bamboo huts, with tiny, airless rooms and hard mud floors. Cooking is done the traditional way, over a *chula*, fed with firewood (*lakri*), a smoky and dangerous affair. The only furniture is usually a stool or high wooden bed; there is no running water, let alone a WC.[22]

Making a Living

What does everyday economic life involve in the villages surrounding the gas plant? We took a cross-section of non-*Londoni* households in Kakura and Karimpur and asked them to tell us how they made a living.[23] Our informants were revisited at regular intervals throughout the year, allowing us to build up a picture of their livelihoods over the seasons. The material we gathered shows that even among households which are sharecropping relatively large amounts of land (a couple of acres), making a living is a highly precarious affair.

Several issues cut across each of the case studies. The first is that cash supply is vital for ongoing viability, but that only the richest families, who have UK connections, manage to stay in credit. This means that people are constantly borrowing money and/or rice in order to keep themselves afloat. As the case studies show, life is a constant round of borrowing, repaying and borrowing again. Social connectedness is key: those with links to *Londoni* families can sometimes access several thousand *taka* as 'help' rather than a loan. Others are part of long-term borrowing relationships, with neighbours, the local shopkeeper or relatives, often having to pay interest on their loans. Most if not all of the poorer households we spoke to were caught in a continual cycle of debt, which they could never completely clear.

Crucially, the case studies indicate that the need for cash is increasing. A major factor is the shift from sharecropping, in which the sharecropper needs no capital outlay besides the costs of production, to the rental *rongjoma* system in which money is given upfront to the owners rather than a proportion of the crop paid back after the harvest. As several farmers told us, absentee landlords prefer this system to sharecropping land, as they receive cash rather than paddy, which they don't need if they're living in the UK. What the case studies also reveal is that sharecropping often involves long-standing relationships between landowners and sharecroppers. *Rongjoma*, however, involves a more commercial transaction, and has to be renegotiated every year.

Other changes have also increased the need for cash: the use of mechanised pumps (which need to be hired) for irrigation is an example, as is the increased use of fertiliser and insecticide for fields which farmers told us used to be more productive before the gas field was built. Here, the changes to the seasonal inundation of land by the river and the 'drying out' of the soil which was discussed earlier are relevant. The spiralling cost of basic necessities was a major factor in 2008, when the research was carried out. As several of the case studies indicate, many families had drastically cut their intake of basic foods during the 'price hike'. These families were not only well below the 'poverty line' (if this is defined as spending more than two thirds of one's income on food), they were periodically facing complete destitution, for all of their income was spent on food, with nothing left over even for clothes. Again, the 'help' of others appears as crucial for the survival of these families.

A second finding is that many of the households we interviewed were engaged in agriculture at some time of the year alongside other ways of earning an income. Day-labourers, professional beggars, Chevron employees, all were periodically sharecropping small plots of land in order to feed themselves. Rather than a decisive shift away from agriculture, what we therefore see is a shift towards mixed livelihood strategies. Having said this, many people told us that the outlays involved in agriculture meant that it wasn't 'worth it'.

Finally, the case studies show how, while making a living for poorer people in Duniyapur is intrinsically bound up with social relationships, migration overseas and the increasing dominance of the cash economy means that these relationships are shifting: old-style obligations and exchanges are being superseded by the market economy.

MAKING A LIVING : CASE STUDIES

The first two case studies are of sharecroppers who live in Kakura. From the amounts of land that both are sharecropping, which are well above average for the village, one might suppose that these households would be more comfortable than those that have no access to land. However, as both cases show, they are continually struggling to balance their costs with the meagre outputs of cultivation. Environmental changes, the reduction in paddy and grazing land due to the gas plant and the roads, and the prevention of the seasonal inundation of water from the Kushiara River, have also had an important impact. Let us start with Lefus Miah.

Lefus Miah (Kakura)

April
Ten years ago I cultivated a small amount of land, but got good yields. Before, the rains came regularly, now they're irregular, so

we have to pay money for water [i.e. to irrigate the land, especially for the *boro* crop].[24] It used to cost about 150 *taka* to cultivate 1 *kiare* of land, now it's 400 *taka*. We also used to get straw from the fields which we used as fuel, but now you can't find it so we have to buy kerosene, which is 60 *taka* for a litre. Before, we ploughed the land with cattle; I had five bulls that I used for farming. Now we don't have any cattle due to the scarcity of fodder for them (which used to be available from the fields). I'm currently sharecropping 10 *kiare* of land, but the cost is 20,000 *taka*, so it's not profitable.

Q. Why do you farm if it's not profitable?
Because there's no work available locally. If I wanted to work at Chevron, I'd have to pay a bribe. We can't say anything against them. If we did, we'd be beaten.[25]

There are nine people in my household and I'm the only source of income. We need 8 kg rice per day. If we got 100 *maunds*[26] that would be enough to cover our needs, but we only get about 80 *maunds*. I don't have any *Londoni* relatives who can help me.

I had a loan from FIVDB:[27] 3,000 *taka* that I used for buying ducks. They all died. Then I had to repay the loan with 3,200 *taka*, so I had to sell some of the paddy. How is it possible to run a family? We barely survive. I don't buy anything extra; I just cover the expenses of eating and getting by. For over a year I haven't been able to buy any meat. I had 5 *maunds* of rice left after the harvest, so sold 3 and bought some fish. Our main food is dhal, dry fish and vegetables. We've had to cut down on the dhal, though. Before, we had half a kilogram; now we only get 250 gm, which isn't enough.

I also borrow money in advance of the harvest from neighbours. In order to pay for the inputs for cultivation I borrowed 3,000 *taka*, which I'll pay back at harvest.

August
This year I've rented 3 *kiare* of *rongjoma* land. I've paid 1,500 *taka* per *kiare* to the owners, who are from Mustafapu and Nadampur – one of them is a *Londoni*, who I've got good relations with; I've been his sharecropper for a long time.

This month I'm planting rice seeds in my 3 *kiare* of land – that costs 1,800 *taka*. I've employed some labourers to help me. In July I sold 20 *maunds* of paddy and got 12,000 taka, which I used for these planting costs and meeting the everyday costs of my family. I haven't taken a loan.

I don't have any close relatives in London, though my father-in-law has some relatives there. No-one helps us. Poor people help themselves.

Due to the price hike, it's very difficult to survive, since we can't afford to buy things. Luckily I don't have to buy any rice, but I buy everything else. I used to buy 1 litre of oil a week, now I can only afford to buy half a litre. We've also cut the amount of lentils we eat by half. We live on dry fish and vegetables.

I have to feed my labourers too, plus pay them 150 *taka* a day. All are local.

October

This month I'm not doing that much. I've cultivated the *aman* crop; you don't need much fertiliser for that, just water.

Of the 12 *kiare* I cultivate, 8 are *rongjoma* and the rest are from sharecropping. One of my sons is learning mechanics in the bazaar; he doesn't have a salary yet, but his boss pays for his meals.

I'm thinking of selling a cow to meet our everyday living expenses.

Of the hundred ducks my wife bought (from the FIVDB loan) only eight survived. I'll sell them when we need to raise some cash. My wife is also rearing two goats.

We didn't buy any new clothes at Eid. I borrowed 300 *taka* to buy extra food: rice, lentils, oil and flour, so my wife could cook special pitha.

December

I'm not doing anything at the moment, I'm unemployed. I haven't got any land to sharecrop. I thought I'd get some *rongjoma* land, but it costs 1,200–1,500 for 1 *kiare*. Last year the yields weren't good. I don't know how I'll raise 1,200 *taka*.

Altogether I cultivated 12 *kiare* of land last year (8 *rongjoma*) but after all the costs we only got 35 *maunds*, which isn't enough for all year consumption. At best, it's enough to subsist for six months.

The next case study is of another sharecropper from Kakura, Toshna Miah whose wives supplement the household's meagre income by making bamboo baskets to sell in the local market. Toshna Miah's comments also illustrate the exhausting balancing act that sharecroppers/small farmers are forced to perform, calculating the food needs of their families versus the yields from their modest harvests. As his comments on gaining access to fertiliser (for which he claims bribes have to be paid) also indicate, the corruption of state officials plays a role in maintaining rural poverty. Note that Lefus Miah made similar comments about gaining employment at Chevron.

Toshna Miah (Kakura)

This year I'm sharecropping 8 *kiare*. We have six people in our household: two wives and three children. I'm an old man, so my wives have to help earn money: they're selling bamboo baskets this year to help out.

We need 2 kg of rice for each meal. But we can't afford this, so have to make do with 1 kg. I also have to borrow money from my neighbours and relatives – as an advance on the harvest. This year I've borrowed 5,000 *taka* plus 6 *maunds* of paddy.

We have three meals a day, but one of those meals is just a name. In the morning we eat plain rice without any vegetables or curry. It's cheaper to buy 20 *taka* worth of dried fish.

To make the baskets we have to buy the materials, which is getting increasingly expensive. My wives make about eight baskets a week, which we sell in the market. We get about 300 *taka* from that, which is a great help. From 8 *kiare* of sharecropped land, we only get three months' worth of rice. The remaining nine months of the year are miserable. We have to borrow money, otherwise we wouldn't survive. If we can't pay the interest on the loans in time then we have to pay double the interest. This is the system around here and is what happened to me this year. That means that I have to use most of the harvest to pay back my loans, so I don't know how to run the household.

In 2004 the floods badly damaged my house, which was completely inundated and we had to take shelter elsewhere. The crops were damaged too. I had to borrow 10,000 *taka*, which I'm still repaying.

The gas field has caused us many problems. The amount of land available has decreased; it's also become infertile. We used to get fish from the fields but now you hardly ever see them.

October

I'm spreading manure over the land before Eid ... I had to spend a lot on fertiliser. I may need some insecticide too. I had to fertilise this land twice. The first time [that I bought fertiliser] I got 7 kg of fertiliser (1,200 *taka*), now I have to spend 1,400 for the same amount. Now I'm hearing that the dealers don't have any. I only got it from Gola Bazaar by offering a bribe. Without fertilisers we don't get high enough yields, so can't pay back our loans.

For Eid I borrowed 500 *taka* from a man in Kakura, so that we could have some good meals.

December (the dry season)

I'm not doing anything this month. My owner's land is near the North Pad. I've got a pump for *boro* production, but I can't get water from there, so am anxious about cultivating the *boro* crop. I'm really feeling worried.... This year my *aman* yields were poor, though people whose land is in the South Pad did well.[28] I had 3 *kiare rongjoma* and 5 sharecropped. After all the costs, I got 20 *maunds* of paddy. But I could barely cover the outlay. I had 16 labourers working for me, and had to pay them a *maund* each, plus 150 *taka*. So I had to take a loan just to pay them. I eventually got 20 *maunds* of paddy. I sold two and a half *maunds* for 500 *taka* per *maund*. The rest of the paddy we subsist off over the year.

Q. Why were the yields poor this year?
The fields were heavily waterlogged. It was also hard to get fertiliser in time. There wasn't any available from our union, so we had to go to Gola Bazaar to get it, and had to pay 20 *taka* per kilogram. So we couldn't put as much fertiliser down as needed, and the yields were poor and the plants attacked by insects. That meant I had to gas the plants (i.e. apply insecticide) three times, which cost more.

Last year I had to borrow 24,000 *taka* for cultivation. I promised to pay 2 *maunds* paddy per thousand *taka* as interest. I've paid the interest, but not the original 20,000 *taka* as yet.

Q. Why is it more expensive to get rongjoma land this year?
The owners realised that you can produce 7–8 *maunds* per *kiare*. If 1 *maund* of paddy costs 500 *taka*, then 7 *maunds* are worth 3,500 *taka*. They get 3 *maunds* as their share, which is worth 1,500 *taka*, which we poor people can't pay.

Q. How will you repay the loan?
The landowners appreciate that the yields weren't good this year. I've borrowed from various different people who understand my situation. Everyone knows that we farmers are in trouble. I'll repay those who need the money most first.

The following comments drive home the fact that the transition to a cash economy exacerbates inequalities between the rich and the poor. As Toshna Miah tells us, poorer farmers can barely manage the costs of *rongjoma*, which have been raised by richer farmers who are able to pay more in competition for scarce land. The roads also benefit the rich while making life harder for the poor.

March 2009

I've got 10 *kiare* of land as *rongjoma*, which has put me in debt. Now I'm waiting for rain. I had to pay 10,000 *taka* for the 10 *kiare*. The owners wanted 1,500 per *kiare*, but I refused to pay it. The owner lives in London – he said that the cost of everything had gone up. One of our villagers, who's a local doctor, contributed to increasing the costs of *rongjoma* by offering 2,000 *taka* per *kiare*, higher than other people were paying. So the owners have raised the prices. The doctor is a rich man. He has a power pump and can cultivate both *aman* and *boro* from the same plot of land. But we don't have irrigation equipment. We only cultivate *aman* on the *rongjoma* land and not *boro*, as it needs too much water.

I mortgaged the land for one year. I have to pay 10,000 *taka* plus 12 *maunds* of paddy by the end of the year. We poor don't have any alternative. We take a loan just to repay the last loan. This is how we survive. I owe 20,000 taka and am trying to work out how to repay it. I borrow money from villagers and have never been to an NGO. NGOs lend 2,000-3,000 *taka*, and ask you to repay on a weekly basis ... so it's better to go to village people.

It's not profitable for me to cultivate *boro* along with *aman*. I don't have a machine [i.e. pump]. I wish I did. The area is surrounded by roads and the water doesn't pass. Before, the river water used to come over the land and it was fertile. Now even for *aman* production there isn't enough water. The embankments and roads are good for the people who use them, but we hardly ever go to Sylhet so what's the use of roads? We don't need roads, they're for the rich men. Now they can get their vehicles right up to their houses. Now because of the road, 1 *kiare* of land is worth 3,000 *taka*.

While the next case study shows similar issues concerning the careful balancing of production costs and outputs with household consumption, it also indicates how the need for cash is prioritised over other concerns. For Tajol Miah and his family, begging is an important component of their livelihood and, as we see, can raise significant amounts of cash, making it more productive than cultivating land.

Tajol Miah

Tajol Miah says he's growing old and doesn't have much energy left for work. He has five daughters, one of whom is disabled. The household depends on her earnings as a beggar, plus the 2 *kiare* of land which they sharecrop, which is suitable for *aman* production only. From the sharecropped land, they got 20 *maunds* of paddy in 2008 which they subsisted from for four months. He spent 2,000 *taka* on seeds, and borrowed 5,000 *taka* for other production costs. His daughter goes out begging 2–3 days a week, earning 50–200 *taka* a week. As he puts it:

> We could earn more, but my daughter can only be persuaded to beg a few days a week. Nowadays around here people give you food or other things, so to do our begging we go outside the village, to places like Shah Jalal's mosque, Sharan Paran mosque in Sylhet City and the like ... People don't want to give money if they see my daughter with me: they say I'm an able-bodied man, so why do I need to beg? So we've changed our strategy, using our daughter to get more sympathy. But as we're far from home we have to stay in a hotel which is expensive, plus food. Ramadan is a good time for us, when people go to mosques ... we see it as a chance to catch them.
>
> For each meal we need at least 2 kg of rice. We never have any side dishes, just the rice. We don't buy vegetables, as we can't afford them.

August

Tajol Miah is sharecropping 8 *kiare* of land; he's planting this month. For the planting he uses seven labourers who he pays 150 *taka* plus meals. The land owners are *Londonis*, with some of the household remaining in Karimpur; he's been cultivating the same land for the last eighteen years. He's had to take loans to cover production expenses and has built up debt of 20,000 *taka*. He and his daughter can earn around 200 *taka* a day from begging. They mostly do it in Gola Bazaar, where people don't know them.

The next two case studies are of households with no access to land. Both live in Kakura. For these households, their daily life revolves around simply trying to get enough food to eat.

Somir Uddin

Somir Uddin is in his thirties with a wife and four children. They live with his mother-in-law; his father-in-law is dead so he takes responsibility. He's a rickshaw puller, earning about 150 *taka* a day; it costs 30 *taka* to hire the rickshaw. His mother-in-law sometimes works as a servant. He says:

> I can't pull a rickshaw every day. Some days I've had to starve, as I haven't earned any money. I try to borrow money, but don't always manage. There are two ways you can get a loan: you can borrow rice or cash. I pay back the loans by reducing our food intake. We borrow from relatives who we know well. Me, my mother-in-law and my wife try to get work during harvesting. My wife and mother-in-law work in the village [as agricultural labourers] while I find work outside. The women get 4–5 *maunds* of rice and sometimes some old saris.
>
> I can't remember the last time I ate meat. For the last three days we've had a snack in the morning, followed by a meal of rice and dried fish at midday and in the evening ... When I get some money we eat two meals. If I don't earn anything, we don't eat.

Lila Begum

Lila Begum is a widow. There are four people in the household, including her son, who is a day-labourer, working on the land and road construction. On average he earns 100–150 *taka* a day. She told us:

> Yesterday my son went out very early to find work. We didn't have anything to eat, so waited eagerly for his return. We waited until the evening, but still he didn't come. That night I had to go to a neighbour to borrow 1 kg of rice. We cooked this and had it with dried fish. The following morning we ate the leftovers. For lunch and dinner we followed the same pattern. This happens to us every day, every month.

When we monitored the food that Lila Begum's household ate over four days, we found that for two of the days they ate twice.

For the other two days they had one meal of rice and dried fish or rice and vegetables and nothing else.

The final case study in this section also shows that simply getting enough food is a major issue for day-labourers. When work is scarce, or the prices of basic commodities rise, as happened drastically during the 2008 price hike, households have little choice but to reduce their calorific intake, sometimes severely.

Bilat Pal

Bilat Pal is a Hindu day-labourer, with two daughters and one son. He earns 150 *taka* a day, but only gets work about 20 days a month, mostly repairing and building houses. The household needs 3 kg rice a day, which costs 100 *taka*. The rest of the money is spent on basic foods. Household members gave us the following information about their food consumption:

Before the 2008 price hike	*Now*
Monthly 4 litres oil	1 litre
Daily 1 kg potatoes	250 gm
Monthly 1 kg dhal	250 gm
8 eggs	4 eggs
Milk	nothing

The household borrows from a shop in Bander Bazaar to buy necessities. When Bilat is paid at the end of the month, they repay the loan. If there's a crisis, he borrows from money lenders in Nadampur, who ask for 20 *taka* interest for every 100 borrowed. He doesn't like to borrow from NGOs because of their strict terms and conditions.

*   *   *

That the rural landless in Karimpur and Kakura face a daily struggle to meet their basic needs is not so surprising in a context where land is a dwindling resource, the costs of rice production are rising and inflation soaring. What these case studies drive home is the extreme insecurity these households face. The returns from agriculture are never certain: floods, insects or the late arrival of the rains can mean one's investment is wasted and the only way to survive is by taking on more debt. Cash is increasingly vital, but it is only those with connections to *bidesh* that have enough of it. Within this context – of continual shortfalls and the ever present threat of hunger – it is small wonder that the rural poor seek connections to those who can provide what development discourse describes as 'safety nets', either via loans or 'help'. I shall be exploring these issues, and the moralities which underlie them in the next chapter.

In the last part of this chapter, however, let us turn to a new possibility for secure income and connectedness that has arisen in the last few years: the gas field. As described earlier, in 2005–7, when the plant was under construction, many local people were hired as construction workers. With monthly wages averaging 4,500 *taka*, and regular employment, the workers – many of whom came from Kakura – experienced an immediate and significant rise to their living standards. These days of plenty were not to last however, for once the construction work had been completed the labourers were laid off. Today, only a small number of local people have employment at the gas field: estimates varied from between 50 to 100; this number fluctuates according to need. Yet rather than being employed directly by Chevron, these labourers are employed by contractors.

Indeed, while for the landless and land poor of Kakura and Karimpur a job with Chevron is highly desirable, offering security of employment, possibilities of overtime and promotion, sick pay, holidays, pensions and so on, the possibility of ever gaining such employment is highly remote, for even if they were to be hired, it would be via labour contractors who offer no such perks, often fail to pay salaries regularly, and require social connectedness, based on patron–client relations. Indeed, to the huge chagrin of local people, many labourers today are brought from outside Duniyapur and its environs, some from as far afield as Pabna. People's claims to work, which draw upon a model of entitlement based on their geographical connection to the locality, and their 'rights', thus mean very little. Indeed, appeals to 'Chevron' to give them work, fall on deaf ears for it is labour contractors, not the multinational which controls employment, and these contractors rely largely on social networks and informal methods of control. For Chevron, this makes possible 'an easy flow of labour' as the community relations officer at the gas field told me (Interview notes, 2008), and is a prime example of what Jamie Cross (2011) has termed the 'ethics of detachment' of contemporary multinationals. As we shall see, it is also easier to control labour when it is drawn from distant areas rather than villages adjacent to the gas field, where local people have a strong sense of rights and in the past have been politically mobilised.

WORKING AT THE GAS PLANT: CONTRACTORS AND 'THE EASY FLOW OF LABOUR'

According to the 'Baseline Survey' produced by consultants for Unocal,[29] one of the main demands that were made in a 'FGD' (focus group discussion) in Nadampur in 2004 was that, if built, the gas field should employ local people. Indeed, alongside anxieties concerning the loss of land, safety and the appropriation of natural resources by a foreign company was the hope that the plant might be the start of something new and positive for the area: industrial development, providing secure employment and business opportunities. Alongside images of the '*shondar desh*' (golden land) is another, equally desirable landscape: of 'development': reliable infrastructure, *pukka* houses, a dependable power supply and industrialisation. During our discussions in London, for example, one man said that he had no problem with industrialisation *per se*, but if this was to take place, *he* should profit from it, not a foreign multinational. Another man, a local councillor in the north-east, emphasised that in his view the gas plant made a 'great visual impact' on the area and its construction had led to better transport links and so on. He was proud to see development taking place in his homeland, he went on; he hated returning home and being reminded of how in Bangladesh things weren't 'up to scratch'. Similar attitudes are shared in Duniyapur. Of course it's good if the village becomes like a town, the matriarch of a middle-income Nadampur family replied in response to my questions; then there'll be development and the lot of the poor will improve.

The early days of constructing the gas field bore out these hopes. Many hundreds of people,[30] such as San Mahmud, were employed as daily wage labourers, helping to build the plant and surrounding infrastructure. This included a small group of women, who worked on the roads. While wage levels varied, most people recall receiving around 4,500 *taka* a month, or 200 *taka* a day. In contrast to the skilled labour at the plant, recruited directly by Chevron at national and international levels, none of these labourers were employed by Chevron, but via contractors, who tendered for the work at the plant's inception. Once given the contracts, Chevron enlisted them as private 'companies' or *enterprises*.

As soon as the work was finished, the majority of labourers were laid off. Today, the men we spoke to who had been made redundant claim that the reason for losing their jobs was that they didn't pay bribes to the labour contractors, or were not connected to the locally powerful leaders who gained contracts with Chevron. As Parry (2001) has pointed out in his work at the Bilhai Steel Plant in India, the point of such rumours is not necessarily that they reflect the objective truth, but rather that they reveal a model of how the world *should be* (Parry, 2001). In this case, the rumours reflect a belief that local people should be compensated for the damage to their livelihoods with secure employment at the gas field, which is equitably distributed in a transparent way, not doled out via the social networks of labour contractors. The complaints we heard are thus as much about the informal nature of employer–employee relations and local politics as they are about their failure to gain employment, which as one man put it, 'is our *right*' (Focus group discussion, Kakura, 2009).

> The leaders appropriated all the benefits. Chevron offered a high salary but the leaders [who were also labour contractors] didn't pay us much. Since the leaders controlled the jobs they became really powerful and had the authority to replace anyone who objected. At the beginning lots of villagers worked for Chevron … now only 50 or 100 people are working. People were sacked for a simple reason: they weren't recruited by Chevron but by the local leaders. These local leaders' followers and relatives got the jobs …
>
> When I worked for the gas field I got 7,500 *taka* a month in cash. Now I don't have a fixed income. (Ex-Chevron labourer, Karimpur, 2009)

> I worked for a year and a half in the gas field, then I was sacked. I worked as a mason; I used to get 4,800 *taka* a month. One day I was working and the next I was told I wouldn't be needed again. When I asked why I was told I had to speak to Mr X of X Enterprise [i.e. the labour contractor]. Since then I've been passing my time doing nothing. I expected to get another job, but I didn't … I hoped to get a job as a rickshaw puller, but they said you're a mason, you don't know how to pull a rickshaw. Since then I've had a loan from the Grameen Bank and am trying to do some small business things. (Ex-Chevron labourer, Kakura, 2009)

Many people have a similar story. Safety training was given, identity cards issued but then the work supply dried up. One man told me how it had cost him 500 *taka* to get his photograph taken for his card in Sylhet Town; a week later, he was laid off. The situation has caused deep resentment: the widespread perception in Duniyapur is that since Chevron is using local resources, it should provide work. In an early focus group discussion that we held in Kakura in 2008, one man put it like this: 'The gas field roads go straight over our hearts, so we should be given priority for work.'

While some local leaders were given contracts to supply labour to the gas field, our research showed that of fifteen enterprises contracting labour in 2009, only about half were 'local' (i.e. from the immediate vicinity), while the rest came from outside the immediate area, some bringing labourers from many hundreds of miles away. These labourers, who are all men, are housed either in purpose-built accommodation close to the gas field, or in houses owned by *Londonis* in the surrounding villages. Each enterprise has different areas of work. One company has the contract to supply security guards, another supplies drivers, while others provide catering. The wages and contracts of these men are different, according to their jobs.

The advantages to Chevron of hiring labour in this way are easy to appreciate. Since the contractors recruit and pay the workers the company does not need to have any direct dealings with them. They are thus a reserve army *par excellence*, un-unionised and with no form of redress from the company, which offers none of the ethically irreproachable standards of employment that it reserves for its own staff, who come from outside the area or are foreign.

The use of contractors also means that labourers can be controlled, since they are hired informally by their patrons and are therefore unlikely to challenge the authority of their *malik* (owners, or boss), due to their 'loyalty', as one contractor put it. As a contractor from distant Pabna explained:

My own people are unemployed during the rainy season as we have only one crop a year in our part of the world. So I bring them to the gas field ... the whole thing is based on trust. We all have to trust each other. Say, for example, if I bring people who aren't good, or who are impudent, then Chevron won't give me another contract. If I recruit people from my own village then I don't need to worry, because my villagers won't be rude to me. They'll do as I say. Also, they'll go to me with whatever they need, like for wages, borrowing money or sending it back to the village or whatever. So that's why I recruit my own people. If you want to be a contractor you have to have repute and trust, which I do my best to maintain.

A practice used by many contractors to secure their workers' loyalty is the payment of a deposit to the contractor by the worker as 'security' before the period of employment has started. If the worker becomes demanding or difficult, or leaves without finishing his or her work, the contractor can simply withhold the deposit.

Having said this, the labour contractor system can bring security for employees, as explained by this worker, who had come from hundreds of miles away to work at the gas field.

> I enjoy working with my own contractor, who I know and who's from my own village. We came in a group of about 20–25 workers, and as we're all from the same village we feel more safe and comfortable in this place where we're outsiders and there are white people around. We know the *malik*, it's like our own company. And if we work with our own contractors we get privileges and favours. Plus my family at home don't need to worry about me because they know where I am and what I'm doing even though I'm in a new place. (Interview notes, 2009)

Other workers were more negative. While all welcomed the employment, we heard stories of contractors taking a 'cut' of their wages, which are paid to the contractors at fixed rates by Chevron; others told of late or outstanding payments. This is a particular problem for landless labourers for whom, as we have seen, the daily balancing of cash supply and food needs is so precarious. Abdullah told us:

> I've been working for nine months but I haven't received any salary yet. I get 100 *taka* (a day) as a food allowance, and have saved up some money which has been a great help. I'd leave if I could get a better job, but I'm staying to get my unpaid salary. If I leave now I'll never get hold of the money.

Another labourer added:

> There's meant to be a system [i.e. a contract] but it's not implemented. We're employed verbally and the employers can sack anyone at any time. Because of this, us labourers are exploited and cheated. (Interview notes, 2009)

These complaints aside, there can be little doubt that the vast majority of poorer people in the area are only too keen to gain employment at the plant, or on its borders: in road maintenance, for example. Whether or not they are employed by labour contractors, the benefits are enormous. As the community relations officer told us, workers can earn up to 8,000 *taka* a month including overtime, which, he remarked 'just involved standing around and gossiping' (Interview notes, 2008). The shift work is regular, from eight in the morning until four in the afternoon, training in safety given, with regular breaks, and so on. Indeed, *inside* the gas field, it is another world: of high security, safety procedures, clocking in, uniforms and modernity.[31]

For the small number of local women employed as labourers, the effects of a regular income can be enormous. Kept strictly apart from the men, these women work in small teams on the roads and other sites surrounding the gas field, always supervised by a man. Unlike their male counterparts the women come from local villages. While some had stories to tell of verbal abuse from their supervisors, most embraced the opportunity to work and the regular income they received (a daily rate of 180 *taka* was reported). Again, these women were chosen by local labour contractors, influential local leaders who now had the power to distribute employment opportunities.

*   *   *

That the economic effects of the gas field are complex is obvious: some people, largely those who have gained work as contractors or the small minority who are working as labourers in and around the plant have gained from the incomes to be had via regular employment. Others, in contrast, have suffered from land dispossession and the knock-on effects of losing 50 acres or so from the pool of available agricultural land. The environmental effects, complex and multifaceted as they are, have exacerbated the shift from an agrarian economy which was based upon social contracts, the use of the commons by the poor and, for some, sustainable agriculture, to one which is more commercialised and hence less inclusive of the very poor, who struggle to find sufficient credit to rent land or mechanised pumps and can barely afford to pay for chemical fertilisers, let alone fish at the market in Enatganj.

What we also see is how while people may aspire to a world in which their rights are met and resources distributed equitably, the realities of Duniyapur are very different. The rural poor want old style development, in the form of industrialisation, jobs, infrastructure and social security. What they have, instead, is a system of entitlements based around old-fashioned patronage, even in the *über* modern world of Chevron's gas field, where jobs are largely only available via social connections to contractors. That the 'good' social capital on which they have relied for generations is failing and inadequate is clear: processes of migration and commercialisation mean that patrons no longer need clients; the old ways are becoming frayed and unsuited to the brave new world of neoliberal Bangladesh.

And yet claims based on social connections must be made, for in lieu of formal employment or an equitable welfare state this is the only way in which the poor can gain entitlements to scarce resources. In the next chapter I turn to this claim making in more detail, showing the vital importance of social connections to the survival of Duniyapur's poor, and the moralities which underlie this particular 'system of entitlement'.

4
Our Own Poor: Social Connections, 'Helping' and Claims to Entitlement

RENUMA BIBI

She is waiting for me inside the house, perching on the hard, high bed in her greying widow's sari. In the twenty-odd years that I've known her she's always been this thin, the skin stretched tight across her cheeks, her arms so emaciated it's a wonder they don't snap. The last time we met, a good seven months ago, she had a funny turn as she left the *bari*: stumbling back to her small house across the bamboo bridge, her body shaking uncontrollably. She hadn't eaten all day, she said, couldn't hold food down. A month earlier, her adult daughter Lila had suddenly died. Lovely Lila, with her bright laugh and bow legs; she always seemed so alive. When I was doing my doctoral fieldwork in the late 1980s she was often in the *bari*, helping with the cooking or cleaning. She wasn't a servant, I was told, but *kutoom* (a relative). In exchange for the domestic 'help' she provided, she'd take home a bundle of rice, get a hot meal or even an old sari, a different form of 'help' (*shahajo*) moving in a different direction.[1] How old was she? People's ages are hard to tell in rural Bangladesh, where no-one records birthdays and poverty so quickly strips women of their youth. Late thirties, perhaps, or older? She'd collapsed in the latrine – *bhut* (ghosts) Renuma Bibi thinks – leaving her mother with no-one to care for her, and besides the charity of her relatives, no source of income.

That is why Renuma Bibi is here. Or rather, *I* am why she is here. As I enter Shuli's *bari*, tired and hot from the walk back from Karimpur, she rushes towards me, throwing her arms around my waist and wailing. Even during my doctoral fieldwork, when I was more competent in Sylheti, I struggled to understand the broad dialect and broken-toothed diction of some of the older people in the area. Now, rendered stupid by lack of practice, I can only grasp every third phrase. But I get the gist. Renuma Bibi is lamenting her sorrows, eyes rolling back in her head, shoulders shaking. And, as with so many of the rural poor, there are many sources of grief:

the death of Lila's father in Britain thirty years earlier and the appropriation of his documentation by ill-intended brothers who sold it on for profit, meaning that Renuma Bibi has never been able to claim a British widow's pension; Lila's unhappy marriage to her cousin across the river and subsequent return to her mother's gappy shack; their unstoppable slide into the mire of poverty Bangladeshi style: loans that can't be repaid, fragments of land sold, floods that wreck whatever few possessions one has, illness requiring expensive medicines, more loans – a life spent weathering the everyday crises that, if only there was a bit of money, would be mere inconveniences. And now her cousin, Abdul Pathan who has grown rich since I knew him as a young, returned migrant from Saudi in the late 1980s, is attempting to appropriate her house.

What Renuma Bibi is telling me, Shuli and her mother explain, is that in his quest for more property to rent to the migrant labourers who have gravitated to the village in search of work, Abdul Pathan is attempting to steal her house. I should make a case against him, they continue, call a *shalish* (meeting of elders to decide over local grievances and disputes, approve of marriages, etc.) and tell everyone the truth about who owns the house. For them it is a lineage matter: both Renuma Bibi and Abdul Pathan are cousins, part of the powerful Pathan lineage.

The family women are right. For the reason that Renuma Bibi has been waiting all day for my return from Karimpur and is now throwing herself at my feet and sobbing is that six years ago I paid £800 for her house to be built.

Should I have done it? During my 1980s fieldwork, as a relatively poor British postgraduate, the only occasion I gave anything away was on my departure, when my saris, mosquito net and lantern were carefully redistributed to poorer people in the village by the women of my household. Then began a long process, spread over many years, when I gradually became like a *Londoni*, visiting every couple of years and assuming the role of patron and helper to his or her less fortunate relatives and the local poor. The role of cash dispenser is now *de rigueur* for returning *Londoni*; Shuli's brother, who lives in Burnley told me that he gave away tens of thousands of pounds during his last trip home. Other *Londonis* regularly send money from the UK, not just to support their relatives, but to help destitute, non-related neighbours. One man I met in north London funds the education of several children from poor households in his village.

As the years have passed I have therefore given up on the methodologically sound but emotionally challenging position of not giving charity to the poor of Nadampur, for as an honorary family member, the role of patron has become increasingly unavoidable. The year before paying for Renuma Bibi's small house to be built I'd had an unexpected windfall; when I heard of the problems she and Lila were experiencing it seemed only decent to help. Now, I regularly give cash to the many women who appear in the *bari* when I'm visiting. It's only £5 or £10, I tell myself; it'll make a huge difference to the recipient's monthly budget, why not?

The question returns us to an examination of the different systems of entitlement in Duniyapur and the moral orders which underpin them. While in the last chapter we saw how the lives of the poor are dominated by constant struggles over resources – land, fertiliser, medicines, food – I shall now turn to what might appear to be a 'traditional' system of entitlement, namely patron clientage and charity which is based on social relations that stretch not only within and between villages, but also transnationally, between Duniyapur and the UK, and rely upon moralities of kinship and 'helping' (*shahajo*). Yet rather than being 'traditional', these tenuous forms of entitlement and the claim making they involve are products of contemporary circumstances. The transformation of some families via transnational migration, the Bangladesh state's inability to provide formal social protection and the presence of multinational companies that appear to dispense largesse yet fail to provide employment are all central.

Underlying each of these factors are the obscene global inequalities that not only allow multinational energy companies to profit from natural gas in Bangladesh while the villages adjacent to the gas field are unconnected to the gas supply, but for British expatriates to earn hundreds of times more than the rural poor they support, and yet who, in turn, are often at the bottom of the economic hierarchy in Britain. In this sense, the politics of entitlement in Duniyapur is grafted onto a geo-political hierarchy in which secure access to particular places brings individuals the possibility of transformative power, not only in terms of their socio-economic position in the *desh* but also in their ability to temporarily turn around the fortunes of those they help, for, as we have already seen, a gift of a couple of thousand *taka* (about £20) is more than some people earn in a month.

These inequalities, and the culture of giving and receiving, or, in Sen's terms, the system of entitlement, in which they are played out are the context in which the 'gifts' donated by Unocal and Chevron – be these t-shirts, slab latrines or new houses – have been received by the local population. Rather than being 'pure' gifts these 'community engagement' donations are deeply implicated in social relationships, dependency and obligation. Analysis of the culture and political economy of giving and receiving in Duniyapur thus returns us to Mauss, as well as recent anthropological analyses of the 'development gift' (Parry, 1986; Rajak, 2011; Stirrat and Henkel, 1997). As we see in the next chapter, within the systems of entitlement and moral orders that exist in Duniyapur, Chevron's development gift is neither the formal compensation that people believe they should have in exchange for the company's extraction of local gas, nor the socially embedded gift of the patron to his or her 'own poor'. Instead it is entirely different, located in moralities that deny both social connection and formal compensation.

First, let us return to moralities of charity and patronage and the claim making these involve. In throwing herself at my feet and lamenting, Renuma Bibi is not only expressing the profound sorrow and distress caused by Lila's death, but also making a claim, for within the system of entitlement by which she survives, social connections to wealthy patrons (Katy) plus her membership of the powerful Pathan lineage are among the few resources she has at her disposal. These social connections are what both Bourdieu and Putnam would call 'social capital'. Yet while Bourdieu was primarily interested in how social capital (knowing the right people) furthered the interests of the elite, in Duniyapur connectedness to social networks that spread across transnational and local space is vital for the survival of the poor, an observation made by other researchers in Bangladesh (Purvez, 2004; Wood, 2005). And while in Putnam's formulation, social capital is presented as civic good, a resource that the poor need more of, in Duniyapur as elsewhere it is also mired in unequal power relations and dependency (Huda et al., 2008; Wood, 2003).[2] As Kabeer writes:

> Where people lack the means to meet their daily survival needs, they will only achieve security of livelihoods by binding themselves into highly asymmetrical relationships, receiving a variety of resources essential for their basic needs in return for a variety of resources which reinforce their patron's dominant status. (2002: 11)

In Duniyapur these relationships are transnational as well as localised. In *Londoni* villages the politics of *place* dominates social hierarchies, for those who have access to the UK or other wealthy countries have become the indispensable patrons of those left behind (Gardner, 2008; Gardner and Ahmed, 2009). Meanwhile, while the very poor seek social connections to patrons located in *London*, the less poor seek connection to *London* via their social links to those already there, for access to foreign countries is obtainable not just via the hard cash needed for documentation, fares and so on but, crucially, via social networks and social connectedness. For those who are successful, connection to the UK or US brings access to formal systems of entitlement associated with the 'modern', or 'developed' world: legally contracted employment, social security, health care, formal education and so on. And yet it is only via claims to informal systems of social connection (or 'social capital') that these formal connections and entitlements can be secured.

I shall return to the transnational relationships and exchanges that shape so much life in Duniyapur in a short while. For now, let us turn to a closer examination of the moralities of giving and receiving that underlie the requests for money made to me by both friends and strangers.

ISLAMIC MORALITIES OF GIVING: QURBANI EID, DECEMBER 2008

The butchers have almost finished. In place of the two bullocks that only an hour ago were innocently chewing hay in the yard, a bloodied mess of flesh, skin and bones is heaped on the ground: the discarded horns and hooves the only tangible evidence of the creatures they once were. Happily, I missed the actual slaughter. I have, however, been watching the team of butchers skilfully skin the animals and slice them up. Now the young men of the family are piling the meat onto the banana leaves laid out on the sandy ground, ready for their ritualised distribution.[3] Already a few *gorib* (poor people) have arrived in the *bari*. They sit patiently on the steps, their children running excitedly around. In an hour or so about fifty or sixty people will have accumulated in the courtyard, each with a plastic bag or bowl ready to receive the meat. When I chat to them I find that rather than being 'local' poor from Kakura, as was the case in the Qurbani Eid I observed in 1988, all are recent in-migrants to Nadampur, living largely in colonies and makeshift huts on land near the school and coming from far away places such as Boirob (to the West of Bangladesh).

Once the meat has been cut into chunks and divided into small piles, the *bari* men move along the row of *gorib* waiting on the steps, handing each person a small amount of the *mungsho* (meat). The rest is sorted into various *deg* (large cooking pot): some for dinner this evening, and some for nearby relatives, including 'our own poor': kin who have fallen on hard times and for whom attendance at the distribution would, I'm told, be inappropriate, a cause of *sharom* (shame). One such person is a well-dressed woman who arrives during the sacrifice, her 5-year-old daughter wearing Western-style jeans and a spangly top. The women of the house greet her warmly, for this was once her *nani*'s (maternal grandmother) *bari*. Since her childhood in the nearby village of Syedpur, she tells me, her family have slipped into poverty; her husband is a lowly ticket collector on a launch. They live in Dhaka, she adds. To my surprise it transpires that this morning she and her daughter travelled the 300 or so kilometres from Dhaka in order to receive their share of the meat, which is duly wrapped in plastic bags and stored in her handbag, ready for the journey home. For while charitable donations are given to both related and non-related poor, the differences between them are jealously guarded by high-status lineages such as the Saiyeds, Pathans and Khans, for whom it is not poverty *per se* which brings shame, but association with the habits of *chotomanoosh* (low-status people: see Gardner, 1995)

Once the non-related *gorib* have their portion, they take off in a large and happy group, heading towards the other *baris* in the village who are known to be performing Qurbani sacrifices. This year the spoils are somewhat reduced: the British recession and slipping rate of exchange of the pound sterling against the Bangladeshi *taka* has had a noticeable effect on how many bullocks can be bought with the money remitted from the UK. Last year her sons sent enough money for six bullocks, Amma says. This year there are only two paid for by British money, plus another one paid for by a cousin (and member of the *bari*) in the US. For the cousins in the *bari* next door, there are none.

Qurbani is of course not particular to Duniyapur or Bangladesh, but is the Islamic festival of sacrifice of sheep, cattle, goats or camels, performed at Eid Al-Adha, in order to share their meat between family, friends and the poor. Ideologically, it is related to the injunction of *Zakah*, one of the five pillars of Islam in which a proportion of an individual's wealth is distributed each year to the poor.[4] In Nadampur in the late 1980s this involved a proportion of the *dhan* (unthreshed paddy) from the harvest, which was donated to the mosque, plus the more generalised practice of giving to beggars who wandered from *bari* to *bari* asking for alms, a practice which continues today. A related practice, which I describe in detail elsewhere (Gardner, 1995) is that of the distribution of *shinni*, in which food such as *pitha* cakes (made with rice flour) *shandesh* or other delicacies are distributed by a household in times of celebration or when special prayers are required, such as during children's exams, the birth of a child and so on. *Shinni* can be paid for transnationally and offered on behalf of household members living abroad; from what I have observed it is distributed among relatives and neighbours, rather than being a charitable donation to the poor.

In rural Bangladesh these spiritual underpinnings to charity have a spatial dimension in which one's 'own poor' tend to be those from the vicinity of one's village. This was what the *Londoni* men we met in the UK were referring to when they spoke of their desire to help their 'own people', for 'degrees of relatedness', and thus the extent that claims can be made and a sense of obligation experienced are calculated according to actual kinship links as well as spatial proximity (Gardner and Ahmed, 2009). In our research in Biswanath we found that 'help' was offered first and foremost to blood relatives, and then to village 'insiders' who, even if unrelated, were seen to be locals with long-lasting relationships to their patrons. Meanwhile 'outsider' in-migrants (*abedi*), who did not have the social connections, were not able to obtain any help beyond distributions at Qurbani Eid, funerals or other ritual occasions. I shall return to the geography of obligation and, in particular, its transnational dimensions, in a short while.

GETTING CONNECTED: GIVING AND RECEIVING AS DUTY AND ENTITLEMENT

That the morality of giving is matched by a morality of receiving should come as no surprise to anthropologists schooled in Mauss, for as we know, The Gift is never free, but involves ongoing social relationships and an obligation to give back. All gifts must be reciprocated; if they are not, social ties are denied. As Mary Douglas puts it: 'each gift is part of a system of reciprocity in which the honour of giver and receiver are engaged' (1990: viii). In the schema suggested by Mauss, societies move from an 'archaic' 'system of total services' (Douglas, 1990: 5–6) based on gifts, to a modern, fragmented society in which gift giving is superseded by commercial relations. Elaborating on this evolutionary model, Parry (1986) argues that in societies featuring an advanced division of labour and world religions with transcendent values, 'pure gifts', often in the form of charitable donations, can be thought of as aesthetic acts. A good example might be the various websites that offer the global Muslim audience the opportunity to practise Qurbani by making an online donation to pay for sacrifices that take place in cyber-space rather than 'one's own poor'.[5]

What we see in Duniyapur is, however, more nuanced. Here, Islamic moralities and practices such as *Zakah* and Qurbani structure and provide an ideological framework for certain forms of giving, but *all* gifts are underscored by localised social relationships in which giving creates and recreates both hierarchy and connection. Indeed, hierarchy and connection are two sides to the same coin; neither can exist without the other.

If there is no 'pure' gift in Duniyapur what is reciprocated by those who receive charity and 'help'? In what we might think of as 'traditional' patron–client relations in Bangladesh, the donations/'help' given by patrons is reciprocated by clients in the form of labour, political loyalty, devotion and so on. Within this context, giving and receiving are part of a long-term relationship, in which the expectations of both parties are reasonably clear. For poor women such as Renuma, the economic support offered by her wealthier kin, which is never regular or wholly predictable, but comes in the form of informal gifts, whether these are second-hand saris, a bundle of rice, or, indeed, a new house, is part of a long-term relationship in which she reciprocates the gifts she receives with domestic labour, prayers and performances of devout subservience or *maiya* (love, adoration). Small wonder that she insists that the nature of the relationship is one of kinship, by continually reminding me that that I am structurally her maternal niece and my children are her grandchildren, for kinship is the basis on which she makes her claims.

That one is entitled to 'help' from particular categories of people but not others, and the ways in which this adheres to status and hierarchy was vividly illustrated to me by Joyoti, the sister of Abdul Pathan. Like Renuma Bibi, Joyoti and Abdul Pathan are distant cousins of Shuli in the Pathan *gushti* (patrilineage). The day after Renuma Bibi visited, Joyoti came to see me. Divorced and living with her son in a separate house in her brother's *bari*, Joyoti may not be as wealthy as Abdul Pathan and his wife, but neither is she living the hand-to-mouth existence of the sharecroppers and landless informants whom we heard from in the last chapter. Nor indeed does she face the destitution of her cousin Renuma Bibi, for, however strained their relationship might be, her brother has an obligation to offer her a degree of economic support.[6] I was therefore surprised when, after the normal greetings, Joyoti requested money in order that she could buy medicine for her bad chest. What about Abdul Pathan? I asked; surely he would pay for the medicine? Only the day before I had visited his *bari*, which, in contrast to the family's mud and thatch cottage of the 1980s, was now an imposing *pukka* house, with rows of colonies on either side. Given his wealth (not to mention his plans for Renuma Bibi's house!) that his sister should now be requesting charity from me was irritating, to say the least. After she had departed (empty-handed) I turned in exasperation to Shuli. Was Joyoti not ashamed to be asking me for money? After all, she wasn't even *that* poor! Shuli's reply was instructive. There's no shame in asking a relative for help, she explained. You're part of our lineage, which is why Joyoti can ask you. What would be shameful is what *chotomanoosh* (i.e. low-status) people do, which is to approach strangers.

As this minor incident shows, for people who are members of higher-status *gushti*, receiving the 'gift' of charity is socially sanctioned if it takes place within the content of established social relationships and relatedness, but perceived as dishonourable if the donor is a stranger; this is the behaviour of the low-status people of Kakura, or of beggars: remember our Kakura informant in the last chapter, who took his disabled daughter to distant towns in order that he could beg away from the shame-inducing gaze of his neighbours. As I mulled over Shuli's response, I realised that in many ways this is the reverse of what is expected in Britain, where social protection is formalised by private agencies and the state. Here in Britain, availing oneself of loans, medicine or social security payments from strangers (the state, banks, charitable foundations) is socially acceptable, but asking a distant relative or friend for money usually isn't, for unless they are members of the same household, adults are not supposed to make claims on the economic resources of others.

From this, we can appreciate how moralities of giving are paralleled by moralities of receiving. Yet, in contrast to Mauss's North American potlatches or the reciprocal prestations of Melanesia in which givers and receivers compete for honour and status, in Duniyapur giving is underlain by extreme economic inequality and social hierarchies which don't always reflect economic class, and in which things are given in different ways to different people, according to their membership of networks of relatedness. Thus while gifts create and reaffirm social relationships, they also create and reaffirm social class, for connectedness takes place via hierarchy. Poor relatives are given 'help', in the form of loans, cash and material objects such as saris, whereas the unrelated poor are given the ritualised charity of distributions at Eid or funerals, or a handful of rice or crumpled *taka* bill in the begging bowl. Their claims are far less powerful than those of people who are socially connected enough to be classed as 'our own poor', though it should be noted that this is a highly flexible categorisation and may include local but non-related people as well as kin. Small wonder that what the unconnected poor of Kakura desire from Chevron is secure connectedness in the form of permanent jobs. Yet for these and other ultra-poor people lacking social connections to Chevron, the UK or local leaders, neither their claims to formal entitlements (jobs, compensation, 'rights') nor informal ones ('help', the protection of patrons) meet with much success.

Let us turn to the relationship between relatedness and social support and the ways that 'help' flows across transnational space. Once again, we see the crucial importance of connections to the UK and other foreign countries for those remaining in the *desh*.

MAPPING RELATEDNESS, MAPPING SUPPORT

As a result of their contrasting histories Karimpur and Kakura have different patterns of intra-household relatedness. In Karimpur, the most successful *Londoni* households settled in the village a few generations ago. Coming from Nadampur, these households are generally members of the Saiyed and Pathan *gushtis* and retain strong connections with their relatives across the fields. Within Karimpur there are extreme inequalities between this handful of households who own (or owned) land and have relatives in the UK, and the rest, who largely have no or little land. These wealthier households are a vital source of support, or 'social protection' as development discourse would have it, for the poor and destitute households which surround them. Some of these households are related, but many who receive *shahajo* (help) from wealthy neighbours aren't; indeed, many are Hindus who have been sharecropping the land of their Muslim patrons, borrowing money from them and so on, for many generations. *Shahajo* thus spreads outwards, from a duty towards close or not so close kin, to neighbours with whom long-term relationships of support often exist, an observation we also made in Biswanath (Gardner and Ahmed, 2009.)

For the wealthy, the ability to 'help one's own poor' is a source of pride, as well as a moral imperative. Explaining how his family's religiosity and honour meant that people looked to him as a leader, Samsun Khan told us:

> Look at my big pond, near the main road. In the dry season, when lots of the smaller ponds dry up I'm happy to let anyone come and use it, whether they're Muslims or Hindus. Being a Muslim, I'm happy to see people feeling comfortable using my water. This is my achievement. (Interview notes, 2008)

That his loss of land to the gas field and subsequent dispute with Chevron have led Samsun Khan and his family to relocate almost permanently in Sylhet Town is not only a personal tragedy, but has also impacted upon his poorer neighbours, including the many Hindu families in Karimpur, for whom he was in the role of patron, providing leadership and 'help'.

Alongside these more hierarchical relationships are those that exist between relatives at a similar economic level, from whom small loans of cash can be taken, food borrowed in times of extreme shortage, and general support given.

In Kakura, however, our research showed far fewer connections between households. Rather than being members of several large, localised patrilineages as found in Nadampur and Karimpur, people from Kakura arrived in the area from different parts of Bangladesh without *gushti* connections. Like the inhabitants of Nadampur's colonies, they are *chotomanoosh* and therefore cannot access the generous *shahajo* of *Londoni* relatives, since not only are there very few *Londonis* living in the village, but also no household in Kakura is related by marriage or blood to the UK connected *gushtis* concentrated in Nadampur or Karimpur. As Lefus Miah told us in the last chapter: 'I don't have any close relatives in London. No-one helps us. Poor people help themselves.'

This is not to say that people in Kakura are without patrons or sources of support. Some are the long-term sharecroppers of landowners in Karimpur and Nadampur (or were, until the land was appropriated by the government for the gas field); others have been working for households in those villages for several generations. Such relationships are not, however, set in stone but continually renegotiated. Indeed, on my last visit to Duniyapur I heard of a quarrel that had taken place between the people of Nadampur and Kakura which had resulted, I was told, in people from Kakura being 'banned' from Nadampur. Perhaps this was why no-one from Kakura was present at Shuli's house at Qurbani Eid. Instead the meat was distributed to a new group of 'our own poor': in-migrants living in colonies and shacks on the edges of the village, who effectively provide a new reserve army of labour for the village.

COPING WITH SCARCITY: LOANS, DEBTS AND MORE LOANS

What does *shahajo* involve, and in what way is it so vital for the poor? Fatema and Masud asked people in the study villages to tell them how they coped with periodic crises, as well as their day-to-day strategies for making a living.[7] Like the case studies cited in the last chapter, what our informants' answers reveal is that access to cash is vital for the survival of households; this comes either in the form of *shahajo* or loans, which may or may not involve interest. Social connections are key to both: those who have connections with *Londonis* are able to secure far greater amounts of *shahajo* than those without, although unless the *Londoni* is a very close relative, help is never guaranteed. The cases also indicate how the poor are highly vulnerable to a range of calamities. The flood of 2004 was one such event which, while leaving the large, *pukka* houses of *Londonis* largely unscathed, destroyed the mud and thatch homes of many of the poorest people in the area, especially those living on the most marginal, low-lying land. Illness and accidents – common occurrences for people suffering from long-term malnutrition and working in manual or semi-skilled jobs without insurance or safety regulations (especially truck, bus and rickshaw drivers on the country's treacherous roads) – are another 'everyday' disaster. As we shall see in the next chapter, landless households' inability to pay for medicine without taking loans is a major disincentive for using the Smiling Sun clinic financed by Chevron.

Kudi Khatun, is a widow from Kakura, heading a household of two sons. In response to a question about times of economic crisis, she told us:

In 2000 my younger son was badly injured in an accident and had to be taken to hospital in Sylhet Town. He stayed there for six months and was off work for a further six months. I had to borrow 50,000 *taka* to pay for the expenses. Most of the money was borrowed from neighbours and relatives. In 2004 my sister got married and we had to borrow 10,000 *taka*. A *Londoni* gave us 4,000 *taka* as *shahajo*. These two events ruined us. We ended up owing 30,000 *taka*. We borrowed from neighbours, who lend out money for profit, though I wouldn't call them professional money lenders. The people who lend have a bit of surplus cash, perhaps from abroad.

Lila Begum is another widow living in Kakura, again with adult sons. In the last chapter she described how her household was forced to borrow food from neighbours if her son failed to find work as a day-labourer. Unlike Kudi Khatun, Lila has no connections with *Londonis*:

Three years ago there was a flood. Our house was ruined, so we built a temporary shelter on the road, where we stayed for three months.[8] As this house was right on the road we had to move again, to a spot lower down. It was so hard living in a temporary shelter like that. In the end we built a permanent house on our own land, at a cost of 60,000 *taka*. Half of this was given by neighbours and relatives as *shahajo*; the remaining 30,000 was a loan. We try to pay it back whenever we can.

Shanifa and her family live in a mud and thatch house in Kakura, which often leaks in the rainy season. Two years ago the house was damaged during a bad storm and had to be rebuilt. As she told us:

It's hard to find anyone more destitute than us in the whole of Bangladesh. My husband is sick – continual fever and starvation makes him worse, so he loses weight and becomes even more ill. Eventually he'll die. He's living on medicine, but I can't afford to pay for it all the time. I need 4 kg of rice a day to feed everyone in the household. Our bellies aren't interested in whether or not we've got the money, we have to eat whatever the situation. It's not just rice. It's also dhal and vegetables. How I manage I really don't know. It's Allah who manages.

Shanifa has been a member of Grameen Bank for ten years. In 2004, after the devastating floods that destroyed crops as well as homes, many people in Kakura were close to starvation. Since Shanifa's house was wrecked she had to borrow money from the Grameen Bank to rebuild it; but has found the loan difficult to repay under the strictures set down by Grameen. Indeed, many people told us that they did not like borrowing from NGOs due to the conditions attached: a fixed amount normally has to be repaid every month and the money used for 'income generation' rather than everyday necessities, whereas loans from relatives, neighbours or money lenders do not have these restrictions. Some gave us the impression that they shopped around for different types of loan, depending on what was needed, the extent of their social connections, and how the loan was to be used, an example of how NGOs can widen the array of choices that people have.[9]

Despite their wariness of formal micro-credit schemes, our data shows that many people regularly borrow from NGOs to cover their everyday costs or to tide them over in times of crisis. In contrast to their better-connected neighbours, such as Joyoti and Renuma, who are part of one of the most powerful *gushtis* (lineages) in Nadampur, the ultra-poor such as Shanifa in Kakura, who lack the social connections necessary for informal 'help' are forced to resort to formal loans from NGOs, despite the restrictions involved. Indeed, membership of NGOs was presented by many of our informants as appropriate for low-status *chotomanoosh*, not people with *gushti* connections.[10]

Many people borrow from a range of sources and often have to go to second and third parties in order to repay the original loan. A Hindu householder from Karimpur told us:

> Last year my wife became ill and I had to borrow 35,000 *taka* for medicine. Most of the time I borrow money from Mohammed Khan, a *Londoni* [who lives in Karimpur]. But I also had to borrow from neighbours. The interest rate is 10 percent. I still owe 14,000 *taka*. When I can't repay a loan I have to borrow from someone else to pay it back. I borrowed 14,000 *taka* from Grameen Bank and with the interest added on, it's reached 20,000 *taka*. I'm now hiding from them, to avoid them …

The following comment, from a shopkeeper in Karimpur, shows how the circulation of loans, in goods or money, is continual, relying upon trust and notions of relatedness:

Most of my customers don't want to pay cash. They're *Londonis* [i.e. related to people living in the UK and partially or wholly dependent upon remittances]. Once their money comes in, they pay me back. [Because of the price hike] everyone has reduced their shopping [so] ... I can't make a profit. But despite this, I run my business. All my customers are relatives. One day they'll pay me back.

The next three informants are in households with varying degrees of connectedness to overseas migrants, both in the UK, and the Middle East. It is significant that the poorest, Fazul Khan, has the most tenuous connection and is unable to make significant claims on the largesse of his sponsor, but must rely on *Zakah*, and the most comfortable, Hazrul Miah relies on a secure and close connection: his brother, who works in Saudi Arabia. Fazul Khan, a day-labourer in Kakura, told us he received 3,000 *taka* at Eid, from an 'aunt', who is a distant rather than a close relative:

My *Londoni* relatives don't help me all the time. During Eid they send a little money and at times of dire need they help. They're not close relatives. They provide money as part of *zakat*, not like a regular remittance.

Abdullah Uddin, from Karimpur, who owns a small amount of land and sharecrops a bit more, has a better connection: *Londoni* relatives who can be called upon in times of need:

I have three nephews in London. My wife's relatives also live there. They don't help me regularly, but when we're in need they help out. For example, when my daughter got married they contributed 50,000 *taka*. The rest of the expenses were covered by us.

In contrast, Hazrul Miah, from Kakura lives in a joint household with four brothers, one of whom is in Saudi Arabia; he sharecrops his brother's land and has 2.5 *kiare* of his own land:

My younger brother lives in Saudi Arabia. He helps me a lot. Whenever I need money I ask him for it and he sends it. He gives me 60,000 *taka* annually. My cousin lives in London, but doesn't help me. My brother-in-law works in Saudi Arabia. He sends money to my sister and clothes and other gifts to us. We were badly affected by the flood in 2004. I wrote to my brother who sent some money. As he's my younger brother I can't ask him for more. Whatever he feels comfortable in giving, I take. When in 2006 my wife had an operation, her aunt in London helped us, too.

TRANSNATIONAL CONNECTIONS: 'HELP', PLACE AND MIGRATION

The stretching of duty across geographical space is an important way in which transnational communities are bound together. In Duniyapur if one has the right connections this can lead to securing financial and material aid. For the lucky and best connected, it may also lead to securing foreign sources of capital and security via migration. As we have already seen, for British Bangladeshis the degree of duty that they have towards those in the *desh* is directly related to the closeness of the kinship connection. Members of the same household are not necessarily guaranteed a regular flow of money, however: Shuli's brothers in Burnley send money to their mother and siblings when they can, but the demands of young families and setting up their restaurant business in the uncertain economic climate of 2008–9 meant that often little or nothing was sent. Our research in Biswanath showed a similar trend: regular remittances from the UK were falling off; with wives and children based in the UK, the pattern was increasingly for irregular 'one-offs', in times of particular need or to help in starting up a new business. Of the stall-holders and shopkeepers we spoke to in Biswanath Town in 2005, for example, ten out of sixteen told us that they had been given start-up funds by *Londoni* relatives (Gardner and Ahmed, 2009: 24). For others, once nuclear families were reunited in the UK, remittances to Bangladesh based relatives had completely stopped (2009: 24).

On their visits to the *desh*, *Londonis* are expected to be bountiful with their gifts and *shahajo*. A Newcastle auntie always arrives with a suitcase filled with saris; some are expensive garments from the UK or Dubai, for close relatives. Others are cheaper or second-hand, for the poor. In the UK, I was told by Shuli's brother how these days he couldn't afford to visit the *desh* because he was expected to distribute so much largesse; he estimated that he had spent £50,000 in the last ten years during visits home. Such generosity is not exceptional; if anything it is greater in areas such as Biswanath where there is more wealth. Here, we heard of UK-based relatives building houses for close kin, paying for their children's education and funding migration overseas. This, plus the hand-outs of oil companies anxious to secure the goodwill of local communities (of which, more later) mean that it is hardly surprising that my visits to Nadampur should bring poor women out in their droves, in the hope of receiving a 100 or 500 *taka* note or worn sari.

While for the ultra-poor connectedness to *Londonis* or other overseas migrants can bring material support, for the less poor connections to *bideshis* also bring the possibility of that most desired of outcomes: the migration of a household member overseas, preferably to the UK. There are two ways in which social connections can bring this about. The first is that wealthy patrons can lend or give the financial capital necessary for securing papers and plane tickets to overseas destinations. The second is that, in the case of *Londonis*, connectedness can lead directly to routes into the UK, usually via marriage, plus jobs and accommodation once there. Here, then, social connections lead to embodied connections (being there!) with prized foreign places, which in turn bring access to economic capital, and, in the case of the UK, the social protection provided by the state in the form of pensions, unemployment benefit, schools and a free health service (Gardner, 2008).

How does this work in practice? While migration to the Middle East can sometimes be arranged with strangers (i.e. agents: *dalal*) this leads to great risk for would-be migrants.[11] In contrast, migration to the UK is only possible via social networks. As the examples show, global economic inequality, which leads to a hierarchical ordering of migrant destinations, each accruing different levels of possible risk and reward, is negotiated via social relationships, themselves hierarchically ordered.[12]

The preference given to particular destinations is continually changing and depends to a large degree on global economic conditions. Although in the late 1980s in Nadampur many young men were migrating to the Middle East for temporary employment, by 2009 the global slump, which had affected destinations such as Dubai particularly badly, meant that the Middle East was no longer seen as a particularly desirable destination. Another reason is that the wages to be earned there are not high enough to enable one to invest in property or businesses at home, given the levels of local *Londoni*-influenced inflation. In addition, the Middle East is often perceived as a risky destination in which would-be migrants are cheated by agents, or go as insecure 'illegals'. Migrants to the Middle East are thus from the more vulnerable lower-income households who lack the social links to get to the UK yet are prepared take the gamble of investing savings or credit on temporary labour migration. This is usually organised by an unrelated agent, who may or may not be trustworthy. Out of the six 'Dubai' households in our research in Biswanath, for example, three had made minor gains from their migration and owned small amounts of land, the rest had failed to make any money and were landless.

Mr Rahman's case is typical. Today he lives on *khas* (government) land, the house and fields that he once owned having been sold to finance his son's migration to Libya in the early 1980s. The hope was that the son's remittances would enable them to buy more land. He was unable to earn sufficiently high wages to do anything but pay for his family's basic subsistence, however. When he became ill and was unable to work the remittances dried up altogether.

Toshna Mia is another villager who was unable to profit from his migration. Like another three men in the village, he was the victim of fraud. Unfortunately his experience is common. After working in a small garment business in his twenties, he saved enough money to migrate to Saudi Arabia, where he stayed for six years, earning around 20,000 *taka* a month, most of which was quickly consumed on subsistence needs by his family back home. After meeting an agent in Saudi Arabia who promised that he could arrange for him to go to Germany, Toshna Mia paid 2 *lakh taka* (200,000) and gave the agent his passport. As often happens, however, the man cheated him, stealing both the money and the passport. Caught without a passport by the Saudi police, Mr Mia was duly deported. Back in Bangladesh, and without the foreign earnings on which his family now depended, Mr Mia soon found himself in debt so decided to go to Singapore. Travelling on a tourist visa, he was unable to find work and was quickly caught by the police and deported. Today he has returned to his garment business in the village, and is slowly paying off his debts.

As these cases indicate, migration to the Gulf or to South East Asia is a risky enterprise. The work is usually arduous and unpleasant, and may not reap earnings high enough to make the original outlay of capital worthwhile. Even if a migrant goes to such destinations legally, he remains vulnerable to fraudsters, exploitative working conditions and the possibility that he simply won't be able to earn enough to make it all worthwhile. This is especially the case in the context of the rampant escalation of property prices in *Londoni* villages.

In contrast, Britain is seen as a secure and profitable destination. Rather than attempting to enter the UK through a high-risk strategy of illegal migration, arranged by a non-related stranger, villagers gain access to Britain through people who are related to them. This involves either being 'brought' to the UK as a close family member or marrying someone with British citizenship. Relationships with successful *Londonis*, plus one's eligibility as a potential spouse, are therefore all-important. Once in Britain one's security is far greater than in the Middle East, for there is an existing network of Bangladeshi businesses to work in, often run by people to whom one is related. There is also the social protection provided by the British state: health care, education for one's children, benefits for the unemployed and pensions for the retired. Even if by British standards a household is living below or on the poverty line,[13] from the perspective of Bangladesh – where extreme insecurity and desperate poverty mean that those without assets may struggle to satisfy their day-to-day calorific needs – it is seen (by those still in the *desh*) as enjoying plenty.

Crucially, entry to the UK today is generally only possible via the social connections required for the arrangement of a marriage with a British bride or groom.[14] In many, but not all cases these are with cousins. The case of one family in Karimpur is instructive. Of five brothers, four are now legally settled in the UK. The oldest went as the dependent of his uncle in the 1970s. The next, Ahmed, was married to his patrilineal cousin in the late 1990s, and their younger brother to another patrilineal cousin in 2007. The middle brother, who remains in Bangladesh, has been looking for a British bride, but by 2008 had had so little luck (due to his short stature and dark skin colour, according to his somewhat unsentimental sister) that the family had decided to find him a Bangladeshi bride. Meanwhile two sisters from the same family have been married to Middle Eastern migrants, and in the *bari* next door, the daughter of their older sister, who is married to another patrilineal cousin, has been married and settled in the UK for several years, this time to an unrelated and highly educated man from Dhaka.

New social relationships therefore draw on existing connections, in order not only to further bind families and people together through marriage, but also to establish firm links between places (see also Charlsey, 2005; Shaw and Charsley, 2006). Yet while the marriage may be desirable for both parties, those in Bangladesh often have more to gain than those in the UK. Transactions – going from both grooms and brides to their new in-laws at marriages – are often very capital intensive. Ahmed's family told me that they had spent a vast amount of money on gold for his new wife, despite the fact that she was his close patrilineal cousin and had been born on the same *bari*. Here, then, inequality between places has either created or shifted inequalities between marital partners; the normal onus on the bride's family to pay dowry has given way to transactions based on the inequality between places (Huda, 2006).

The desire for transnational marital connections to be made by Bangladeshi-based relatives can also lead to strains and fissures in family relationships. The arrangement of such marriages can therefore be a risky business. The marriage might well end in disaster; there are many stories in circulation in Nadampur of *Londoni* girls refusing their grooms or mistreatment of Bangladeshi brides once in the UK. Things can also go wrong before the marriage is contracted: prospective marriage partners rejected, overtures from one party met with perceived snubs, umbrage taken. Mr Ali, a Biswanath businessman, described how his household had fallen out with his British-based uncle and aunt over the arrangement of a marriage between his brother and his British cousin. While he and his brothers were keen for the marriage to take place, both the aunt and her daughter resisted the alliance, arguing that a Sylheti groom would not be suitable for a British-born girl. Allegations of the misappropriation of money quickly followed and today the British-based wing of the family no longer sends any form of support.

As this example shows, attempting to make social connections can bring rewards, but there are also risks involved. Crucially too, some people desire and need connection more than others. What strategies do they use to make their claims? As we see below, it very much depends on who they are.

STRATEGIES AND CLAIMS OF CONNECTION

In the last chapter I briefly discussed Amartya Sen's (1982) perspectives on famine, which he argues result from *entitlement systems* that give some access to food while excluding others. Building on the notion of entitlement, I suggested that in Duniyapur one might discern two systems of entitlement, one based around formal claims and inclusion in the benefits of global capitalism via a functioning state, employment, social welfare and so on, and one based around informal social connections, which entitle those with sufficient connectedness to a share of resources in the name of charity, 'looking after one's own' and patronage. In reality these 'systems' are not completely distinct; people's allegiance to them shifts according to context. A *Londoni* might denounce patronage and nepotism in the Bangladeshi government, for example, while feeling duty bound to help a distant cousin find work in his restaurant.[15] Yet despite this ambivalence and the blurriness of reality, each 'system' is underlain by distinct moralities and practices. In this chapter we have heard something of the moralities of the informal system of patronage. As we have seen, the *extent* to which entitlements can be claimed depends upon degrees of relatedness, whether this is in terms of actual kinship or geographical proximity (Gardner and Ahmed, 2009). Crucially the *ways* in which such entitlements are claimed are informed by the moralities of which they are a part.

In the case of Mr Ali in Biswanath it was the moralities of kinship, duty and obligation that were appealed to in his attempts to arrange the marriage of his brother. Here, his household's claims of entitlement to marriage with their UK cousins were made on the basis of relatedness rather than charity. The risks of such negotiations are manifold, for if not done with tact, a claim might be experienced as a 'demand', the result being strained or even ruptured relations. I was reminded of this one morning while visiting a family in Nadampur whose son had married a British cousin. The bride's mother was visiting from Manchester, and a huge row was unfolding. The women of the house, the groom's sister and mother, were berating their son's mother-in-law (and aunt) for her daughter's behaviour on her last visit to the *desh*. Why had she brought such insubstantial presents? And why had she only stayed a day, when, as a cousin, not to say a daughter-in-law, she should have stayed for weeks? Did she not love and honour them? The shift of power, away from Bangladeshi husbands and towards British young women, and what this might tell us of the relationship between gender and place is worthy of a chapter in itself. Here, however, the pertinent point is the way that my friends were framing their dissatisfactions on the basis of the duties of close kin, in a context where they clearly needed and desired the connection far more than their *Londoni* daughter-in-law/cousin.

In the second example, the claimant's entitlement to resources controlled by others is even more tenuous. Here, the claim is made on the basis of charity, and framed almost as a lamentation, though not usually so melodic or ritualised as those described by James Wilce (2003). The scene I'm about to describe has been played out in numerous versions over the twenty years that I've been visiting Nadampur. It's often women's business, the tales of tragedy and the sympathetic (or not so sympathetic) comments they evoke. These tales may have a particularly Islamic flavour. As others have noted, in many Muslim societies suffering and devotion are closely aligned; women's narratives are therefore often framed in terms of the pain and torment they have experienced (Gardner, 2002a; Grima, 1991). My concern with the performative aspects of tales of loss and suffering is not meant to negate the objective experiences that the tales describe, or indeed the emotions of grief and distress which they express, though, as Wilce (2003: 40) points out, emotions are themselves ideologically and culturally constructed and contingent on history. Rather, my purpose is to reflect further on the ways in which people in particular structures of entitlement use a variety of strategies to make claims on others.

The women are sitting in the cooking area at the back of the house: essentially a bamboo lean-to with a tin roof, where Shuli, Amma and whoever is currently employed by them as a *kamla beti* (servant girl) spend long hours cutting vegetables and scaling fish, or stirring giant *degs* of rice and *torkari* (curry) over the *chula* flames.[16] As is often the case, the group is not confined to Shuli's immediate family: the empty rooms at the back of the *bari* have been inhabited for a while by a distant and impoverished cousin, his wife and children, who largely spend their days helping out in Shuli's house, while neighbours, sisters and aunties constantly drop by.

Today everyone's attention is focused upon a middle-aged woman in a frayed and dusty sari. She is seated on the low stool by the door which is reserved for children, household members and servants, rather than the high bed in the communal living area, where close relatives and neighbours of equal status are invited to gossip and share *paan*. The woman is from Kakura, I'm told: Hasna Bibi, mother of Abdullah. As she recounts her story in a low monotone, that from time to time tips into lament, her audience gaze at her sorrowfully, only occasionally interjecting an exclamation of 'Ya Allah' or 'How much sorrow there is in the world!'

What is clear, even to my imperfect Sylheti, is that disaster has struck Hasna Bibi. Last week both her adult sons were killed in a bus accident on the road to Sylhet. Her grief is unimaginable, but her current plight is even more pressing. As a landless widow, her sons were her only sources of income. Without them, or close relatives who can help her, she is in danger of starvation. Her narrative, made to unconnected women in the next door village, is thus her only resource: just as beggars parade their cauterised stumps or blinded eyes, severely traumatised, bereaved or abused women who have no status left to lose wander from *bari* to *bari* in search of sympathy and alms.

To interpret such narratives *solely* in terms of claims over resources would be a gross simplification. Stories are inherently social acts, drawing people together and making sense of life communally. As Michael Jackson writes:

> Stories make it possible for us to overcome our separateness, to find common ground and common cause. To relate a story is to retrace one's steps, going over the ground of one's life again, reworking reality to render it more bearable. A story enables us to fuse the world within and the world without. In this way we gain some purchase over events that confounded us, humbled us and left us helpless. In telling a story we renew our faith that the world is within our grasp. (M. Jackson, 2002: 245; cited in F. Ross, 2003: 332)

As anthropologists have described, in contexts of structural and physical violence, stories can be important ways for personhood to be reconstituted, and experiences shared with others. In situations of extreme pain, whether emotional or physical, words and speech are often erased; pain destroys language and one is rendered 'speechless' (Scarry, 1985).[17] As Samsun Khan put it: 'The day they took my fields I lost my words' (Fieldnotes, 2008). The finding of words is thus a vital part of healing, as recognised institutionally by the hearing of testimonies in Truth and Reconciliation Commissions (see F. Ross, 2003).

Here, though, in understanding the role of story telling and lamentation for the dispossessed in Bangladesh, it is worth remembering that the social or emotional connections made through the sharing of pain usually lead to some form of material support. After her story was told Hasna Bibi was given some food and a small bundle of *chaal* (husked rice) by Amma and sent on her way. Clearly, her entitlement over household resources was very slight, for she was only connected to her audience through the threads of human empathy and the Islamic injunction to charity. In other cases, the claims by the very poor are made more assertively: Renuma's lamentation was met with substantial material support by Shuli and her mother; she is, after all, a cousin.

Sometimes though, there may be discord in the ways that the claims are interpreted. While the claimant may have a strong moral sense that he or she has an entitlement, the person to whom the claim is made may reject it out of hand as an unreasonable 'demand'. As we saw in the instances of the relatives of *Londonis* asserting their connections rather too strongly, making claims can be a risky business, leading to a rupture of social connectedness rather than its fruition into material or social rewards.

The way in which the people of Kakura are constructed by their neighbours in Nadampur illustrates this point. After four years of visitations by oil company officials and consultants, often accompanied by the 'gifts' of logo-embellished t-shirts, sweets for children and promises to improve conditions in the village, Kakura's inhabitants are now increasingly angry at the lack of material help they say they have received from the outsiders. Indeed, I was advised not to visit because of the unreasonable demands that my friends said would be made on me. The vociferous claims of the village's inhabitants are given all the more emotive force by the strong sense that the permanent jobs and connectedness to Chevron they believe to be their right never materialised. In this context it is worth remembering that, despite the wealth with which they are increasingly surrounded, in 2008 many people were going hungry. Not only does the village have no school, it is not even connected to the electric lines that run from Karimpur to Nadampur. Yet when claims to entitlements are made, the result is that they are deemed (like children) to be 'very demanding'.

As this implies, the making of claims can be a risky business, for as a strategy of denial, those with control over resources are apt to label the claimant troublesome or even dangerous. In Wilce's (2003) brilliant description of the poetics and politics of lamentation he shows how women's complaints may lead them to being labelled 'mad' (*paghol*), a condition remedied by their being chained up or beaten to exorcise the evil spirits that have caused the errant behaviour. Perhaps the stridency of Kakura's claims and complaints is why I was told that the village had become increasingly criminalised. This was explained to me in Nadampur as the result of the population's previous employment by Chevron, which, it was implied, had made them overly needy for cash. It was no longer safe to walk around the area unaccompanied I was told; one should lock one's doors. By the end of our fieldwork in 2009, Shuli told me that the village had cut off its connection with Kakura, preferring to employ its new group of 'own poor', who charged less for a day's work and did not make such unpleasant demands.

No-one illustrates this better than San Mahmud, who we met at the beginning of Chapter 3. Lingering by the gas field's security fences, San Mahmud mutters and grumbles over his treatment by Chevron. They promised work, he says, but now refuse to help him.

Taking everything, they gave nothing back; the local leaders sold them down the river; while the rich line their pockets, the poor go hungry. No-one listens to him: not the security guards who stand watch by the gates, the workers who pass on their bicycles or in their jeeps, or the village men who stop by the *chai* stalls for a leaf of *paan* and a chat with their friends. He's a lunatic, they say, a well-known Kakura thief, whose incoherent ramblings should not detain anyone for a single moment longer.

*   *   *

While the rural poor struggle to assert their entitlements to food and other basic needs using the language of social connection, kinship and charity, and uttered as lamentations, pleas or angry denouncements, billion-dollar multinationals seek entitlement to something else: natural resources. How are their claims made? Financial and technological prowess clearly dominates in the gaining of contracts with national governments. In the next chapter I turn to the ways in which Chevron makes moral claims over its entitlement to extract and profit from Duniyapur's natural gas. As we shall see, the discursive practices and underlying moralities of these claims are very different from those of the people of Kakura. Using the globally fashionable development-speak of 'partnership' and 'empowerment', Chevron claims that its presence is ethically irreproachable and that it is fully entitled to do its work. Moreover, poverty and politics become submerged in the techniques of development. Let us consider Chevron's programme of 'community engagement'.

5
Claims of Partnership and Ethical Connection: Chevron's Programme of 'Community Engagement'

It's spring 2008. I'm distracting myself from essay marking by Googling 'Chevron'. I've already printed out various financial reports concerning the company's incursion into Bangladesh, plus a corporate press release on the opening of the Bibiyana Gas Field. Now I click on a link to the company's 2007 *Corporate Responsibility Report*.[1] The cover is illustrated by a familiar Bangladeshi scene: a fisherman, his back to the camera, casts a net from his boat, which has come to rest in a thicket of water lilies. The only discordant note, unsettling the romantic imagery of the traditional wooden boat, the barefoot fisherman and lily strewn waterway, is an industrial fence that dissects the horizon to the left of the picture. I recognise it instantly as the fence which surrounds the gas field. It's the next click, though, which causes me to gasp with surprise, for there, on page 2 of the vast oil conglomerate's annual CSR report is a young man whom I will call Khaled, who I have known since he was a child. Khaled, according to the blurb: 'is one of several villagers who run family-owned fishing businesses near the Bibiyana Gas Field. He participated in the Livelihood Program, a partnership between Chevron and Friends in Village Development Bangladesh, that supports local micro-businesses.'

It's an appealing image, zooming from the ether onto my screen: Khaled's smiling face in the foreground, while in the pond behind a ring of fisher-folk stand waist deep in water, their hands grasping a net filled with dancing fish. My own photos of Khaled and his family, taken since he was a child in the late 1980s, were never so artful. Rather, they were either formal portraits, in which after changing into their best saris or *lunghis* my subjects would stare unsmilingly at the camera, or hurried, amateur snaps of everyday work and life, which I promised I would keep to myself, for only *chotomanoosh* with no status to imperil and precious little *sharom* (shame) would allow themselves to be seen working in the fields, fishing or washing pans in their worn everyday clothes.[2]

Like all pictures, that found on page 2 of the 2007 CSR report tells a myriad of stories. The most obvious, perhaps, concerns *scale* (Tsing, 2005: 58), the telescoping from what appears to be the vast, global operations of transnational corporations, whose names receive millions of hits on internet search engines (google 'Chevron' and you will receive over 8 million results), to a real person, living in a small village in Sylhet, whose circumstances have, through an odd coincidence, become the subject of both the writings of a British anthropologist (read by several thousand?) and the marketing brochures of a multinational oil company (read by millions?). To this extent, Khaled's appearance on my computer screen merely confirms what I have been describing since my doctoral fieldwork in the 1980s: not so much the way that the 'global' impacts on the 'local', but how neither can be separated from the other, for, in this instance, the 'local' is globalised via the PR machinery of the corporation and the worldwide web, while the 'global' has appeared in Nadampur in the guise of not only the gas field, but also the professional photographers whose job it is to produce glossy representations of contented recipients of development assistance (or CSR) for global consumers. Even this is too simplistic: as we saw in Chapter 2, the villages in Duniyapur have always been 'global', with long-standing migratory links to the UK, the Middle East and South East Asia, and deeply rooted historical connections to the global economy.

These interactions between global and local scales, or 'the grips of worldly encounters' that Tsing (2005) calls 'friction' underscore every chapter in this book. Here, I wish to focus on one element of the encounter, whereby via a range of development-oriented programmes and 'community engagements', a specific type of interconnection and exchange has been taking place within and beyond Duniyapur with resonances, meanings and effects at all scales. This leads to particular stories which are told in particular ways: Khaled's happy face is one image among many others which form part of a corporate narrative of successful community engagement, ethical business practice and 'partnership'. As I suggested at the end of the last chapter, these stories are an important aspect of Chevron's claims over Duniyapur's natural resources: they have the moral right to extract gas, it is implied, since they are 'partners' with the community.

Yet while Chevron officials work hard to control the story, carefully ordering particular forms of knowledge and directing specific performances as evidence of success, there are other discordant narratives in circulation, drawing upon different types and ways of knowing, which undermine the company's claims. What emerges is a struggle between different actors over what success involves, what knowledge one needs to judge it, and, crucially, how it is represented. Let us return to Khaled, whose picture in the 2007 CSR report illustrates the following blurb:

> in the lowlands surrounding our natural gas project in Bibiyana, Bangladesh, we work closely with community members, local leaders and non-governmental organisations to create programs that support family businesses, improve health care services and schools and create jobs for residents. (Chevron, 2007: 2)

While not factually incorrect, this statement is far from undisputed. Or, put another way, it is merely one representation among others. Indeed, while Khaled's picture is a photographic representation of his features, taken one sunny morning in early winter beside a pond filled with fish that Chevron had helped fund via its Alternative Livelihoods Programme, the image both reflects and distorts the truth, focusing on some elements of the scene while blocking out others: the play of light on water, the dancing fish and grinning 'community member' turned artfully into something not quite real. Not surprisingly, the story behind the photograph is more complex and messy than page 2 of the *CSR Report* would have us believe. Yes, Khaled said with a grimace when I next met him, he *had* seen his picture in the Chevron report. The whole affair was a bit embarrassing; he'd been out in the fields overseeing the work of the Patnis in his pond (Hindu fisherman, some of whom live in Nadampur) when a group of Chevron people had approached from the road. One had a camera, and started to take his photo, giving him no time to change into clean, smart clothes. Did they not ask his permission? The question made Khaled laugh. Why would big Chevron people need *his* permission? They can do what they like, can't they?

Like many people in Duniyapur, Khaled's attitude to the programmes financed by Chevron is ambivalent. During our research we met people who said they had benefited from them, and others who said they hadn't. In what follows I am less interested in the verifiable truth of the claims made in the *CSR Report*, and more in the way that each group makes their claims and the different moral orders involved. My focus is therefore not so much upon whether or not the programmes funded by Chevron as part of their community engagement programme 'work' or are 'a good thing', but more upon how claims to programme success and community partnership are made.

In this endeavour I owe much to David Mosse, who has written perceptively of the 'social relations of success' in aid projects, showing how, rather than being an objectively verified state, a project's success is socially produced, the result of carefully managed representations of reality, using particular formats and forms of knowledge (Mosse, 2005). In his description of the visits of VIPs and other prominent public figures to the Indo-British Rain-Fed Farming Project in the mid 1990s, for example, Mosse describes how, in a similar way to Khaled's image in Chevron's 2007 *CSR Report*: 'everyday life gives way to project, time, space and aesthetics. The village is organised to resemble the project text so as to be pleasingly read by outsiders' (Mosse, 2005: 165).

If the story of Khaled's appearance on page 2 of the *CSR Report* raises questions concerning the representation of successful community engagement, it also returns our attention to unequal power relations between individuals, groups and places. In the last chapter we saw how 'giving' and 'receiving' are important social acts in Duniyapur, providing safety nets for the vulnerable, producing social identities and recreating/altering social hierarchies. While giving and receiving are deeply implicated in local and transnational inequality and difference, they also create and recreate the connectedness that most people need and desire. Rather than being 'free' or a 'pure' gift, charity or 'helping' in Duniyapur are woven into a thick and often protective cloth of relationships, expectations and moralities.

What happens when the expectations of those who 'give' arise from a different moral order from those who 'receive'? Or when, rather than aiming at connection, the 'givers', or 'donors' as they become when the scale zooms outwards to incorporate a transnational aid agency or oil company, want not *connection* as evidence of their effectiveness, but *disconnection* or, in development-speak: 'sustainability'? In what follows I suggest that Chevron's relationship with Duniyapur involves forms of connection that are quite different from those we heard about in the last chapter.

The company is of course tangibly connected to Duniyapur, via the physical presence of the gas field and its connection to the gas supply, as well as its roads and signage. The company also makes claims for a formalised connection with the local villages, which is described as 'partnership' in its PR literature, and is largely mediated by the NGOs it has contracted to carry out its programmes. Chevron is not however, socially connected to the area as a patron, or indeed, an employer of local people. Indeed, by adhering to the international discourses of 'sustainability' and 'helping the poor to help themselves' via individual entrepreneurship, access to micro-credit and so on, its programmes aim ultimately at *disconnection*, for within development discourse the ultimate aim and proof of project success is the donor's ability to disconnect, withdrawing funding while the projects that have been initiated replicate themselves: such is the essence of 'sustainability'.

To explore this in more detail, let us turn to recent work within the anthropology of development on the 'development gift.'

EXTRACTIVE INDUSTRIES, CSR AND THE DEVELOPMENT GIFT

In their seminal article 'The Development Gift', Stirrat and Henkel (1997) argue that, despite international development orthodoxies of 'partnership', with their implications of equality and sameness, what development gifts actually do is mark difference and hierarchy. This argument is brilliantly developed by Dinah Rajak, who has used theories of the gift to analyse not the development gifts of donors, but CSR programmes carried out by the Anglo-American mining company in South Africa. Rather than business and markets being amoral, as suggested by Mauss, Rajak argues, CSR brings morality into business practice, allowing mining companies to extend moral authority over the places where extraction takes place via moral discourses that stress partnership, responsibility and so on. Not only do global codes of ethics act as a form of governmentality (Dolan, 2007), they also naturalise neoliberal tenets of entrepreneurship and the role of the market while eliding questions of power and ecology. Rather than being a 'moral bolt on' to offset the harsh realities of neoliberal capitalism, CSR is therefore intrinsic to its workings. Yet while CSR discourses of 'partnership', 'empowerment' and 'participation' allow the company to avoid charges of patronage, on the ground, the politics of the gift remains, sometimes forging alliances and reducing conflict with the people surrounding the mine, but always with the power relations of giver and receiver intact (Rajak, 2011).

The similarities between Rajak's South African case and Duniyapur are noteworthy. Yet there are also important differences for in Duniyapur Chevron has very little vested in forging long-term relations of patronage with its 'communities'. It does not employ many local people, and besides a handful of 'local leaders' does not have a relationship with the majority of the population. Indeed, it has contracted various NGOs to be its intermediaries with programme beneficiaries; it is NGO fieldworkers, not Chevron officials, who visit the villages, while Chevron's community liaison staff are rarely seen outside the high-fenced confines of the plant. Moreover, despite their rhetorics of long-term commitment, they – like other multinationals – will withdraw from Bangladesh if conditions get too difficult: if the government becomes impossible to work with, for example, or the risk to reputation caused by national activism against its presence too great. While espousing moralities of 'partnership', its policies thus demonstrate what Jamie Cross (2011) has termed 'detachment as corporate ethic'. On a practical level there is very little to motivate the company to establish lasting connections with the local poor. Indeed, on a moral level to have personalised relationships would turn it into a local patron, which would blow the moral virtue it has accumulated.

To further complicate matters, the exigency of the pure gift, with its promise of moral salvation, is not the only motivating factor behind programmes of community engagement, for the gift of community engagement involves contradictory objectives. While one is to donate a 'pure' gift, another involves the expectation that the gift be reciprocated in the form of public displays of gratitude which enhance the company's international reputation. As the Director of External Affairs told me, the main aim of community engagement is 'reputation'. The *raison d'être* of the gift is therefore multifaceted: to gain the compliance of communities *and* to create corporate merit via a narrative of ethically upstanding corporate standards. Community engagement thus attempts the tough gymnastic act of successful manoeuvres on both the local and the global scale, or, put another way, of being both a pure gift creating spiritual virtue and a reciprocated gift creating social relationships, not of long-term patronage but rather short-term links with local leaders who allow the company to operate in the area. Part of this contract involves an expectation by Chevron that through its programmes a certain sort of 'community' will emerge, in which exploitation, desperate poverty and injustice are swept from view via schemes such as micro-finance, village development committees, training schemes and so on. These schemes aim to create, via 'the community', a local population of self-reliant entrepreneurs, an ideological project that lies at the heart of neoliberalism (Li, 2007; Ong, 2006). Let us turn to the programmes.

CREATING CORPORATE MERIT: THE INVENTION OF PARTNERSHIP AND COMMUNITY

As we have seen in Duniyapur, while gifts/charity/*shahajo* (help) mark difference, so too do they mark relatedness and links in social networks; within the local moral economy rather than being denied or hidden under the rhetoric of 'partnership', hierarchy and dependency are to be expected. The global donor, however, wishing to chime with Northern discourses of equality, participation and democracy, with the inevitable stress on partnership,[3] eschews any suggestion of patronage or dependency in its literature. In its statement of 'The Chevron Way',[4] for example, Chevron explain its: 'Vision ... To be the global energy company most admired for its people, partnership and performance.'
Specifically:

Partnership
We have an unwavering commitment to being a good partner focused on building productive, collaborative, trusting and beneficial relationships with governments, other companies, our customers, our communities and each other.

The rhetoric is remarkably similar, though perhaps not as punchy as that of Oxfam:

Oxfam is a vibrant global movement of dedicated people fighting poverty. Together. Doing amazing work. Together.[5]

There is of course an important difference. While Oxfam is an NGO (or a 'vibrant global movement') registered as a charity in the UK, Chevron is a transnational energy company, whose remit is not to fight poverty, but to mine oil and gas, or in their words, to 'provide energy products vital to sustainable economic progress and human development throughout the world'.[6]
When and why did transnational energy companies start using the language of NGOs and donor organisations, with their tropes of sustainability, progress and 'human development'? Moreover, why

is Chevron seemingly offering development gifts to the communities surrounding the location of its 'real' work, the extraction of natural gas? Is this simply an exercise in public relations, a co-option of language and representations which satisfy contemporary global moralities concerning codes of conduct for extractive companies in the neoliberal twenty-first century? Indeed, is the analogy of the 'development gift' even appropriate? Rather than starting life with the aesthetic ambitions of the 'pure' gift, in which at the outset there is no discernible relationship between giver and the receiver (cf. Parry, 1986; Stirrat and Henkel, 1997), the gift of the oil company, let us call it the 'community engagement gift', starts life with relationships between givers and receivers already in existence, albeit with some 'work' to be done on making them rather more cordial.

Yet while a narrative of success aimed at global consumers is relatively easy to manage, the tale gets increasingly tricky to tell to the residents of Duniyapur, whether they are located in Bangladesh or the UK, not only because they are better placed to spot the gaps and silences in the narrative, but also because most of them do not accept Chevron's claim over Duniyapur's natural resources. Anti-multinational activism informs both types of manoeuvre: placating local criticism and bad feeling is crucial if the gas field is to be kept working, for security is a major risk,[7] while corporate reputations damaged by negative publicity on the internet or in international media can lose millions of dollars of business. For Chevron Bangladesh, the community engagement gift therefore aims to do many things: create 'partnerships' and produce and perform project success for a global audience using the tropes of acceptable development discourse while also placating local people and quelling local agitation against the gas field's operation.[8] Its claims to entitlement are thus made at the local, global and transnational scale. It's little wonder that, as these divergent narratives rub up against each other, sparks sometimes fly.

That there are multiple and sometimes contradictory objectives in development work has been noted by several anthropologists of development (see Grillo and Stirrat, 1997; Mosse, 2005). The motivations and ideological underpinnings of CSR are similarly complex, though rather than its main objective being 'improvement' *per se*, whether state or donor sponsored (Li, 2007), as Steve Wilson, CEO of Chevron, Bangladesh, candidly put it in an interview: CSR is 'business driven' (Interview notes, 3 December 208). Chevron will never be a major funder or practitioner of development in

Bangladesh, Wilson continued, for this is the role of the government. This was not to say that community engagement is a minor part of the company's operations. Not only could the programme in Bibiyana become a 'showcase' of good practice, but 'the risk to reputation' is taken very seriously. 'Blow-outs', resistance movements and accidents in protected forests all lead to problems with the media and government which have to be micro-managed, leading to weeks, months or years of work.

In offering its gifts Chevron is therefore asking for substantial returns: the compliance of the local population, a shining reputation at regional and global levels, and the production of a certain kind of 'community'. Before making its *gift* of community engagement, the company therefore had first to create the right type of community.

CREATING COMMUNITY

In her ethnography of colonial, state and donor improvement schemes in Indonesia, Tanya Murray Li argues that such schemes must be understood in Foucauldian terms as a form of governance. Unlike explicit forms of discipline, governance operates by educating desires, aspirations and beliefs, which people often don't even notice happening (Li, 2007: 5). By rendering what are essentially political problems (such as extreme poverty, or the loss of livelihoods to industrial development) as 'technical' issues with a range of technical solutions, projects of 'improvement' govern by the back door. Li's approach chimes closely with Ong's analysis of the relationship between distinct forms of knowledge/technology and neoliberal regimes. In particular:

> *Technologies of subjectivity* rely on an array of knowledge and expert systems to induce self-animation and self-governance so that citizens can optimise choices, efficiency and competitiveness in turbulent market conditions. Such techniques of optimisation include the adherence to health regimes, acquisition of skills, development of entrepreneurial ventures, and other techniques of self-engineering and capital accumulation. (Ong, 2006: 6)

Within schemes for improvement, a key part of the process is 'problematisation', whereby a problem is identified and a solution offered. The techniques of problematisation change over the years: PRA is currently in vogue, though as Mosse and others have shown, it is fraught with difficulties (Mosse, 2005; see also Cornwall and

Pratt, 1999). Another element in contemporary schemes is the role of experts, who: 'focus more on the capacities of the poor than on the practices through which one group impoverishes the other' (Li, 2007: 7). In Indonesia Li describes how World Bank 'community development' schemes drew from romanticised notions of a previously existing 'natural' community that the project would restore via particular techniques (the setting up of committees etc.). Meanwhile poverty was diagnosed by the World Bank team as resulting from undemocratic structures and corruption rather than socio-economic relations, the solution being the introduction of neoliberal practices of competition and accountability. In sum: 'To govern through community requires that community be rendered technical. It must be investigated, mapped, classified, documented, interpreted ...' (Li, 2007: 234).

Seen in this light 'community development' is an anti-politics machine *par excellence* (Ferguson, 1990; Li, 2007), distracting attention from the true causes of poverty, offering technical solutions to political problems, and governing, not through discipline and authority, but the implementation of new administrative structures, edicts and bureaucratic structures, all underlain by implicit neoliberal ideology. Let us examine the ways in which Chevron's programmes have created an image of a particular form of 'community' in Duniyapur, with adherent technical solutions to its problems.

Like the World Bank project in Indonesia, the first stage of Chevron's community development programme involved the hiring of consultants and experts to 'map' the area that was soon to be referred to as 'Bibiyana' (a name I never heard during my fieldwork in Nadampur). As Naser Ahmed, the Director of External Affairs, writes of the early days of 'community relations' in Duniyapur:

> We told them that we were more interested to know about where their strength lay, what their capacities were, before we set out to address their needs. Our goal was always to forge a partnership with the local community to play a part in the overall development of the community. Therefore we felt the need for a strategic approach to our development plan. We conducted several studies with the help of local research organisations. We first carried out a survey to assess peoples' perception of the company. And then we went for a baseline study to assess the socioeconomic condition of the locality. The latter gave us indications of the critical needs and capacity of the community. (Chevron, 2008: 11)

Later came the inevitable PRA exercises in which problems were diagnosed and the field of action delineated (Li, 2007: 246). The knowledge gained from these exercises was written up in more reports, and the 'problem' (the loss of livelihoods to the gas field/ poverty) transformed into 'project goals'.[9] As in all development projects, the solutions offered by the reports were technical in nature; once speaking the language of development it is virtually impossible to break free of the vernacular. As a result of these 'scoping exercises', project objectives began to materialise, all of which found the solutions in strengthening community and individual capacity. After participatory assessment and planning, community groups were to be formed, with organisational capacity building taking place; training in literacy and other 'productive' skills would be offered, alongside technical, supervisory and marketing support. As a community relations official explained of these early days of planning: 'Before we came, there was *nothing* here ...' (Interview notes, December 2008, emphasis mine).

According to an early report, the main project objectives were:

> to develop productive skills through training and education for economic emancipation of the vulnerable groups in Bibiyana and provide input support to enable effective utilisation of the acquired skills

and:

> to bring into being a supportive environment and a systematic process of improving livelihood through providing access to quality services, community mobilisation and increase viable and sustainable opportunities through educational interventions and production and marketing assistance to the disadvantaged people.[10]

Key to these objectives was the setting up of Village Development Organisations (VDOs) which would involve committees of 'local leaders', who alongside NGO field officers would choose beneficiaries for the credit and training. While being offered supplementary training in accounting and book-keeping, these VDOs are, like those in Li's World Bank Community Development Project in Indonesia, modelled on a notion of natural communities, in which leaders speak for, and know, 'the people', and in which the role of development is to strengthen and modernise these structures, provide training and improve access. The nature of relationships *within* communities, in which the elite (i.e. 'the local leaders') essentially dominates and exploits the labour of the poor, is conveniently ignored (see also Pattenden, 2010).

Alongside these mapping exercises, with their technical language and objectives, the area, referred to by several of the Chevron executives we interviewed as 'our community', is physically demarcated via Chevron's Road Safety Awareness Programme. Part of this involves large billboards which have been erected along the Sherpur to Nadampur road to advocate road traffic safety. Using local children as their models, each sporting a Chevron tee shirt and hard hat, the billboards are the first sign that one is entering 'Chevron Country'. It was these billboards that I first saw on visiting Nadampur in 2005. Appearing immediately after turning off the highway onto what used to be a dirt track leading for 5 or 6 miles towards Kakura and Nadampur, the signage seems not so much to advertise traffic safety as the presence of Chevron. A few miles later we passed a group of women labourers working on the side of the road. Within the context of rural Bangladesh, their appearance was extraordinary, for they were wearing hard hats, work boots under their saris and safety goggles. It seemed as if we had crossed the borders of a new country, a mini-state run by a transnational extractive company (cf. Ferguson, 2005).

I shall return to the relationship between projects of improvement and governance in a short while. For now, let us shift focus from the ways in which Chevron has created community to the 'gifts' it offers.

THE COMMUNITY ENGAGEMENT GIFT

Like pre-colonial European scavengers approaching 'the natives', twenty-first-century transnational oil companies approach the 'communities' surrounding proposed mining sites bearing gifts of appeasement (see also Sawyer, 2004: 9). In the early days of Unocal, before the plant was built, these gifts were the equivalent of sweeties offered to recalcitrant children: t-shirts with the company logo and other items of clothing featured large. Later, the offerings became more sophisticated. This was partly in response to the demands made by local people. Before the plant was built Chevron was negotiating with four 'Demand Realisation Committees',[11] each of which had a list of stipulations. As I have already described, a hospital, a school, the supply of gas, a fertiliser factory, a power plant, improved roads and – of course – higher rates of land compensation, were top of the wish-lists. With the exception of the roads that linked the North and South Pads to the main road at Syedpur, few of these demands materialised, not least because some fell outside of the realms of what was legally possible for a foreign company operating within Bangladesh. The supply of domestic gas, for instance, was not something that Chevron, contracted by the government to extract the gas, and lacking ownership of pipelines or the means to convert the gas for domestic usage at source, was ever able to provide. Nor, as we have seen, was the company able or willing to take the place of government in providing schools or hospitals. There were, however, other gifts, which neither stepped on the toes of the government nor contradicted the discourses of 'sustainability' and 'helping the poor to help themselves' which the company now took up. They were also cheap.[12]

Some of the gifts were aimed at the poorest. Slab latrines were distributed to households without hygienic sanitation.[13] Tin roofs and concrete pillars for low-income housing were also supplied, sporting the Chevron logo. The company could not provide piped gas, but it distributed smoke free *chulas* (stoves).[14] These, like other gifts, have come with a price tag attached: the 'community' should contribute to their upkeep. In the case of the stoves, for instance, when it appeared that people were not caring for them properly, they were 'sold' to recipients at a cost of 200 *taka*,[15] in order to instil a sense of ownership.[16]

Other gifts came with similar conditions attached. Again, within current development moralities of creating self-reliance rather than dependency, these were aimed at producing a sense of ownership. Two 'Smiling Sun' medical clinics were built, run by the NGO SSKS, and partly funded by the donations of *Londonis*. These provide diagnostic services but not medicine, with a further programme of outreach health workers, and an ambulance which could take patients to the nearest hospital in Sylhet, though at a cost. Our research in 2008 showed that the poorest households in the area did not use these services since in their view there was little point in having a diagnosis if they could not afford the prescribed medicines and, if in dire need, the fare of a CNG[17] was lower than that of the ambulance. While not actually building a school, the company has provided support for four high schools in the area, via the funding of teachers and teaching materials, the distribution of school uniforms and providing several hundred scholarships for pupils each year (Chevron, 2008).

The clinics and scholarships are part of Chevron's objective of creating 'sustainable' development and community partnership in Duniyapur, which in turn allows it to make claims over its moral right to extract gas in the area.[18] This objective is often repeated in its literature, for example:

Chevron Bangladesh will always consider itself a partner of the local people of Bibiyana in the community's effort to improve their socio-economic condition. The company would like to strengthen this partnership with a view to achieving sustainable development in the locality. (Chevron, 2008)

Our goal always was to forge a partnership with the local people to play a part in the overall development of the community. (Chevron, 2008: 10)

While some people told us they appreciated the gifts, others told us that the costs were too high or that they were excluded from the benefits. As one man from Karimpur put it:

Chevron has established a community hospital but we don't benefit from it. What's the point if all the expenses are borne by us? First you have to pay 40 *taka* to register, then you have to pay 20 *taka* for every visit. None of the medicine is free. Once I used the ambulance, but to get to Sylhet it cost 1000 *taka*. (Fieldnotes, 2009)

I should reiterate that these more negative responses do not mean that there are no benefits for local communities: our visits to the clinic found it being used by largely satisfied patients. Rather than examining in simplistic terms whether Chevron provides the services that it claims as part of its community engagement strategy, the anthropological question is both more subtle and more interesting: why, when Chevron and FIVDB clearly provide a range of services and programmes, do some people state that: 'They give nothing?'

One answer to this question is that the *aim* of sustainability, in which benefits are not simply provided 'for free' and the donor eventually withdraws from the relationship, is not shared by local people, who feel that since Chevron is using 'their' gas, it should provide a range of benefits in compensation; even better, it should connect to the population properly by providing them with the benefits of global capitalism and neoliberal development via employment at the gas field, not to say connection to the gas.

Seen in this perspective, rather than donating a 'gift', Chevron is making (or failing to make) a payment. As another man put it: 'This company has been looting our gas while paying nothing to us villagers' (Fieldnotes, 2008).

In the following analysis, made by a member of a VDO, Chevron is placed at the centre of the 'big disease' of poverty and disenfranchisement, responsible for its cure, not as a 'partner'. Within this perspective, Chevron is positioned as an alternative to the state, responsible for providing 'big cures'.

> Say you have a big disease and Chevron is giving us a Paracetamol. If the disease is big the treatment should be big too. You need a big doctor, diagnosis, operations, expensive medicine, good care and so on. But Chevron wants to satisfy us by providing Paracetamol? (Fieldnotes, 2009)

I shall return to these divergent understandings and expectations of Chevron's role later. For now, let us return to the idea of sustainability which underscores the programmes. The key phrase in this context, which was repeated to me by officials in Chevron, is emblazoned on a banner inside the offices of the Alternative Livelihoods Programme which the company funds, and is of course a mantra of current development practice – it is: 'Helping the poor to help themselves' (see Gronemeyer, 1999 on 'helping').

The ideal of self-sufficiency, close cousin to the goal of 'partnership', seems morally unquestionable. Who, after all, wants to create dependency? Shouldn't resources be used to 'empower' people to do things for themselves? As Steve Wilson told me, the locals of Duniyapur 'are a proud people', who eschew hand-outs and want to be helped-to-help-themselves: 'You know … "give a man a fishing rod" …' (Interview notes, 3 December 2008).

It is this ethos which underlies the Alternative Livelihoods Programme, funded by Chevron and managed by a local NGO, Friends in Village Development Bangladesh (FIVDB). The programme was initiated with the explicit aim of avoiding the situation that had arisen after land compensation was given in the North Pad in the 1990s. As the Head of External Affairs recounted, at the time Unocal had simply paid the landowners compensation. Rather than improving the situation however, the policy had led to anger. The first problem was that the landowners had quickly spent the compensation money and now had no means of livelihood. The second was that a large number of people, who used land but don't own it had lost their livelihoods but been given no compensation. The Alternative Livelihoods Programme (ALP) was devised to meet their needs.

Like the majority of NGO programmes in Bangladesh, credit is the cornerstone of the ALP.[19] One of the main activities of the ALPs, which are administered by VDOs, is loans and savings programmes, made available to small-scale entrepreneurs who use the credit to fund a variety of livelihood activities: goat rearing, broiler farms and fisheries are examples.[20] The programme also provides training, with an explicit aim of sustainability. VDO members are trained in accountancy so that they will eventually function without the support of FIVDB, and borrowers are trained in goat rearing, beef fattening, etc. There is also an adult literacy programme in Kakura, and a sewing programme for local women, in which training is given on sewing machines and a market supplied for the pieces of embroidery that the women produced. The Director of External Affairs at Chevron Bangladesh told me that the goal of these programmes was 'empowerment'.[21]

Like most NGO programmes, these activities have met with varied outcomes in the different villages. In Kakura NGO workers told us that the extent of poverty has meant that fewer people have been able to take up the loans, or to repay them.[22] Indeed, NGO workers told us that here, in particular, there was a strong feeling that Chevron should 'give' and not expect repayments. There have been mishaps (many people reported that their ducks had died) and disappointments (the sewing programme was not really a success)[23] as well as achievements: informants who had used the loans to diversify their livelihoods or offset a crisis, for example. Our interviews with recipients provide many examples of people who feel their lives have been improved by the ALP programme. Our research never intended to appraise the programme, however, and nor is that the purpose of this chapter. Hits and misses are the stuff of development work, however they are narrated. Rather than focusing simplistically upon 'success' or 'failure', the anthropology of development should analyse the taken-for-granted discourses and practices, seeking to delve beyond what is supposed to happen to the 'unintended consequences' (Ferguson, 1990) or, as David Mosse puts it: 'What is of interest is less the relationship between policy and implementation, or dominance and resistance, and more that between hidden and public transcripts' (2005: 7).

Alongside the inevitable hits and misses, the ALP and other Chevron-funded initiatives have the avowed aim of producing self-reliant entrepreneurs with access to markets, education and health care services, all of which they must contribute to in order to avoid dependency and create local self-reliance and self-discipline. Yet what all of these programmes fail to do is address the social and political relationships which create poverty, treating it instead as a technical problem which can be 'solved' via technical remedies such as credit or training. Like the clinic or school programmes, the Alternative Livelihoods Programme is not largely aimed at the poorest, for one needs land for beef fattening, broiler farms and fisheries. Instead, Chevron's community engagement gift(s) come, like a Trojan horse, containing the imperatives and norms of neoliberal capitalism: individual entrepreneurship, self-reliance, access to credit and meritocratic reward are among its hallmarks. With the stress on credit, training and improving access to markets for those with the greatest capacity, the programme neatly replicates the unspoken norms of neoliberal capitalism, described by Ong as populated by 'free individuals who are then induced to self-manage according to market principles of discipline, efficiency and competitiveness' (2006: 4).

Moreover, as Jonathan Pattenden describes in South India, where the government and international donors have been strongly pushing the creation of Self-Help Groups (SHGs), ideals of 'self-help' fail to challenge the distribution of resources between classes in rural areas. Civil society organisations are thus depoliticised by international and national policy agendas, by working with and aiming funds at 'communities' rather than identifying the poorest and working directly with them. Rather than addressing the true causes of poverty – class relations and, in India's case, the withdrawal of the state from development – SHGs:

> provide low cost, highly visible anti-poverty initiatives ... that help forestall social instability in the context of 'jobless growth' and stagnation in the rural sector. Far from being a tool for redistribution between social classes, SHGs appear to facilitate the maintenance of the status quo. (Pattenden, 2010: 509)

PERFORMING/NARRATING SUCCESSFUL COMMUNITY ENGAGEMENT

While the gift of community engagement involves the technologies of ideological governance and is aimed at creating a compliant community of 'partners', the objective of *reputation* can only be met via public performances and narrations, which celebrate the giving of the gifts. It is during these performances that the 'payback' of the community engagement gift becomes most explicit. While successful community engagement is generally performed in sites within Duniyapur, the importance of the performances for Chevron lies in their transformation in the global arena via reports and other literature which narrates success for an international audience, for it is here that their claims for the moral right to extract resources matter the most.

The ways in which project 'success' is constructed is the focus of David Mosse's ethnography *Cultivating Development* (2005). Arguing that the ethnographic question for the anthropology of development should not be *whether* projects work but *how* they work, Mosse suggests that rather than policy, development interventions are driven by the need to establish and maintain relationships. In order to enrol a range of supportive actors, projects need interpretive communities, with managers frequently spending more time disseminating evidence of success than dealing with the tricky everyday problems of implementation, since: 'development success is not objectively verifiable but socially produced' (2005: 172). VIP visits, project literature, brochures,[24] videos are all part of the performance, for 'success is not guaranteed, but produced through processes requiring constant joint work' (2005: 168).

Such performances of success are central to Chevron's Community Engagement Programme in Duniyapur, and are, I suggest, aimed primarily at the 'interpretive community', the global audience of Chevron. This audience is not the same as Mosse's 'Indo-British Rainfed Farming Project', which was primarily made up of policy makers, donors, colleagues within DFID and the government of India. Instead, it largely comprises Bangladeshi state officials, Chevron's international executives, competing corporations and the company's shareholders. More generally, the company seeks 'good PR', both in terms of public relations within Bangladesh and internationally.

A key event in the performance of success is the 'handing over ceremony'. Indeed, 'handing over' lies at the very heart of community engagement: the moment when the gift (and its payback) is made public. School rooms or NGO offices are prepared for these events, banners erected, local, national and international dignitaries invited. The community is represented by a selection of 'local leaders' and grateful recipients; the gaps in attendance will never be known to those outside Duniyapur. Once assembled, speeches are made, photographs taken, usually of the moment of 'hand over': the computer, sewing machine or stipend physically changing hands.[25]

I am not suggesting that these performances are devoid of emotional content or coldly calculating and insincere. There can be little doubt that, as well as constructing success, handing-over ceremonies produce real feelings of warmth and connection, themselves generative of a sense of success. Indeed, the role of emotion, whether positive or negative, has received little if any analysis in the anthropology of development. There can be little doubt, however, that these events are carefully managed, a fact that has not escaped many locals. I was laughingly told by several people, for example, that the bull selected as an example of the Beef Fattening Programme had in fact been bought from outside the area. Whether or not this story is true is beside the point. Rather, the rumour highlights the way that such events stage success and edit out failure. Crucially, it also shows how performances of success are undercut by contesting versions of reality. As James Scott writes of 'everyday forms of resistance' in Sedaka, Malaysia: 'Those with power ... are not, however, in total control of the stage' (1985: 26). While Scott is writing of class relations rather than the relationship between a multinational energy company and its 'communities', similar observations can be made in Duniyapur.

Performances need an audience if they are to be meaningful. While the assembled locals and dignitaries are important participants, handing-over ceremonies require a global audience if they are to have their full impact on 'reputation'. Why else would a small bridge, recently built in Karimpur sport a brass plate with the words: 'Bibiyana Friendship Bridge', when no-one in the village besides, visiting transnational *Londonis*, reads English? Local performances of success are thus turned seamlessly into heart-warming stories of partnership and community and disseminated via Chevron's PR machinery, the reports and newsletters to be downloaded at a click, received through the post for shareholders, or handed in hard copies to visitors and colleagues. For example:

> Buffie Wilson, wife of Chevron Bangladesh President Steve Wilson recently made a visit to the village of Karimpur, located next to the Bibiyana Gas Field in Habiganj. Her visit heralded a brand new beginning for the families of Champa Begum and Jotsna Dev. Both women lost their homes during the devastating flood of 2007 and in standing by the community, Chevron gave them the chance to restart their lives afresh by rebuilding their homesteads. Their

homes were officially presented to the proud new owners in a simple, heart-warming ceremony and Ms Wilson was accorded a rousing reception. Champa Begum and Jotsna Dev finally found a reason to smile after last year's floods wreaked havoc, chaos and devastation in their lives.[26]

In another example, a satisfied recipient of training and credit gives testimony as to how the ALP has turned his life around:

I just feel exhilarated when I go to my vegetable farm. I have learned how to plant and grow vegetables and I have made sure that there will be no insect or pest attacks on my vegetables as I have learned to apply appropriate insecticide at the appropriate time. The villagers who also received training along with me are also successfully applying the scientific method of farming and getting good results ... All my efforts are being directed to the one and only goal, which is farming ... By fulfilling this dream I will drive away poverty from my family. (Matin Khan, cited in Chevron, 2008: 40)

A final example shows how even land acquisition, the subject of so much bad feeling and agitation in the area, can be turned into a story of success, in which land losers celebrate their contribution to national interests and improvement:

About fifty acres of land were acquired for the development of the Bibiyana Gas Field. Of which about eight acres ... used to belong to my family ...

Even though our land was acquired in the national interest, I personally think that each of us has been immensely benefitted. The standard of living in our area has risen and the value of land has gone up. People of the area are also held in high esteem because of the project ...

It is by the Grace of Allah that the development work has reached a successful end. I have lost my land, but after taking into consideration the activities centering on the field, and the future possibility of development of industries, one realises that the Bibiyana serves the greater interest of the local people ... (Haj Md. Moinuddin, cited in Chevron, 2008: 43)

Success is narrated through numbers as well as 'human interest stories'. Through reports, newsletters and PowerPoint presentations, achievements are celebrated via the recitation of numbers of stipends given, training received and so on. Again, the effect is to reduce problems of poverty, injustice and disenfranchisement to technical issues that can be solved via concrete, quantifiable measures such as training or access to small loans. As I shall suggest in the next chapter, competing forms of knowledge have played a major role in contestations over the role of transnational mining companies in Bangladesh. These different and at times violently opposed discourses involve different and incommensurate ways of knowing: rumour competes with the 'hard' quantitative data cited in corporate reports; qualitative anthropological research with baseline surveys. Within the construction of community engagement success, however, the net effect of so many numbers is an impression of project aims successfully achieved, though no account is given of how such calculations were made.

FROM THE GIFT OF COMMUNITY ENGAGEMENT TO THE CORPORATE GIFT: THE JOURNEY ENDS

Finally, let us consider the material goods produced by the company. These also transmit messages of community partnership and support, and are presented to visitors to the company offices. Here the 'gift' finally comes to rest after its complicated journey. Originally offered in the form of development aid by the oil company to 'the community' in return for performances of partnership, community development and the 'disadvantaged people of Bibiyana' being helped-to-help-themselves, the gift is converted into value via corporate narratives of success which are conveyed globally via PR literature and further materialised in the shape of mugs, calendars, pieces of embroidery and even packets of tea. These are then passed in a quite different direction, 'upwards' to the urban and cosmopolitan consumers whose approval the company seeks. A close examination suggests that many of these gifts are aimed at urban Bangladeshi recipients, to whom helping-the-poor-to-help-themselves is perhaps a less appealing theme than national pride and economic development.

The packaging of these gifts is their very point. For example, on the front of the packet of tea we read: 'Tea, from the garden of Chevron's neighborhood'. On the back, we're told:

Lackatoorah Tea Estate of National Tea Co. Ltd., one of the oldest tea gardens in Sylhet has been growing quality tea for the people both home and abroad for the past 125 years. Chevron, one of the world's leading resources and project development companies, has been contributing significantly to the development of Bangladesh's energy sector.

Here, the colonial history of the tea sector and its obvious parallel with the presence of Chevron and other foreign companies is elided under an image of economic productivity and contribution to national development. Similar nationalist sentiments are carried on the company calendar. Again, it is Chevron's partnership with Bangladesh the nation rather than with 'the community' that takes centre stage. Each month of the calendar is illustrated by a beautifully shot photograph of people carrying the Bangladesh flag, with a poetic quotation underneath. For example, July:

> You reside eternally in the spirit,
> O my homeland; for you
> We are adorned with new energy

On the cover of the calendar, we read:

> Human energy, leading Bangladesh with energy and spirit ... In Bangladesh, where the people are known for their resilience, Chevron seeks to identify the spirit that guides them and their actions. Bangladesh's national spirit is best exemplified by its people's desire to build a better tomorrow, to strive forward by attaining economic growth and to go beyond the odds with the overriding power of aspiration and hard work. All Bangladeshis play a role in this progressive thrust towards the future by bravely facing myriad adversities and by actively contributing to the realisation of collective goals.

* * *

It is important to remember that the motivations behind programmes of development/ improvement are complex and at times contradictory. The realities of improvement projects are complex; not only is a range of actors involved, each with their own understanding of 'development' or CSR (field officers, policy makers in Dhaka or Washington and so on), but at any one time an individual may hold various and even contradictory views of what they are doing. Reducing the gift of community engagement, and the moralities which underpin it, to neoliberal governance or, in more crude terms, as a way of 'buying off' local resistance to the gas plant, misses the more nuanced and complex ways in which business advantage, neoliberal moralities and PR tactics interweave with a range of ideological stances, dreams and aspirations. When asked what motivated him, for example, a high-level executive in Chevron Bangladesh told me that for 'work' it was the wish to promote the 'reputation' of the company, whereas at a personal level, he, like so many of his compatriots, wished to harness the might of Chevron to 'do good' for the national betterment of Bangladesh, an aspiration that the company seeks to evoke via the calendar and other corporate gifts. As noted earlier, such gifts are aimed at urban and professional Bangladeshis, who visit the Dhaka offices and bear such gifts away, not the global audience accessed via the worldwide web, for whom the idea of 'partnership' with 'empowered' Third World villagers is so seductive.

The gift of community engagement is thus linked to a variety of moral orders or, in Foucault's terms, 'regimes of truth', which appear in different guises at different points along its journey and are both hidden and explicit. Neoliberal ideology figures large. The creation of a certain sort of community, made up of entrepreneurial and self-reliant consumers, is key to much of the ALP and the moral injunction to be 'sustainable'. Nationalist morality also plays a part, and is used by the company to suggest that, as a partner with the nation, it too seeks economic development and improvement. Yet while similar to Arjun Appadurai's 'scapes' (Appadurai, 1990) in that they are overlapping, unbounded and not reducible to a single location, these moral orders, and the narratives they involve, become meaningful at different points in the journey of the gift. Sustainability and helping-the-poor-to-help-themselves resonates deeply with the moralities of First World consumers, employees and opinion formers primarily located in the North, for whom questions of ethics and certain forms of morality are placed at the centre of 'good' business practice as well as personhood. That Chevron needs to promote its activities on the international and national stage as morally 'good' is not simply about governance, but also about the moral orders in which its CEOs and other high-level executives operate.

Yet this moral order, so closely linked to the neoliberal project, is often at odds with the moralities of giving and receiving within Duniyapur and its transnational social fields. A similar observation was made elsewhere in Bangladesh, where recipients of a BRAC programme which aimed at self-reliance and empowerment of the ultra-poor turned to NGO workers to act as patrons, thus recreating the very conditions of dependency which the programme sought to break down (Huda et al., 2008). As this indicates, 'helping the poor to help themselves' is a tall order in a context where the state is ineffective in its provision for basic human needs and access to material resources only comes via one's connection to others. In the absence of free secondary education, medicine and roads, not to mention sources of regular employment, is it surprising that the landless inhabitants of Kakura and Karimpur are unreceptive to the injunction to 'help themselves'? Indeed, the aim of self-reliance is out of step within a context where livelihoods are patched together via a web of social relationships which are sometimes supportive and sometimes exploitative yet nonetheless are vital for survival. While fishing rods may be desirable, they are not much use without being connected to the family who own the pond, or the money lender who provides the capital to buy feed and fry for the fishery.

In what follows I describe a specific 'worldly encounter' (Tsing, 2005) when these different moralities and forms of connection were made explicit. As we shall see, each type of morality is linked to a claim: by Chevron, to be socially disconnected and yet also 'partners' in order to access gas, and by the poor, to be socially connected to powerful and protective patrons, for material survival. The encounter took place in the UK rather than in Duniyapur and involved an attempt to transform the transnational gift of *'shahajo'* into the community engagement gift of 'partnership'.

PARTNERSHIP REQUESTED: CHEVRON COMES TO THE UK

In 2010 Chevron's Director of External Affairs came to the UK to meet members of Duniyapur's transnational community. His purpose was somewhat unusual: to set up a foundation which utilised the charitable donations of expatriates from Duniyapur for community development activities in the area, rather than the largely individualised contributions, which, as we saw in the last chapter, can amount to thousands of pounds per person per year. The plan was that Chevron would match these funds: for every hundred or thousand pounds raised by the *Londonis* the company would contribute an equal amount. This innovative scheme was thus directly aimed at sustainability, creating a charitable foundation which eventually would rely only upon the funding of expatriates with a long-lasting stake in the development of their 'homeland' communities. It potentially marked an important transition in transnational relations: from personalised, individual links between *Londoni* patrons and *deshi* clients, to a more formal type of giving, closer to the 'development gift' than the socially connected *shahajo*. The need for donors to gain status and local recognition was acknowledged by the plan: scholarships, community facilities and so on would be named (The Md. Uddin Bridge, for example).

Partnership with members of the Bangladeshi diaspora was key to the project. While these partners might be from the actual villages of Duniyapur, the plan was also for a wider set of alliances from civil society groups in the UK and US, in which the donors would have no pre-existing social links with Duniyapur. Similar projects organised by BRAC have been successful in attracting the enthusiasm of a younger generation of British Bengalis, who often have only limited links with poor relatives in the *desh*. For many *Londonis* from the various villages in Duniyapur the transition from *shahajo* to formalised donations organised via the NGO that Chevron planned to commission for the work was, however, viewed as highly problematic. While some welcomed the idea, many others in the consultation meetings we attended were vociferously opposed. What would be the *point* one man asked; he already gave large amounts of money to people in his village, and was contributing to the building of a mosque in his British neighbourhood; the fund would be yet another obligation. Another *Londoni*, who had taken steps to raise funds for a hospital with non-Bangladeshi members of the Rotary Club explained why he didn't want to be involved. It was all very well asking non-Bangladeshis to contribute, he said, but he couldn't ask his compatriots for charity: not only would he get ensnarled in the complex politics of his community in the UK, which could put him at risk of rumours of misappropriating the funds, but his request for donations might be misinterpreted as begging; it simply wouldn't be appropriate to ask his neighbours and relatives in Britain with whom he was of equal status for money. Moreover, partnership with Chevron might risk his good name.

As the above implies, the politics of giving and receiving in Duniyapur, both in the *desh* and transnationally, is highly complex. The transition from the gift of patronage to the development gift is not simple, for each form of giving is embedded in a significantly different moral order. This is not to say that individuals are unable to engage in both forms of donation; as the fund has developed during the course of writing this book it is clear that this is not the case. Rather, not only are transnational villagers already committed to a range of personalised obligations in the *desh*, from building a village mosque to paying for the education of poor clients, in which a move to impersonal donations doesn't make much sense, but also the work of *fundraising*, a practice that is seen in Britain as morally 'good', might be interpreted differently within the transnational community, where by requesting money one risks accusations of corruption/malpractice and of being perceived to be in the role of low-status receiver rather than high-status giver. This danger is exacerbated by the involvement of Chevron, which is viewed within Duniyapur and transnational communities in the UK with ambivalence and suspicion.

The partnership that the fund needed if it was to be successful, at both a practical level and in terms of how it would be positioned within Chevron's narratives of successful community engagement, as another example of uncontroversial and mutually beneficial connectedness to satisfied locals, was thus harder to achieve than the programme's creators had originally hoped. Indeed, from the perspective of the British villagers we met, Chevron's needs seemed greater than theirs. They already had excellent relations with their home villages; many had established reputations as community leaders and patrons, whose moral standing was continually reproduced via their generosity to their 'own poor'. They did not need 'partnership' with Chevron in the funding of community development programmes. What they required, they told us, was accountability over environmental issues, appropriate grievance procedures and dialogue. In the long term, the men we interviewed hoped to see substantial development in the area: proper roads, factories that created jobs for local people and the supply of gas, 'something to be proud of', as one man put it.

NEOLIBERAL GOVERNANCE, MORALITY AND THE COMMUNITY ENGAGEMENT GIFT

In his critique of James Scott's *Seeing Like a State* (1998), James Ferguson takes issue with Scott's suggestion that global capitalism creates homogeneity, uniform grids and simplification in the same way as the state, the only difference being that global capitalism is motivated by profit rather than planned improvement. If sub-Saharan Africa is taken as an example, Ferguson argues, there is scant evidence of the creation of homogeneity. Instead, the 'global' reach of neoliberal capitalism is limited to small patches of investment, usually in the form of resource extraction, 'hopping' rather than 'flowing' from London to specific mining enclaves made safe from endemic violence by private security firms for transnational mining corporation employees. The result is that 'useable' Africa ends up with secured enclaves in countries such as Nigeria and Angola, while 'unuseable' Africa gets a hodge-podge of NGOs patching over the gaps left by failed states (Ferguson, 2005: 380).

Bangladesh is not the same as Angola or Nigeria. The state hasn't yet failed, though its coverage of basic services for its citizens leaves something to be desired, to say the least. There are, however, resonances with Ferguson's argument. The programmes and investments into infrastructure and human development made by Chevron only stretch to the limits of 'their neighbourhood', as they put it, as do the road safety campaigns, the improved sanitation and income generation programmes. As Steve Wilson told me, Chevron is not a development organisation *per se*; that would be to interfere with the government, for whom good relations are crucial (Interview notes 3 December 2008). Yet to argue, along the same lines as Ferguson (2005), that *all* Chevron is doing in its CSR programmes is creating an enclave of security via small-scale investments aimed at winning community acceptance in order that the company can carry out its business, is too simplistic.[27] Indeed, governance is attempted, though not necessarily achieved, through complex means, which are both explicit in the candid explanations of Chevron staff, and less transparent. The gift of community engagement is thus both a conscious and unconscious attempt at governance and control, while simultaneously drawing upon contemporary Northern moralities of ethical business practice, human rights and so on. Yet while the tropes of 'partnership' and 'empowerment' are constantly used, the policies of community engagement do nothing to recognise the true causes of poverty, let alone address them.

'Community engagement' and the discursive techniques it involves can therefore be read as claims by Chevron over its entitlement to profit from the gas reserves of Duniyapur, drawing upon the moral orders of global development and neoliberal ethics to bring legitimacy to its actions. In the next chapter we see how systems of entitlement in Bangladesh can also involve forcible and sometimes violent forms of control by the state and its agencies: this is governance at its most raw.

Combined with this, while entitlements are asserted, others seek to deny them. Indeed, the *attempt* to govern and control is not the same as achieving control. While development and community engagement programmes seek to reduce problems of dispossession and inequality to apolitical technical issues requiring technical solutions, as Li astutely points out, politics often refuses to go away, for the practice of governance is quite different from the practice of politics (Li, 2007: 10–12). In Duniyapur, no amount of training, micro-credit, goat donations or handing-over ceremonies will prevent the messy business of politics from endlessly re-emerging, like a many-headed hydra. The corporate narrative of success, which appears so seamlessly in the reports and PR material produced by the company, only partially covers up contesting claims and alternative narratives, relying not on the knowledge and techniques of development discourse but those of exploitation and protest. It is to these narratives that we shall now turn.

6
Rumour and Activism: Politics Breaks Out

September 2009. It's been a long day. I'm sitting by the *bari* pond enjoying a rare five minutes' solitude. We've spent the morning in Kakura and Karimpur discussing our research 'findings' with various informants, a practice which nowadays is pretty much standard in anthropology. Sharing findings with informants is not just good manners; it also allows people to participate in the research process, 'talking back' and correcting the 'expert'. On a pragmatic level, it adds value to research: mistakes can be rectified, general impressions confirmed, analyses deepened. Like most anthropological research however, invariably a messy, hit-and-miss business, the morning's work has only loosely conformed to these high-minded ideals. We had hoped to hold a meeting in both villages, but found few people around, so decided to split up and visit the case-study households, handing out a printed list of 'findings' to share and discuss. In planning our visit this document had seemed important: when we embarked on the research people had complained that they were tired of researchers/consultants asking questions or requesting that they gather for PRA events and then disappearing in their jeeps without communicating the results. I also wanted feedback for the report I was writing for Chevron,[1] which suggested ways that the company might change its CSR practices in order to better reach the poorest inhabitants of Duniyapur. Since this was written in English and we had only limited time and resources it had seemed appropriate to translate a summary of local concerns rather than the entire report. The 'research findings' had thus been reduced to a one page summary of 'community engagement problems': the effects of the embankments, lack of grievance procedures, concerns over safety and so on.

While the people we spoke to agreed with the 'findings', and told us they were happy to have participated in the research, the morning has left me uneasy. First, what to me was a summary (or checklist) of findings, translated into Bengali, to be distributed in our study villages as a record of the research process, had, in its entry into

Karimpur and Kakura become a list of 'demands'. In retrospect this was hardly surprising since I had told everyone that one outcome of the research was the report I would present to Chevron; this was both true, and more satisfactory than the writing of this book, which would take several years and be of dubious practical use. Since I was white and foreign, most people assumed that I had the ear of the company, or was actually working for them. Inevitably they would be disappointed and feel let down when our findings (their 'demands') fell on deaf ears; I was not optimistic that my report would lead to actual changes.

The second reason for my unease was that during the morning a handful of men had been notably hostile. One had followed us into Karimpur, shouting that outsiders were continually coming to the village, giving out sweets to the children and making promises that they didn't keep. Another had entered Samsun Khan's house while we were having tea with him and accused us of spying for Chevron. Finally, a group of men at the tea stall outside the high wire fences that enclose the gas plant had angrily demanded to know what we were doing. Accusations of spying are a common anthropological affliction; during my fieldwork in Nadampur in the 1980s I was rumoured to be spying for the British High Commission, a logical deduction, given the BHC's habit of carrying out unannounced 'village visits' to check the veracity of immigration applications. Given the number of experts and consultants that had descended on Duniyapur since 2004, most of whom were employed by Unocal/ Chevron, it was hardly surprising that people believed that we too were working on their behalf. Why else would we be there?

An alternative answer comes in the form of a call that Zahir receives as I relax by the *ghat*. It's from Chevron, Dhaka, and the caller, a top executive, is incandescent. Why are we distributing lists of *demands* to be made against Chevron? We are clearly liars, posing as innocent anthropologists when all along we're activists, seeking to stir up community resistance and turn Bangladesh against Chevron. The whole thing is a PR disaster. As Zahir turns on his own PR skills, soothing and calming the executive, the realisation sinks in that our list, part of an exercise that in Sussex and Dhaka seemed an irreproachable aspect of correct methodological procedure, looks very different in the highly charged political context of Duniyapur. While we've been sitting in the muddy yards and thatched homes of Karimpur, someone has faxed the document to the office in Dhaka and before we can utter the phrase 'participatory research methods' we have simultaneously become spies, working against the villages for Chevron, *and* activists, working against Chevron for nationalist anti-multinational campaigners.

On return to Dhaka, relations with the Chevron officials are repaired and my report presented. Here, another slippage takes place: while in the villages the research findings turned political, in the national offices of the ethically minded global corporation they are turned technical. Our findings, or those that I've hoped the Community Engagement team will find useful, are politely countered by reference to the baseline surveys and PRA exercises which, as we saw in the last chapter, create particular sorts of communities, with technical problems requiring technical solutions (Li, 2007). Political questions concerning the access to resources by the poorest, representation on VDOs, etc. are, in turn, countered by numbers: so many scholarships awarded, so many goats donated, so many trainings successfully completed. Meanwhile my Bangladeshi colleagues have a somewhat different experience. More calls are received: not, this time from Chevron, but from friends in Duniyapur. They shouldn't return, my colleagues are warned. Now that they're known by certain people with certain interests to be working against Chevron, things could get nasty.

*   *   *

The story illustrates a number of important points. The first concerns how within the Bangladeshi context, whether in Dhaka or Duniyapur, the living rooms of transnational villagers in Oldham or the offices of Bengali language newspapers in London, no statement concerning the activities of mining corporations is politically impartial. One is either a spy or an activist, for or against. As Stuart Kirsch points out with reference to political violence in West Papua, observation can never be neutral; within fraught political contexts anthropologists have to take sides (2002: 68). Yet while politics is everywhere, public relations operations in multinational energy corporations facing a global audience make great efforts to suppress them. As we saw in Chapter 5, the practices of corporate social engagement and the celebrations of project success and community partnership that these involve neutralise politics via the anodyne language and techniques of development. Within this context the apparently apolitical transcripts of consultancy reports, surveys, project objectives and programme outcomes can be understood as a specific exercise in power, a form of governance in which the entitlement systems that cause poverty are not interrogated, the status quo remains unquestioned and neoliberal ideologies asserted.

While the last chapter focused on how the policies and politics of CSR attempt to turn issues of unequal access to resources, dispossession and the structural violence of hunger into technical problems that the company has the power to solve, I now turn to the politics that is erased by the carefully managed PR literature. These were there from the outset and have never gone away, for, as Li reminds us, the reach of governance is limited, for 'men in their relations, their links, their imbrications are not easy to manage' (2007: 17).

Within Bangladesh as elsewhere, the politics of resource extraction is not only 'local', but national. While the never ending compulsion to find new territories, or the 'spatio-temporal fixes' of neoliberal capitalism (Harvey, 2003) push corporations such as Unocal/Chevron into countries such as Bangladesh, they then encounter the tricky nature of weak and/or unreliable states, which do not always act in ways that satisfy global codes of ethics. Even if the state is partly cooperative, creating a hospitable environment for foreign investors with tax breaks, Free Economic Zones and so on, other forces, both within and outside government, may counter such efforts. Narratives of project success and partnership are thus muddied by the actions of the state and its officials, who may act in ways that contradict the ideals of 'partnership' and harmonious community cooperation propagated in the discourse of community engagement.

These accounts of partnership and project success are also countered by alternative narratives, generated by different groups, of exploitation, imperialism and resistance. Such 'counter-discourses' arise within the context of a weak and untrustworthy state, as well as the global histories and relationships that have helped create particular political conditions within Bangladesh. They can thus be read as critiques of global hierarchy as well as commentaries on local/national conditions. They are also powerfully articulated claims of national entitlement over natural resources, radically undermining the claims made by Chevron.

Within these different claims, alternative ways of knowing and different forms of expression are central, as are the analytically separable moral orders which underlie them. In the ethics of social science, we were involved in an apparently 'objective' participatory research exercise, sharing 'findings' with informants. Within the politically fraught context of Duniyapur we were circulating a list of 'demands' which fitted with people's knowledge of the history of the gas plant and opposition to it, as well as the 'micro-political-economy' of local relationships, resources and entitlements (Leach, 1991; Li, 1996). Back in the air-conditioned offices of Chevron, we were using the language of development consultants, presenting a list of recommendations, solutions to technical problems that the corporation with its teams of experts and vast resources would surely solve. Here, knowledge of surveys, PRA exercises and numerical targets and 'outputs' is utilised. Meanwhile, national activists based in Dhaka draw upon their knowledge of global political economy and subaltern history.

I am not suggesting that these genres are completely separate: borrowings, translations and cross-references often take place. Not only do some people participate in multiple discourses, but new narratives and ways of telling are constantly merging and emerging. What we do see, however, is how particular types of narrative arise from particular political contexts. The narratives that follow can be interpreted as stories, or ways of sharing experiences with others and reconstituting personhood (see Gardner, 2002a: 27–36). The role that stories play in contexts of violence, dispossession and suffering has been observed by various anthropologists who have tended to emphasise the potentially healing role of 'giving voice', and of connecting personal and internalised experiences to the collective (see for example Mattingly, 1998; Myerhoff, 1992; F. Ross, 2003). Other work emphasises how identities are constructed in the act of story telling, and pain made sense of. Crucially, telling a story is inherently social: narratives only make sense within their social context (Mumby, 1993). Much of this pertains to the stories of protest, capitulation and corruption that follow. There is another aspect, however. As we shall see, stories can function as political tools, used to undermine the claims made by others over power and resources. Let us turn to the rumours of corruption that figure in almost every story told in Bangladesh about the country's natural resources and the role of multinationals in exploiting them.

RUMOURS OF CORRUPTION

In the accounts that follow, rumours of corruption figure large. While these take different forms according to where they originate, all can be read as critiques of the teller's place in an unequal world where power is routinely abused as well as commentaries on the contradictions of uneven development.[2] Later I shall recount rumours and stories that involve catastrophe and fatality, revealing people's deep unease about the environmental effects of the gas field, as well as their physical vulnerability. These stories express and perpetuate fear for some (Kirsch, 2003) while providing sources of black comedy for others. For both groups, the stories are used to position themselves in relation to modernity. To this extent, rumours can be thought of as 'wide awake dreaming', in which fact and fiction are intermingled as people try to make sense of what may have been a traumatic past and work out possible future outcomes (Turner, 2004: 238).

That corruption figures so large in the rumours that circulate about Chevron and its beneficiaries tells us a great deal about the relationship between people, the state and modernity in Bangladesh, where, as I have described, access to resources for rich and poor alike is largely through relationships of patronage and kinship. To get anything done, one must know someone. This as much the case for the middle classes wanting to ensure a last minute ticket on a Biman flight or a university teaching job as it is for the rural poor wanting land to sharecrop or a small loan to buy food. Yet despite widespread acceptance of the need to use social networks and contacts for individual or group advantage, within villages, as well as national politics, allegations of corruption are a prime means of framing complaints and attacking enemies. In 2008–9 this may have been exacerbated by the caretaker government's 'anti-corruption drive', in which large numbers of politicians and business people were imprisoned under corruption charges.[3]

As Daniel Jordan Smith has shown in his compelling ethnography of practices and discourses of corruption, in Nigeria people live simultaneously in two worlds in which, on the one hand, the expectations of reciprocity and patronage remain, while on the other the ideals of modern governance and citizenship are aspired to. As he writes: 'The Nigerian state is at once a neo-liberal institution claiming the full range of powers and responsibilities typical of a modern nation state and a prize to be captured and shared according to the principles of patronage' (2007: 13). While everyday fraud and deception in Bangladesh are not perhaps as extreme as in Nigeria, the comparisons are striking, for in Bangladesh too: 'everyday practices of corruption and narratives of complaint they generate are primary vehicles through which [people] imagine and create relationship between state and society' (2007: 5–6).

In Bangladesh it is not just the state which is imagined via discourses of corruption, but also aid agencies, multinationals and NGOs, all of which contribute to and are constructed by freely flowing 'ideascapes' (Appadurai, 1990) of good governance, democracy and transparency. The latter, in particular, is a powerful trope in the narratives of villagers and Dhaka intellectuals alike, a compelling signifier of twenty-first-century global morality. Yet as West and Sanders (2003: 12) argue, just as the ideal of transparency is born out of modernity, so are the conspiracy theories that inevitably thrive alongside it. While more grandiose than humble rumours in the way they connect events at different scales via overarching arguments about how the world works and, in particular, the leveraging of power by those in control, like rumours of corruption, conspiracy theories can be read as texts which reveal their teller's experiences of power, modernity and globalisation.

Rumours and conspiracy theories can be understood not only as socially produced critiques of political economy but also, in James Scott's terms, 'weapons of the weak', hidden transcripts which talk back to exploitative or repressive powers. To this extent, rumour can be seen as a political tool which, in places such as Duniyapur, function as 'small arms fire', a form of symbolic sanction against the rich (Scott, 1985: 25), or, more generally, put modernity and its beneficiaries on trial (West and Sanders, 2003: 16).

Yet before we rush to celebrate the emancipatory qualities of rumour, we should bear in mind that it can be used by the powerful as well as the weak. In Bangladesh, rumours and allegations of corruption are used by senior politicians in smear campaigns against their enemies as much as they are used by the poor against the rich. The current government campaign against the Nobel Prize winner Muhamad Yunus, who has been ousted from his role as leader of the Grameen Bank amidst accusations of wrongdoing is a case in point.[4] Such rumours can also be used against multinational companies by disgruntled bureaucrats seeking to gain advantage or wreak revenge, as well as by those with interests in Chevron's continued presence in Duniyapur seeking to undermine the activities and statements of university researchers.

Bearing these points in mind, let us turn to local politics in Duniyapur starting with accounts of the opposition movement against the gas plant.

REALPOLITIK: 'LOCAL LEADERS', PROTEST AND CO-OPTION

Behind the anodyne descriptions of 'local leaders' and 'community relations' found in consultancy reports, lie the messy and complex stuff of real relationships and politics, whether in villages in

Duniyapur or government offices in Dhaka. It is in this context that Li's distinction between the *practice of governance* (when improvement schemes render problems technical) and the *practice of politics* (a critical challenge to the latter) is illuminating (2007: 11–12). In Duniyapur, while the practice of politics did indeed challenge the development of the gas field for a short period in 2005, united opposition was quickly quashed and/or submerged by tactical interference and pressure from a range of sources, dividing the leadership and creating new divisions in the area which continue today. Here, national political interests plus the threat of violence or legal action against those taking direct action against the gas field combined with the divided nature of local politics to extinguish any effective campaign.

Characterised by a constantly shifting vying for resources and interests rather than straightforward factionalism, local politicians in Duniyapur were momentarily united in opposition against the gas field. After the field was built, however, the divisions between leaders were not only transformed, but deepened, for the stakes were now so much higher, with some apparently gaining a great deal and others losing out. Rumours of co-option, 'selling out' and corruption continue to flourish in a context where nothing is transparent and no knowledge complete. As we shall see, Chevron's CSR schemes have also played a role in dividing the opposition and transforming local politics.

What shaped local politics before the arrival of the gas men? While the local elite largely dominated the area, the balance of power was constantly shifting from one individual and group to another, a situation similar to other parts of Bangladesh. Drawing from recent research into local power structures carried out in three villages in Faridpur District, Bangladesh, for example, David Lewis and Abul Hossain show how the image of Bangladeshi rural power relations acting as a constrictive 'net' from which poorer people are unable to break free, is overly deterministic. While earlier work on 'the net' aptly described the exploitative and seemingly insurmountable nature of constricting ties of patronage in the 1970s, in contemporary Faridpur, these ties were far looser, with the rural elite also influenced by decentralised government, increased levels of party politicisation and the presence of NGOs. In each village local politics varied, according to the specific context, with greater or less degrees of elite control (Lewis and Hossain, 2008).

In Duniyapur similar observations can be made. While leaders tend to be drawn from the elite, the support a leader receives is based around people's perceptions of whether or not he represents their interests rather than straightforward factionalism. A candidate for the *upazila* (i.e. local council, controlling infrastructure, food aid and other public works) or *union parishad* (a smaller unit, similar to a parish council) gets votes according to a range of factors. Being members of the same lineage might help but does not guarantee support. Reputation, ability to gain resources for the locality or the candidate's political connections are also influential. People often vote strategically, favouring candidates who are members of parties that they believe will win the national elections. In the 2008 election, for example, Hindus living in Karimpur told us that they were going to vote for an independent Hindu candidate, while people in Kakura had largely decided to vote for the Awami League candidate because they had calculated that if the Awami League came into power he would be in a better position to help them.

Despite the relative fluidity of political power in the area we should bear in mind that the 'local leaders', whether formally elected union chairmen or respected patrons taking decisions on traditional *shalish* (village-level councils, where disputes are settled, marriages approved and so on) are invariably drawn from the wealthiest and/or highest status groups. The poor are not, and have never been, represented at any level. As a Unocal-commissioned report on community relations in Duniyapur points out, their voices aren't heard and no-one speaks on their behalf (Reyes and Begum, 2005: 12). Rather than attempt to change this, or 'empower' the poor, as the company claims, the new structures instituted by Chevron via their village development organisations (VDOs) have done little to increase political representation among the poor, building instead upon pre-existing hierarchies with a romanticised vision of the relationship between 'local leaders' who are expected to speak for 'the community', including the landless and the Hindu minority.

When Unocal embarked on developing the Bibiyana Gas Field in 2004–5, the company was immediately embroiled in the deeply politicised and contentious stuff of everyday power struggles, at both local and national levels.[5] At that time the BNP was in power nationally and locally. For the government the Bibiyana development was a prestige project, which it wanted completed as soon as possible. Unocal was therefore working to a strict timetable, with the objective of inaugurating the plant in 2007. Meanwhile the Awami League supported opposition to Unocal's activities both locally and in the national resistance campaign, a strategy that was to change as soon as the tables were turned and they were in power after the 2008 elections. I shall describe these processes in more detail later.

In Duniyapur the most influential leader in 2005 was Joful Haque, the chairman of the *union parishad*. Joful was a BNP member, with a long history of local leadership. While the other villages also had union and *upazila* representatives, other men had more informal leadership roles. Samsun Khan, for example, told us that his high social status, saintly ancestry and family honour had contributed to his role as a leader in Karimpur, though he was not involved in the formal politics of the *union parishad*. Samsun Khan was soon to become one of the largest land losers: his property is directly opposite the plant; nearly all of his fields were forcibly acquired by the government. While other leaders, who did not lose land, would eventually enter into negotiations with Unocal/Chevron, Samsun Khan has remained one of the fiercest opponents of the plant. It should be noted that his continuing anti-Chevron stance is rumoured to arise partly from the activities of his enemies, who have blocked his involvement in subsequent community engagement activities, thus preventing him from forging more positive relations with the company.

The early days of the development of the gas reserves and the processes of land acquisition involved initially met with united opposition. When they were informed of the derisory price that the government intended to pay for their land, people were swiftly mobilised against the operation, presenting a united front between and within the affected villages. The Reyes and Begum report notes the possibility that even in the North Pad at Dighalbak, where operations had taken place smoothly since the late 1990s, people might unite with the communities of the South Pad against Unocal and repeat similar demands in the form of the rapidly proliferating Demand Realisation Committees (2005: 19).

Recounting this time, Samsun Khan tells of a meeting of over 2,000 people at his *bari*. He and five others formed a committee in order to put their demands to Unocal, and to organise the demonstrations. The committee was led by Abdul Ullah, an individual 'without lineage status' (in the words of one informant) who was quickly making a name for himself. Joful Haque was also prominent in the protest movement. As another leader, Russell Saiyed recounts:

We did many things at the outset: movements, protests, demonstrations. We stopped Chevron's vehicles. The DC promised us he'd meet our demands but nothing happened. If he'd wanted, he could have done a lot to help us. The local UP [*union parishad*] Chairman and members also participated in helping us formulate the demands ... (Interview notes, 2008)

Samsun Khan continues:

We started to protest alongside Joful Haque. The protest movement lasted about six months, from January to May 2005. We stopped government officials and Chevron's people from entering the villages; we stopped their vehicles by building a barricade. We lay down on the roads and went on hunger strike. (Interview notes, 2008)

With community relations at an all-time low and construction of the gas field obstructed by angry and united villagers, Unocal acted swiftly to reduce the conflict. According to the accounts of Chevron officials today,[6] the then Unocal President became directly involved in negotiations to increase the compensation rate; later they would be advised by Reyes and Begum (2005) that their employees might smooth things over via 'cultural awareness training', including lessons in how to make eye contact with the locals, waving at children and not driving too fast.

The government was less subtle in its approach. Armed police escorts were provided for company and government officials, and violence threatened. In one of his visits to the area, for example, the District Commissioner, who was accompanied by armed guards, reminded local people that in similar situations in Bangladesh, troops had been called in and publicly threatened to have the leaders arrested (Reyes and Begum, 2005). Today, people talk darkly of the beatings and arrests that took place during this period. Whether or not these rumours can be verified is beside the point, as well as beyond our abilities as a researcher. Rather, they should be read as contemporary critiques of the powerlessness that ordinary people experience in the face of state might. For example, many of the poorest people's accounts of how their lives have changed since the gas field's construction end in comments such as 'What can you do? If you say anything, you will get a beating' (Fieldnotes, 2009). As Stuart Kirsch shows in his discussion of West Papuan rumours of state-sponsored brutality, accounts of violence render the unseen tangible via language, giving people a means to express their fears and concerns; the resulting narratives are not only a reaction to terror, but can have the negative effect of amplifying it (Kirsch, 2002).

Within Bangladesh, these comments and the fear they express need to be set in the context of sustained human rights abuses by the police and special forces such as the infamous Rapid Action Battalion, plus the high incidence of death 'in cross fire'.[7] In the first five months of 2009 alone, for example, the human rights organisation Odhikar reported that 29 people had been 'extra-judicially killed' by the police and security forces. Odhikar also reported that, in 2008, 149 people were killed by security forces (Home Office, 2009). Meanwhile the U.S. Department of State report says that:

> Although the constitution prohibits torture and cruel, inhuman, or degrading punishment, security forces, including the RAB, military, and police, frequently employed severe physical and psychological abuse during arrests and interrogations. According to human rights organizations, the use of such techniques increased in 2007 after the interim government declared the state of emergency ... Abuse consisted of threats, beatings, and the use of electric shock. According to human rights organizations, security forces tortured 12 people to death. The government rarely charged, convicted, or punished those responsible, and a climate of impunity allowed such abuses by the RAB, police, and military to continue. (2008: 2b, section 1c)

If the state's solution to the 2005 Duniyapur activism was the tried and tested method of violent force (threatened and/or actual), the position of Unocal was less straightforward. While needing to avoid the financial and political costs of failing to complete construction on time, the company did not wish to be associated with the dirty stuff of everyday governance in Bangladesh, for this could damage both their local and their global reputation. For example, while the Reyes and Begum report cautions that UBL (later Unocal) should 'Ensure that company related vehicles and other infrastructure are not used to commit human rights abuses' (2005: 24), the rationale appears to be that this might damage the company's reputation rather than human rights abuses in the name of resource extraction being a bad thing *per se*. As the authors continue:

the company reputation is directly linked to the reputation of the user, or how the vehicles are used. For example, several companies currently face court cases [in the criminal court] because 'their' vehicles were used by the police or army to commit human rights abuses ... (2005: 24)

While clearly sensitive to the realpolitik within Duniyapur, and in other sections advising that the company should not be associated with forcible land acquisitions, this report is a fascinating example of the way in which consultancies commissioned by oil companies render political problems technical, with each section ending in a list of recommendations and 'dos' and 'don'ts'. For example:

Do: be polite but firm, 'soft on the people, hard on the issue'. Explain your position, show compassion and understanding (which is different from agreeing) for the grievances expressed. (Reyes and Begum, 2005: 28)

As Unocal was negotiating an increase in rates of land compensation and entering into discussions with the Demand Realisation Committees, the government was taking matters into its own hands. In another story I was told how under the direction of the government one of the local activists/leaders was taken in the night by the Rapid Action Battalion to their base in Habiganj, thus compromising attempts by Unocal to build 'community relations'.[8]

Just as multinationals cannot necessarily control the governments in the countries where they work,[9] nor are all their employees necessarily working towards the same agenda. Community relations staff may, for example, have particular aims and objectives or views of 'the community' that are not necessarily shared by their colleagues working in security. In another section of the Reyes and Begum report, a 'senior UBL staff member' is quoted as saying: 'Unocal is really the David here and the people are Goliath. If they stand up and demand something in protest they have all the power' (2005: 8). While from the standpoint of local people such a view of power relations verges on the ludicrous, it is worth noting the potential threat that local activism was deemed to pose during this period.[10]

Although I have no evidence that Unocal condoned the use of violence against the activists, it should be noted that they accepted the use of police escorts for their visits to the area and provided accommodation for a specially assigned police force, a tactic that indicates the prioritising of 'security' over human rights considerations. As the Reyes and Begum report states:

> UBL [Unocal] has agreed to provide barracks, located 7 km from the site, and a vehicle for a special police contingent assigned to the area. While such support is not unusual, there is always a risk that, in the event of the use of force, the company will be associated with any abuses. For example, threats of violence have already been applied. *In addition, one high ranking official told us there is no space in the land acquisition process for human rights considerations*, and UBL admits to 'having no control over the police' ... (2005: 23, emphasis mine)

If state threats of violence were risky for Unocal's reputation, other government tactics also had hidden costs for the company. Many of the accounts we collected indicate that pressure was put on *union parishad*-level BNP leaders to stop their opposition to the plant by high-ranking BNP members. As Reyes and Begum report: 'people are aware that pressure was applied by BNP government officials at very high levels to the local BNP leader who organised the community protests. The resulting perception is that UBL is aligned to the ruling party' (2005: 6).

Meanwhile, Samsun Khan, the leader who stood to lose the most from the land acquisition and who was least likely to back down, was, according to his account, approached by the Awami League and offered support to continue his opposition. This strategy, of siding with activists fighting the presence of mining multinationals by the opposition, followed by support for those very multinationals once the opposition party is in government has been followed by both the Awami League and the BNP, whose covert support for the national resistance campaign, the National Committee, seems to depend upon whether or not they are in government. For example, in another story, the reputed Marxist intellectual and activist Nur Mohammad recounted how during the BNP's government Sheikh Hasina and the Awami League had supported activism against multinationals by the National Committee. When the Awami League came into power in early 2009, however, its position was reversed. During a demonstration against the newly elected Awami League government's relationship with multinationals in September 2009, Anu Muhammed was badly beaten by the police and ended up in hospital, only to be visited by both a newly supportive Khaleda Zia, of the BNP, and a somewhat embarrassed Sheikh Hasina, though presumably not at the same time.[11]

Back in 2005, alongside the political pressure from the BNP came the news that after Unocal's intervention the rate of land compensation had been increased. It was at this stage that the leaders, principally Joful Haque and Abdul Ullah began to negotiate with the company who were now promising a range of community engagement gifts. As those leaders, now effectively co-opted by the company, withdrew their support for the protest movement, they started to persuade others to stop too. As Samsun Khan explains:

Then finally Chevron's officials offered to negotiate. They gave us some promises, but now we can see that these were just bullshit. They promised that gas would be provided to the houses, young men would get jobs, electricity would be available: no more darkness. As it turned out, we didn't get anything. Rather, we've been turned into criminals ... I have no words to say about Chevron. The day they grabbed my land, I lost my words.

RISKY RESOURCES: RUMOUR AND DIVISION POST-2005

While Unocal/Chevron was anxiously seeking community compliance to its operations, the 'community leaders' it was negotiating with were risking their reputations in the hope that, via their connection to the company, they would gain access to a range of resources and political advantages. Whether these gains were personal or for the good of their communities depends largely on who is telling the story. Whatever the truth, there can be little doubt that the stakes were high. Chevron was perceived as having the potential to bring large-scale benefits to the area via jobs, hospitals, schools and roads, and those at the heart of the negotiations would clearly gain in status and esteem, not to say the moral virtue of having contributed to the development of their locality. Moreover, there were contracts to be gained for the supply of labour, building materials and so on, adding not only to the personal wealth of the contractor, but also his reputation as a patron.

Yet while expectations of the potential rewards were high, many people were to be disappointed. Not only did the supply of jobs quickly dry up once the construction of the gas plant was completed, but the resources that many people believed to have been promised were far smaller than they had hoped: not a 200-bed hospital, but satellite clinics; not a school, but scholarships; not industrial development and company employment, but the Alternative Livelihoods Programme. In their narratives, leaders who had backed away from confrontation and were now negotiating with Chevron on the shape and size of the company's community engagement gift were placed in an impossible position, for they simply could not deliver what local people expected. These included 'public goods' such as the hoped-for hospitals, power plants and so on, as well as private goods, gained through patronage. As Abdul Miah explains:

> Of all the demands we made to Chevron, we achieved about 5 percent. Our fellow villagers started insulting us because we hadn't achieved their demands. They became very suspicious, saying that we'd been 'bought' by Chevron and were no longer looking out for their interests. I suppose the reason for these suspicions is that I'm working as a contractor for Chevron, so people think I'm their man, not a man of the people. Through my tree planting project I can hire a few women labourers, but not much more, so everyone's dissatisfied with me. Their demands are so high, but I can't recruit 100 people, only 15 ... (Interview notes, 2009)

The backlash seems to have been experienced most severely by Joful Haque, whose attempts to make connections, gain and dispense patronage and seek community engagement gifts from Chevron have led him into a troublesome terrain, for as local accounts of realpolitik surrounding the gas field show, local politicians who seek connections with American oil companies have much to gain, but also a great deal to lose, given their ambivalent, slippery yet invariably powerful role in the local imaginary.

During my 1980s fieldwork Joful was the *union parishad* chairman. A well-connected member of one of the most powerful lineages in the area, with its far-reaching genealogy of lascars, landowners and *Londoni* links, he was at the centre of local affairs. Unlike many local politicians he had a reputation for honesty and political commitment, working to improve the lot of the poor rather than lining his own pockets. The lot of politicians ebbs and flows, according to which party is in government, and by the turn of the century, Joful was no longer an elected union member, but still garnered much local respect, sitting on the local *shalish* (informal decision-making body for a village or number of villages) and so on. When I visited Nadampur in 2006 to find the plant in the early stages of construction I was told that he was busy negotiating the prices of land compensation with Unocal and doing everything he could to help people whose land was to be lost.

By the start of our fieldwork in 2008 the story had changed dramatically. At that time Joful was involved in building the Shining Sun clinic on the side of the Nadampur/Syedpur road, and was one of the main 'leaders' that Chevron was working with. Aside from his family, however, no-one had a good word to say about him. Even within his own lineage, people mumbled to me that he had 'done nothing' for local people, just used his connections with Chevron to benefit himself with contracts, bribes and fat commissions. Not surprisingly, those with the most tenuous connections, geographically as well as socially, were the most critical. Why was the clinic so close to Nadampur, rather than Firizpur or Karimpur? And why was so much given to Nadampur's High School? In the UK rumours were also rife. *Some* local leaders had grown wealthy from their connections to Chevron, we were told; these people had 'sold out', interested only in individual material gain.

It is neither appropriate nor possible for me to comment on the veracity of these complaints and rumours. Rather, we should take these stories as just that: rumours, circulated in order to contest and undermine the power of a local man with strong connections to Chevron. Having said this, during my many visits to the village I never saw any evidence of the new-found wealth of Joful and his family. They are not by any means the richest people in the area, living in a modest, 1970s house, with bamboo partition walls and earth floors. The house that Joful's *Londoni* father started to build in the early 1990s was never completed; since his death, only its foundations remain. Moreover, we were told by his friends that they had lent him money so that he could pay for his son's education: hardly the actions of a man grown wealthy through the largesse and back-handers of Chevron. Yet the rumours and anger persists. During the local elections at the end of 2009, he had gained so little support for his candidacy that he was forced to withdraw

As the rumours of Joful's dubious relationship with Chevron indicate, while functioning within a context wherein access to resources largely comes via personal connections, people simultaneously hold ideals of good leadership, in which governance is transparent and there are no personal gains made. As Daniel Jordan Smith has observed in Nigeria, within the political economy of patronage, accusations of corruption made by ordinary people coexist with their own expectations of benefits from patrons, so that: 'to be without a patron is to be without access to resources, but to be a patron is to be under great pressure to accumulate and share wealth, including through corruption' (2007: 13).

In Bangladesh, as in Nigeria, the moralities of patronage/ corruption are highly complex. While patrons are expected to provide support and favours for those with whom they are socially connected, if they either fail to distribute their personal benefits, or when practices seen in other contexts as benign patronage take place in the more formal terrain of state/corporate relations, allegations of corruption follow.

Perhaps this moral separation between public and private domains is why a particular character figures large in many of the rumours of corruption that we heard in Duniyapur and the UK: the Habiganj *tashildar* (i.e. land registration official and thus in the public domain), a man who is said to have made a fortune from the land acquisition process, taking large bribes (*baksheesh*) with every transaction. Indeed, the complaint that bribes had to be paid in order to gain land compensation ran through nearly every account we heard, souring Chevron's claim that 97 percent of landowners were compensated without difficulty.

One reason for these discordant accounts could be that a considerable amount of the land taken for the gas field was either disputed or not officially documented. As we have seen, this was particularly the case in Karimpur, where land passed from Hindu families leaving for India or Sri Mongal to Muslim settlers from Nadampur. Officially classified as 'enemy property', Hindu land was acquired by the new owners in oral rather than written contracts. In order to 'process' these claims, people told us, they had to pay 10–15 percent of their compensation money to the *tashildar*, who demanded payment for the extra work involved in processing claims on undocumented land. Proof of his new-found wealth was to be found on the man's fingers, the gossip went, where he wore no less than eight gold rings. With no personal links in the area this man is not in the role of patron, but is instead a state functionary. He thus embodies everything that is wrong and rotten about local governance, a thorn to prick the corporate bubble of efficient and fair compensation.

These rumours were repeated to us in Britain as well as Duniyapur for gossip and information flows thickly in transnational communities. As we heard during a focus group discussion in Burnley:

Participant 1: I know some people who had to pay 10 or 15 percent as a bribe to land officials and other things ... I've met

that person who was dealing with these things ... he had eight rings on his fingers.
Participant 2: Yes, I've seen him! (laughs). (Interview notes, 2009)

During the same discussion, the rumours that particular local leaders had profited from their relationship with Chevron which we heard in Duniyapur were repeated. Again, the problem seems to be not so much that money was made, but that it was made by people in official roles, whose responsibility was to be transparent and publicly minded. While this gossip is based in local knowledge and history (e.g. 'I knew him very well ... twenty years ago he wasn't a rich man, but he is now'), our British informants were also keen to contextualise individual corruption within the wider system, with one man commenting:

> I can't personally blame him [the leader under discussion]. I would probably do the same, given the condition that Bangladeshi people in that society find themselves. Where it becomes, I suppose, unethical, is where you have an opportunity – you can give employment – but you chose not to, and you fiddle other people, and you're living at their expense. (Interview notes, 19 May 2009)

Here, the criticism is not that money flowed from Chevron to individuals, but that, as a patron, the person under discussion failed in his duty to redistribute at least some of the benefits to his clients. We also see in this story how Chevron's attempts to deal fairly with local people have been kyboshed by the state and its functionaries.

Whether or not they profited from their dealings with Chevron, the problem for Joful Haque and Abdul Miah seems to be less that they gained via their connections and more that they were not able to distribute the gains to the wider community: after all, other people became 'contractors', and have not been exposed to such public criticism. Interestingly, wider complaints concerning the role of Chevron in the area seem to be subsumed by personalised complaints against these particular individuals, who have come to embody all the disappointments and frustrations that people experienced. In a focus group discussion in Karimpur, for example we heard the following:

> Nowadays no-one's interested in protesting against Chevron. Who will do it? No-one has the courage. Before, we were united

and we acted together. Now our leaders have made a pact with Chevron and don't pay us any attention. What would we gain by starting a movement against Chevron? They would take out a case against us ... we once heard that: 'Gas won't flow, but blood will,' but now nobody says anything. The leaders of the movement didn't listen to us and now they've appropriated all the benefits. They are rewarded by becoming contractors but they don't hire local labourers. If we say anything we'll be thrown into jail. (Fieldnotes, 2008)

Similar comments were made in Kakura:

What can we say about our local leaders? They are guilty ones ... all have appropriated the benefits and are filling their stomachs, why would they think about us? Joful Haque has destroyed our fate, otherwise Chevron and FIVDB would do something for us. The local leaders threatened us, saying that if we got involved in a movement against the gas field we'd be caught, so that's why we're not mobilising ... one of the protesters has a court case against him which still hasn't been solved. We've been scared off, so we don't protest. We went to Joful Haque to get him to help us but he was really rude and forced us to leave. He was our chairman then, he shouldn't have done that. He also had a case filed against him, but got out of it due to his links with the ruling BNP party. (Fieldnotes, 2008)

As this last quote shows, people (in this case, the landless inhabitants of Kakura) believe strongly in the ideal of democratic politics and social justice (a chairman shouldn't be rude and force people with valid complaints to leave), yet have no legitimate avenues of complaint against leaders who fail to live up to the standards of democratic representation and feel unable to take action without the support of leaders/patrons. Rumours of corruption thus both frame complaints against specific individual leaders and can also be read as wider commentaries on the powerlessness of the poor, who are not politically represented and are under constant threat of state-sponsored violence.

Whatever the truth, since the 2005 protest there can be little doubt that the balance of power has shifted considerably in Duniyapur though not in the ways one might expect. Joful Haque, so closely connected to Chevron and thus, in theory, so well placed as a distributor of corporate resources, has become deeply unpopular as a result of what, in retrospect, appears to be a risky strategy of compliance. Meanwhile, the reputation of Samsun Khan is intact but he no longer has a base in Karimpur. As he explains:

> Chevron have looted our land but our protests died due to these two leaders [i.e. Joful Haque and Abdul Miah]. First they mobilised us against Chevron, then they made a secret pact and got the benefits ... due to my conflict with Chevron I became a target both for Chevron and these leaders. They prevented me from claiming my compensation and a number of cases have been filed against me. I had to get out of the village and go to live in Sylhet Town. ... I now feel insecure in Karimpur. (Interview notes, 2008)

For both leaders, their high-risk strategies in their relationships with Chevron: compliance and co-option for Joful Haque, and direct action and opposition for Samsun Khan have led not to profitable alliances and connection, but rupture and disconnection.

Meanwhile the new structures put in place to oversee the distribution of Chevron's community development resources have both accentuated and changed pre-existing divisions, giving a select group of 'local leaders' limited resources for distribution to the poor and needy while excluding others. By doing this Chevron neatly side-steps direct involvement in the messy business of village politics and power relations, leaving it to the 'local leaders' (or 'partners') with whom they have developed cordial relations to collate lists of recipients and distribute project resources accordingly. Once again technical solutions to political problems take place under a romanticised rubric of 'partnership', while realpolitik and the structural causes of poverty are conveniently ignored. Within this context, Robins' observations concerning the legacy of the East India Company are pertinent: 'For many Indians – particularly in Bengal – the Company's story has two profound morals: first, that multinational companies want not just trade, but power; and second, that division and betrayal among Indians enables foreign rule' (2006: 13).

Meanwhile, within the villages the new resources have led to new bases of patronage, new divisions and new sources of complaint from those who are either not included on the VDO's list of recipients, or who did not get as much as they expected. As many people told us, to gain benefits from the Alternative Livelihoods

Programme, one has to be connected to the leaders sitting on the VDO; membership of the VDOs should be decided by election, they said, not chosen by Chevron. In Karimpur, for example, we were told by a landless man that:

> If you want to get a loan you have to get help from the leaders. Without their recommendations the loans aren't ensured. What can I tell you about these leaders? Local politics has become very bad. This kind of politics isn't even found in Dhaka! Whoever protests will immediately be silenced ... Once you've become a leader no-one can talk against you ... who will talk on behalf of labourers? You'll be threatened if you speak out. (Fieldnotes, 2009)

As these and the other quotes from our interviews indicate, generalised complaints about people's exclusion from the resources provided by Chevron, and indeed their place in the global pecking order, tend to be transposed onto commentaries of the qualities of individual leaders. Experiences and feelings of powerlessness, whether in the face of the state or multinational companies, are glossed under dark references to 'beatings' and 'threats' which cohere to people's intimate knowledge of the history of the gas plant and activism against it. Critiques of the state and the presence of multinationals are thus made via local knowledge of actual individuals and events.

In the next section, where I turn to the narratives of national campaigners, we see the opposite process, where critiques are based in an ideological understanding of the relationship between state, society and neoliberal capitalism, the terrain is political economy and the history referred to is national rather than local. In comparison with the poetics of village narrators who speak eloquently of 'losing their words' and having their 'hearts consumed by the fire', national campaigners use the language of nationalism and global exploitation, while drawing upon their detailed, though contested, knowledge of economics. The passion is equally strong, for the core of the story remains the same: the loss of resources to outsiders, the corruption of those in power and the failure of modernity to bring the promised benefits of social justice and economic compensation.

NATIONAL ACTIVISM: WORLD SYSTEMS, ECONOMICS AND CONTESTED INFORMATION

The eastern region of the country is rich in gas, while the northern region is rich in coal resources. The Bay of Bengal in the south is resourceful in gas, oil and many other minerals. The most prospective gas fields in the eastern region are under the grip and control of multinational companies. Though the maritime region in the Bay of Bengal has immense potential for oil, gas and other mineral resources, the maritime boundary of Bangladesh is still undemarcated because of gross negligence on the part of past governments ... The very sovereignty and national security is under threat as the uncertainty surrounding the maritime boundary persists ... The maritime area has been divided into 28 blocks and bidding invited by the preceding interim government on the basis of a model production sharing contract which frustrates the peoples' interests ... Fortunately the interim government failed to complete its plan because of stiff opposition from the people. However, the conspiracy of the international plunderers continues unabated (Shaheedullah and Muhammed, 2009).

Like the narratives of resistance to and compliance with the gas field that we heard in Duniyapur and Britain, the accounts, writings and narrations of national-level activists whom we interviewed in Dhaka and London involve closely argued analyses of power relations and the struggle over resources, which, rather than being local, are national or global in character. Rather than involving rumours concerning particular individuals, the critiques are systemic, either based in the author's analysis of global political economy, or claims of global conspiracies in which multinationals work with corrupt governments and Western aid agencies to plunder Third World countries. Just as the accounts of the dispossessed in Duniyapur unsettle corporate accounts of successful community engagement and partnership, national-level protest and the acute political critiques that it produces continue to undermine the self-representations of multinational mining companies as benign forces for neoliberal development in the South.

As the above quote indicates, accusations of plots between multinationals and corrupt government officials figure large in many of the accounts and protests. Such theories, which connect events and relationships into an overarching system, are, West and Sanders argue, an inevitable part of modernity, flourishing alongside the ideals of good governance, transparency and rationalism. As they note: 'The depth of local wells of conspiracy ideas is as great, it would seem, as the breadth of global transparency claims' (West and Sanders, 2003: 12). Conspiracy theories can thus be read as 'ideological formations' which indicate how people experience power as fragmented and contradictory (2003: 15). A common example of such a theory, which I have heard recounted in the homes of NGO professionals and academics in Dhaka, Bengali restaurant owners in Britain and villagers in Duniyapur, and indeed, is repeated across the Muslim world, is that 9/11 was a Jewish plot, enacted to bring the wrath of America against Islam, a 'proven fact' which has apparently been suppressed by the hegemonic media in the West yet is available for all to read about on the web (Interview notes, Burnley, May 2009).

In the National Committee activists' conspiracy theories the narrative is organised around rationalist tropes of political economy, and regional and global history, and involve careful academic analysis of and contestations over the financial details of Production Share Contracts, tax breaks and energy sales and consumption. As such they use different language and narrative techniques from village accounts, but like the latter, involve both critique of the existing political order, and the ideal of a world order in which democratically elected politicians are answerable to citizens, government information is made public and resources nationally managed, a utopia remarkably similar to that posited by Western donors in Bangladesh. I shall return to the use of different types of knowledge in political struggles later in the chapter. For now, let us turn to the history of anti-multinational/mining activism in Bangladesh, where, as we shall see, the tropes of imperialist conspiracy figure large.

While mainstream political parties in Bangladesh tend to be dominated by factionalism and struggles over resources, radical or alternative political activism has developed over the country's short history from a strong ideological base in Marxism and links to the Soviet or Chinese communist parties in the 1970s to 'single-issue' politics, which use particular issues to generate a wider critique of international relations and Bangladesh's place in the global economy. In 2008–9, the main issues around which organised activism and opposition coalesced were the exploitation of the country's gas and coal resources by multinationals and the fate of Chittagong Port, which was being developed as a Free Trade Zone for foreign investors with input from the World Bank and other donors. The fate of Chittagong Port has been a bone of contention for a while; in 1999 the government's attempt to lease it to an American company for 199 years met with such opposition that the company was forced to withdraw.[12] It was the issue of gas and coal resources, however, that dominated the national agenda during our research, and which had led to the formation of the National Committee in 1998 by Marxist intellectuals such as Anu Muhammed, a Professor of Economics at Jahangirnagar University and Nur Mohammad, who had long led radical leftist opposition within the country.

Nationalism is an important aspect of much political activism in Bangladesh, which is hardly surprising, given the country's history of colonisation and its relatively recent struggle for independence. Accusations of aggressive foreign imperialism are emotive themes, with activists decrying the multinationals presence and the continued exploitation of Bangladeshi resources by foreigners; in this context comparisons with the East India Company are often made, and for good reason (Robins, 2006). Another presence viewed with huge suspicion is India, which is often represented as a dominating imperialist force which must be resisted in order that Bangladeshi sovereignty can be retained. For example, agitation over Indian management of upstream waterways culminated in the 'Long March' to Chilmari in 2005, involving calls for the ending of the Indian River-Link Project which threatened to damage Bangladeshi rivers and was termed a 'weapon of mass destruction' by the leadership of the march.[13] Similarly, one of the main demands of the National Committee is that Bangladesh's sea borders with India and Burma be properly demarcated.[14]

The role of extractive multinationals came under the national spotlight in 1997, after the blow-out at the Magurcchara Gas Field in Sylhet, which at the time was operated by Occidental and is now operated by Chevron. Compensation for this, plus that for the blow-out at Tengratila, operated by the Canadian company Niko, has never been received by the Bangladeshi government, an issue that became the first rallying cry for the newly formed National Committee in 1998. Since then, there has been a steady flow of campaign issues, all involving the exploitation of Bangladesh's resources by foreign mining companies and, vitally, the corruption of Bangladeshi state officials in their negotiations with these companies. The details of contracts and deals with the government and foreign interests are closely attended to: in this respect the main thrust of much national-level protest, like the critiques of villagers in Kakura and Karimpur, is that Bangladesh is being 'sold out' by corrupt leaders, leading to the rallying cry: *Amar desher tel gas amar deher rakta!* (Gas and oil are the life blood of our country, and we must protect them!).[15]

In Duniyapur, local people were joined in their protests by the National Committee and their (then) allies in the Awami League and other parties, plus their contacts at Shah Jalal University in Sylhet. While local concerns were centred on issues of land compensation, for the national campaigners the protest involved rumours that the gas would be exported to India via a pipeline that Unocal would construct.[16] As Nur Mohammad explains later in this chapter, the actual extent of the gas reserves was also disputed, with Petrobangla and Unocal accused of over-exploiting and exhausting the field. A 'Long March' had been held a decade earlier concerning Sylhet's gas reserves, with participants marching from Dhaka to Sylhet.[17] Yet although for a while in 2005 Duniyapur became the focus of resistance, its role was soon usurped by momentous events on the other side of the country, in Dinajpur.

To date, it is plans for an open coal mine in Phulbari, in the north-eastern district of Dinajpur, to be developed and operated by the British-based company GCM Resources/Asia Energy,[18] that has captured most public attention, in Bangladesh and beyond. Like all facts and figures in the charged arena of Bangladeshi mining, estimates of the number of people to be displaced by this project vary from 40,000 to 500,000. Beyond the loss of homes and livelihoods, protest has focused on the environmental damage that would be caused to an area of highly fertile agricultural land. Opposition peaked in August 2006, when a demonstration involving thousands of people was fired on by the police, leaving three protesters dead and many more injured. The strength of opposition to the plan eventually led to the then BNP government withdrawing from their negotiations with Asia Energy. Using the language of national defence and imperial conspiracy, S.M. Shaheedullah and Anu Muhammed, the convenor and secretary of the National Committee respectively, wrote in 2009:

A devastating project in the shape of Phulbari coalmine to guarantee plunder of coal resources in the northern region by a multinational company was pursued many years but this project has been foiled by the life and death struggle of the people. This very prospective coalfield was planned to be handed over to Asia Energy ... a multinational company. True, this sinister move has been quashed by the people's resistance, but the conspiracy lingers on ... So far this agreement [The Phulbari Agreement, which forced the government to cancel the deal with Asia Energy] has not yet been fully implemented. As a result, Asia Energy, which was due to be driven out of the country, has been engaged in nefarious activities involving corruption and crime, home and abroad (Shaheedullah and Muhammed, 2009).

While Asia Energy continues to lobby the new Awami League government, led by a severely compromised Sheikh Hasina, who in opposition in 2006 supported the Phulbari resistance, the ability of 'people power' to prevent what would have been a major deal for the government, including a large power plant which would have produced significant amounts of electricity for the power-starved domestic market, is noteworthy. In this instance, large-scale public protest within Phulbari united with an organised network of seasoned campaigners and intellectuals via the National Committee, which was, in turn, supported by international lobbying organisations such as the UK-based Mines and Communities Network.

Ensuring that no future deals are made with Asia Energy at Phulbari has joined a list of 'demands' that were being circulated by the National Committee at the time we were doing our research, as explained to us during interviews, and set out in blogs, a Facebook page,[19] newspaper articles and so on, while activism has tended to follow the Bangladeshi method of demonstrations, road blockades, marches and *hartals* (strikes) sometimes in alliance with unions and other left leaning organisations. The format of national-level protest is thus similar to that described to us in Duniyapur, with carefully formulated demands, stoppages and demonstrations. And though the detail of the demands is different, involving national rather than local sovereignty, proprietorship of natural resources by civil society, compensation of millions of dollars paid to the government by multinationals and the trials of politicians accused of taking a cut of profits, at heart the concerns are the same: corruption, public access to information, equitable and just contracts, and the protection of natural resources, which should be used for national development rather than foreign profit.[20] Secrecy, rumour, information and disinformation also play a major role in both local and national protest.

LOCAL, NATIONAL AND TRANSNATIONAL LINKS

So far my descriptions of protest against Unocal/Chevron in Duniyapur and the activism and protests organised by the National Committee have treated both as separate, making a neat division between local, national and global. In reality such divisions are blurred or become meaningful only in certain contexts. That villagers in Duniyapur are confined to the 'local' is clearly untrue: as we have already seen, not only are many people highly mobile, but knowledge of events and people flows thick and fast between communities in Britain and *Londoni* families in Bangladesh. While non-migrant villagers may have less experience of different places, with few people travelling much further than Habiganj or Sylhet Town and women often remaining in the locality for many years without travelling beyond it, as citizens of Bangladesh, people take an interest in national and global politics, and are able to influence them via national elections. Just as campaigners in the National Committee are experienced users of the web, using it to put forward their views and publicise their activities on the global arena, so are (younger) British Bengalis with links to Duniyapur adept at blogging and accessing information over cyberspace.

Distinctions should however be made between the different locales of protest. As described above, the concerns and actions of the National Committee have a particularly Bangladeshi flavour: national sovereignty rather than global warming is the rallying cry against coal mining or gas extraction, and while the internet is used to publicise issues and concerns, activism has tended to adhere to traditional Bengali protest methods such as calling *hartals* and 'Long Marches'. This does not mean that leaders have not actively sought international support over particular issues. For example, Anu Muhammed told us that they had made links with international anti-globalisation and anti-mining organisations while he had been lobbying against the Asian Development Bank in Kyoto in 2007, as well as during the Phulbari campaign.

The National Committee is also supported by its transnational members in the UK, some of whom move regularly between the two countries. Indeed, British Bengalis continue to play an important role in Bangladeshi politics. Expatriates in Britain helped fund the Independence movement, for example, and today there remains a strong will within 'the community' to play a role in the economic development of Bangladesh. In their interviews, British-based activists and journalists stressed their input into the creation of the nation-state of Bangladesh. As one journalist and community activist said of the role of *Londonis*:

> We've got a history and we've got proof that we've saved this country and we have created this country [i.e. Bangladesh] ... we can develop a part of our country if we are confident enough. If the government is willing and they give us a chance. (Interview notes, 5 March 2010)

Yet it would be a mistake to assume that location in Britain *per se* determines the way that critiques and concerns are framed. Our interviewees at two Bengali-language newspapers in East London, all of whom were linked to the National Committee and were middle-class professionals, discussed the same concerns and made the same critiques as Anu Muhammed and Nur Mohammad in Dhaka, while focus groups of men with familial ties in Duniyapur who lived in Burnley and north London, drew upon similar issues and complaints as their relatives in Duniyapur. Global imperialism and government corruption *were* discussed, but largely by younger men who had been educated in Britain, while local issues of land compensation and the corruption of individual leaders were the subject of complaint by those who had arrived in Britain as adults.

The fusion of national protest with local resistance in Duniyapur was short lived. While in Phulbari local protesters were joined by national campaigners in an organised and sustained campaign, and after the killing of demonstrators in 2006 the movement eventually broke into the global space of international news and international campaigning organisations, our research found little evidence that, beyond temporary alliances between individual leaders and the National Committee, there has been much in the way of sustained relationships between the groups. Indeed, while corruption, dispossession and the struggle over resources have been the dominant concerns of both parties, the needs of the poor are little attended to by the National Committee, who speak of 'the people', but are largely concerned with macro- rather than micro-political economies. Likewise our informants in Duniyapur shared the nationalist sentiments of the National Committee, yet utilised the notion of sovereignty not in the national context, but in terms of the gas being under 'their' fields and 'their' land.

CONTESTED KNOWLEDGE, INFORMATION AND SECRECY

As I discovered when I naively bore our list of 'research findings' to Karimpur and Kakura, no form of information or type of knowledge is neutral in the fraught arena of gas extraction in Bangladesh; however and wherever it is located, information and knowledge are political. Combined with this, different ways of knowing are hierarchically arranged and associated with different types of power, from CSR's development discourse and its attendant forms of knowledge, to the localised knowledge of politics, power and kinship relations of the poor. These epistemologies, and the moral orders with which they are associated, are accepted, asserted, undermined or ignored depending on who holds them and who is listening. Rumours are part of this process, functioning to undermine and destabilise the established narratives and knowledges of the powerful.

As we have seen, narratives of protest and resistance to multinational extractive companies in Bangladesh in general and the gas plant in Duniyapur in particular involve the shared concerns of corruption and exploitation, yet are organised around different types of knowing and telling. In Duniyapur, intimate knowledge of local history and specific individuals has tended to frame critiques of Chevron and the government. Stories are personalised and rumours of corruption involve actual people. In contrast, the knowledge of the national-level campaigners, and they way they use it, is very different.

Perhaps the most salient feature of the statements and interviews of National Committee members is their use of facts and figures to counter information put out by the government. In recent years, for example, a series of newspaper articles has argued that at the Bibiyana Gas Field the gas reserves are being over-exploited by Chevron, who, it is claimed, intends to extract as much profit from the gas field as possible before withdrawing. Reports such as the one cited in Chapter 3 (e.g. 'Petrobangla allows Chevron to over exploit gas reserves at Bibiyana')[21] are countered by information published by the government and Chevron concerning their estimates of reserves. Talking of the National Committee's role in countering this 'propaganda', Professor Muhammed argues :

A section of 'hired' consultants, bureaucrats, businessmen, media, U.S. Embassy, Indian High Commission, World Bank and ADB began stipulating Bangladesh is 'floating on gas' and it was 'best time to export gas.' And, if Bangladesh misses the chance, later she might not get handsome price in ever-changing international market. They, in addition, opined that Bangladesh can construct her basic infrastructure including necessary components like education or health sector with the money obtained from gas export. NCPOGMPP [i.e. the National Committee] then had to wage war at two levels. First, we had to theoretically challenge this propaganda by making people aware about the exact situation of real gas reserve scenario of Bangladesh, dynamics of internal use and demand, etc. The IOCs exaggerated that Bangladesh had 100 trillion cubic feet of gas while we had only 12–13 trillion cubic feet of gas reserve in reality ... in last several years the amount has reduced to 7–8 trillion cubic feet of gas reserve for internal use.[22]

Alternative figures counter this version of reality. In 2010, for example, it was announced by Petrobangla and Chevron that reserves at Bibiyana had 'doubled'.[23]

As this indicates, information – continually contested, countered, repeated and repudiated – is central to debates concerning the country's energy resources, figuring large in the countless articles published in national newspapers, blogs and internet news sites. To date, none of this information is made publicly available in Bangladesh, although in 2011 an Information Commission is being set up. And while Chevron is a signatory to the Extractive Industries Transparency Initiative, Bangladesh is not. This means that Chevron do not have to disclose information about its contracts within the country. Within the US, the company will be forced to disclose all information on each of its projects, but only by the end of 2012/early 2013.[24]

Within this context, the only thing one can be certain of is that very few of these 'facts' can ever be verified. Given the lack of transparency of the detail of contracts between the government and multinational corporations, plus the secretive nature of the Bangladeshi state, objectively obtained and impartially verified information concerning projected gas or coal reserves, compensation payments, production share contracts, and so on, is highly elusive and, due to the high levels of mistrust in public or corporate information, were it to be made available, it would probably not be believed anyway. With their academic training in subjects such as economics and political science, many of the members of the National Committee thus enter into a war of words, facts and figures with official or corporate sources. For example, activists in both Dhaka and London told me that the production share contract that Chevron have for the Bibiyana Gas Field is 80:20 (i.e. Chevron takes 80 percent of the profits), while Steve Wilson, the CEO of Chevron told me that the company had a 40 percent share. As Anu Muhammed explained:

> They were all secret contracts and very unequal contracts and very damaging to the national economy because by making an economic calculation you can find that ... when you can purchase a unit of gas from a state-owned company, we have to pay more than 30 times that price from a foreign company. (Interview transcript, 20 September 2009)

In an interview published on the 'Bangladesh Watchdog' website, he further discusses these contracts, using the discourse of economics and national finance to make his point:

> Meantime, our successive governments have signed 12 PSCs with different IOCs in recent years. These PSCs have conferred upon them ownership of around 80 percent of total gas explored and the rest 20 percent lies with our nationalized institutions like BAPEX and Petro-Bangla. These multi-national oil giants deal with or regulate our 12 major gas fields in the Sylhet region. If you look at the atlas of Bangladesh and dissect it into east and west, you would notice that most of the oil fields are located at the eastern side or particularly in Sylhet. Now, the multi-national oil giants earn around 3,000 crore taka from these 12 gas fields. If we could spend just one-tenth of this 3,000 crore take to reshape and strengthen our nationalized oil and gas exploration institutions like BAPEX or Petro-Bangla, we did not need to depend any longer on foreigner consultants and imported machineries! Just imagine that because of irresponsibility and malfunctioning by two multi-national oil & gas companies namely Occidental in Magurchara, Sylhet during 1997 and NAIKO in Tengratila, Sylhet during 2006 ... around 500 billion cubic feet gas were simply burnt out or wasted! Around 87.50 acres of land in Magurchara were damaged with 176.97 crore taka losses in total.[25]

Such contestations, which to an outsider anthropologist unschooled in economics can appear to be almost impenetrably detailed, arise from a governmental culture of secrecy. As Anu Muhammed succinctly put it:

Our demand is to make sure that every contract is open and transparent. It's a people's resource ... people should have the right to know what the government is doing to their resources! (Interview transcript, 20 September 2009)

In London, National Committee members made the same point, arguing that the reason the production share contracts with multinationals were so exploitative to Bangladesh was simple: corruption. PSCs were negotiated 'under the table', I was told, with profits being tucked quickly away in Swiss bank accounts. As one informant put it:

We demand from our government ... what is the contract that you sign? And the government won't disclose it ... what happens is that if someone then leaks it out, they [the government] will say 'No, that is false!' (Interview transcript, 20 September 2009)

Later in the discussion, I was told by another activist:

We only argue on leaked out information, but there's no authenticity to leaked out information. (Interview transcript, 20 September 2009)

Leaks and falsehoods, rumours and accusations: all arise from the politics of secrecy and corruption, and all thrive in the never ending struggle over 'truth', which of course is also a struggle over claims for entitlement. In this context it is not merely knowing that brings power, but, more importantly, persuading other people to 'know' the same thing, for in a context where salient facts are kept secret and little can be proven, narrative persuasion is of vital importance. This is why, as I argue in the next chapter, transparency and freedom of information are so vitally important.

For now, let us return to the analysis of rumour.

INFORMATION AND DISINFORMATION: RUMOUR AS A POLITICAL TOOL

As anthropologists working in a variety of contexts have shown, rumours – whether these be of vampires and cannibals, violent attacks by insurgent forces or treaties taking place on the international stage (Kirsch, 2002; Turner, 2004; West, 2003; White 2000) – can be understood as ways that people make sense of, and talk about their place in an insecure world. Never authored by a single person, they fluctuate, change and take on new meanings that may be understood in different ways by different people, they have a great deal to tell anthropologists and historians eager to comprehend the sense that their informants make of their lives and the contexts in which they live them. To this extent, whether something actually happened or not is irrelevant. As Luise White reminds us, rumours offer us a way of seeing the world as their narrators see it. Rumours of vampires in colonial East Africa, for example, reveal the vulnerability of those that tell them and, unlike witchcraft accusations, which arose from tensions in intimate social relationships, expressed new relationships with colonial outsiders. Rather than dismissing rumours, or other stories, as 'incorrect', White argues, hearsay is itself a social fact, for: 'true and false are historical and cultural constructions. They are not absolutes, but the product of lived experience, of thought and reflection, of hard evidence' (White, 2000: 30).

In the next chapter I shall turn to rumours and stories that circulate concerning the safety of the gas field, arguing that the terror of accidental and violent disconnection expressed in these stories can be understood, in part, as reflecting people's despair at their disconnection from the benefits of neoliberal development and their alienation from corporate and state functionaries. Now, however, I want to take a step away from the analysis of rumour as allegory to ask a different question: not 'What do rumours *mean?*', but instead: 'What do rumours *do?*'

One answer might be that, as suggested earlier in this chapter, rumours can be interpreted as 'weapons of the weak', a way of unsettling hegemonic truths or slyly attacking and undermining the powerful (Scott, 1985). There is some evidence of this in Duniyapur, where stories of the corruption of certain leaders are told by poor sharecroppers and labourers, who would probably not repeat such tales to the leaders' faces. The problem with this analysis, however, is twofold. First, it is not only the weak who indulge in, and pass on rumours and gossip. Second, in attempting to explain what rumours do, we also need to ask who believes them. The question returns us to the starting point of this chapter: the way that different types of knowledge coalesce with and/or undermine hierarchy, and, indeed, the use of different forms of narrative in struggles over power and resources. While I am not suggesting that there is no objective truth or verifiable facts, I am arguing that in the context of Bangladesh, where nothing is transparent and corruption is rife, political struggles go hand in hand with contestations over what is and is not true. Ultimately what matters is not what is or is not objectively 'true', but who is heard and who is believed. To this extent the facts and figures of the National Committee, while drawn from a different epistemology and circulated in a different domain, assume the same evidential status as the stories of the *tashildar*, with his eight gold rings, even if ultimately they have different effects.

If rumours concerning his integrity and ability as a local patron have harmed Joful Haque, the rumours that circulate about the corrupt relationships existing between Chevron and government officials damage the thing held dear by those promoting corporate social responsibility: reputation. It was this 'threat to reputation' rather than the (rumoured) depleted gas reserves that might lead to the company withdrawing from Bangladesh, Steve Wilson told me (Interview notes, 2008). Indeed, rumours don't float around in the ether, they are powerful tools which can be used to attack one's enemies. To this extent assumptions of a cosy conspiracy between corrupt governments and multinational mining companies miss the mark. Rather than having imperial power over Bangladesh, companies such as Chevron struggle to maintain good relationships with a tricky and at times capricious state whose officials are apt to act in their own interests. In one story, repeated in the national press and turning viral on the internet in early 2010, Sheikh Hasina's son, Sajeeb Wazed Joy, was anonymously accused of receiving a US $5 million bribe from Chevron for allowing them to proceed with work on a US $52 million compressor plant; apparently no tenders had been received from other companies.[26] This rumour had direct repercussions for Chevron officials hoping to meet with Duniyapur *Londonis* in Britain a few months later, with the latter refusing to attend discussions over the Bibiyana Trust for fear that their own reputations might be smeared by association. The allegations were furiously refuted by Chevron officials. Presented on Petrobangla-headed stationary, they were lies propagated by a disgruntled government official who wished to harm the company, I was told.

While rumours and other forms of narrative can harm corporate reputations, and are clearly part and parcel of the vicious nature of Bangladeshi politics, their effectiveness, like that of the other forms of knowledge and information discussed in this chapter, is closely related to the networks in which they circulate and the places from which they originate. The academic discourses of the National Committee are given a radically different weighting from the localised discourses of landless villagers in Duniyapur, who, in contrast to nationally renowned activists such as Anu Muhammed, have a limited and largely disinterested audience.

This brings me to my final point. While rumours may be used to attack individuals and interest groups, or more generally to critique power relations, not everyone believes them. The success of rumours and other forms of knowing, measured by the degree to which they are accepted as 'true', or their narrative force is, not surprisingly, directly related to the degree of power that the narrator has. While allegations written on Petrobangla-headed stationary lead to the setting up of investigative committees, newspaper headlines and yet another bruising received by a multinational oil company in the rough and tumble of Bangladeshi politics, and the demands of leftist Dhaka intellectuals, with their connections to the internet, the international media and lobbying groups, can lead to contracts being cancelled, the narratives of the dispossessed are rarely heard and are generally dismissed.

Let us turn to the book's concluding chapter, where we see how connection and disconnection are directly related to knowing and power.

7
Blow-out!
Stories of Disconnection and Loss

It was the deepest hour of night, long after the final prayer. Perhaps it was the noise, perhaps the unnatural red light flickering on the walls. Whatever, Miri Bibi awoke with a start, her heart beating hard. Through the thin walls of her hut she could hear the shouts of her neighbours, the bang of doors, the hysterical barking of the dogs. On the wooden platform beside her, the three older children were rousing, sitting up and whimpering with alarm. Pulling her sari around her shoulders and grabbing the baby in her arms, she ran with them into the yard. Outside, the sky was crimson, the flame so huge that it seemed to tower above the village, three or four times larger than the usual flare. All she could hear, in those first few moments, was the hideous roar of the gas.

What they had dreaded was happening: a blow-out, like the ones at Magurcchara and Tengratila Gas Fields where vast explosions had led to widespread environmental damage. If these installations had been situated close to human habitation, as the Bibiyana Gas Field was, the accidents would have certainly led to loss of life, possibly on a horrific scale. Now, regarding the reddened sky and looming flare with horror, Miri Bibi and her neighbours made the obvious assumption. Screaming at the children to follow, she ran from the yard, making for the large pond that lay behind the Saiyed Bari. Here, among the water lilies and weeds, the rapacious flames surely could not reach them.

Written as Third World disaster narrative, the above account appears to lead to an inevitable finale: a terrible industrial accident causing death and destruction. In Duniyapur, however, the story of the flaring ended quite differently. Indeed, it can be told in a number of ways. Here's another version, also authored by me:

On the specified night the planned flaring of extraneous gas took place at the Bibiyana plant. This procedure is 100 percent safe, with no additional risk to the communities surrounding the plant. In order to avoid unnecessary alarm among the population, community leaders were informed the day before the flaring took place.

Whether potential disaster or standard industrial procedure, what happened that night can also be told as a joke. As a Newcastle restaurateur (born and brought up in Duniyapur) merrily recounted:

Everyone thought the flaring was a blow-out! They went rushing out of their houses screaming! One woman was in such a state of panic that she mistook her pillow for her baby, and went running around with it under her arm! The rest of the village jumped in the ponds ...

All versions are true to the extent that they reflect the various stories I was told of the flaring that took place in Duniyapur one night in 2008. All are also clearly fictions, in that the accounts given by different informants are refracted above via my authorship. Objectively, what we can say is that in 2008 a standard technical procedure in which excess gas is burnt off in a controlled flare, led to widespread panic in the villages surrounding the Bibiyana Gas Field. This was described to us by almost everyone in the area as an example of the dangers of the gas field, a terrifying night when they awoke to find the sky 'filled with fire' and ran, in terror, from their homes.

Told as a black joke by British *Londonis*, who use the story to poke fun at their *deshi* cousins, the different accounts of the flaring show how a single event can be experienced and narrated in radically different ways by different actors. The blow-out-that-wasn't-a-blow-out also raises vital questions concerning the relationship between knowledge, narration and power. Take, for example, the response of the Director for External Affairs when told of the mayhem that the flaring caused. This was not supposed to have happened, he explained sorrowfully: they had clearly communicated the planned flaring to the community leaders. Although at the time he was in Dhaka, he too had been woken in the night, not by leaping flames but by the frantic phone calls of people in Duniyapur shouting about a blow-out. Here we see how assumptions concerning the nature of 'community' and 'local leaders' led to what was essentially a breakdown in communications. Assuming that 'local leaders' communicate corporate information to the 'community', Chevron's staff took no further action in their efforts to inform people about the flaring. Meanwhile as one of our informants snorted derisively: 'They informed the local elite by text!' Community relations staff probably did not intend it, but the implication in this statement is clear: important information of an event which was to lead to widespread terror for the population surrounding the gas field was not communicated in a respectful or understanding manner.

If the blow-out-that-wasn't-a-blow-out is a case study in how not to do community relations, it is also an example of the intrinsically lumpy nature of knowledge. Rather than flowing freely from domain to domain, or Chevron offices in Dhaka to the *baris* of landless households in Kakura, it gets stuck in the pipeline, its movement blocked by 'leaders' who are imagined by CSR planners as representing 'the people', but who in reality inhabit complex roles and relationships and who are highly unlikely to disseminate news about flaring to people they have little connection with, especially if they are very poor. As this clearly shows, information and knowledge are, like other resources, not accessible to everyone equally. Instead, their dissemination marks lines of difference and hierarchy. Shuli's household in Nadampur, with their kinship connections to leaders close to Chevron, *were* informed, while those without these connections were not so much left in the dark as left to the spectre of the flare, with its threat of the ultimate disconnection.

Who controls knowledge and information? Throughout the book we have seen how struggles and contestations over resources in general, and the gas field in particular, have revolved around different claims and narratives, each drawing upon distinct and sometimes contradictory moralities and types of knowledge. In this concluding chapter I shall focus on the narratives of rupture and loss told by people in Duniyapur. This returns us to the book's central theme: *connection* and its antonym, *disconnection*. As we shall see, stories of *blow-out* are more than simply accounts of the gas field's flaring, or indeed people's well-founded fears of an industrial accident. They can also be read as metaphors for violent disconnection and rupture, whether from the transformative energy of the gas, with its contradictory possibilities of enrichment and destruction, from the land on which livelihoods depend, or the richly woven web of social connections so vital for everyday survival.

In this final chapter I suggest how stories of industrial disaster and the fear that they express can be interpreted at a metaphoric as well as a literal level, revealing the profound risks that engagement with neoliberal capitalism has involved. Within this analysis, a blow-out is merely the most dramatic materialisation of the uncertain world in which people struggle for survival. As old forms of connection fall away, there seems to be little to replace them for those without formal connections to land or foreign countries in Kakura and Karimpur. Long-term connections to patrons over the fields in Nadampur involved exploitation and inequality, but also some kind of security, however conditional. As the local economy becomes increasingly monetarised and the *Londonis* who once 'looked after their own' return less frequently, and as the industrialisation that has encroached upon local resources has so utterly failed to provide the desired employment, is it to be wondered at that people speak of being 'consumed by the fire'?

'WHEN THE FIRE COMES': STORIES OF TERROR AND THREAT

Her cousin Abdul Karim was a good man, Amma tells me; one of the best. Living over the way in Karimpur, he was known for his generosity and honour, extending help and support to all who asked. When the officials arrived at his home in 2005, he was aghast to hear of their plans for his land. He had no choice: it was to be taken by the government and used to build a large gas field operated by the Americans. For weeks he worried about what was to happen, hardly able to bear the stress. Not only was he to lose his family fields, but he was becoming increasingly afraid about the safety issues. In order to find out what the dangers were, he decided to travel to Tengratila, where there had recently been a large blow-out, with flames reported to have leapt 150 feet high.[1] The scene of devastation that he confronted was terrifying. Returning to Karimpur, he was in a terrible state of anxiety and fear. It was that night that Abdul Karim's heart gave up: he dropped dead from the worry of the gas field.

The story of Abdul Karim's fearful visit to Tengratila and subsequent death from *cinta* – worries – (which I cite as such: a story, told to me in the context of a conversation with Shuli's mother in 2005 about what might happen if and when the gas field was built) is instructive in several ways. First, 'blow-outs' can and do happen in Bangladesh. Second, the risk of a 'blow-out' causes terrible anxiety and fear in the villages close to the gas field. The accounts that follow are thus narratives born from terror, ways of making sense of the chaos, panic and speechlessness caused by Chevron's unexpected flaring. In their statements in which the future is envisaged in terms of disaster, death and immersion in flames, one might argue that our narrators are signalling their sense of powerlessness and vulnerability caused by the gas field; through the telling of these stories of terror, they are also reassembling normality and reasserting their dignity.[2]

> The gas field has had a severe impact on our life. We are scared about the flame, when it comes. Since the gas field has been operating there have been a number of incidents. When the flames grew large we had to leave our house. Recently it happened again. The villagers had to leave because of the heat, the earth walls of our house started to crack, the earth was cracking up too. Me, my children and their mother were literally running around, looking for shelter. It was midnight. Everyone was running around, the children were shouting, looking for somewhere to hide. Some people jumped into the ponds, while others sheltered on the banks. Listen, the day I saw that fire, oh my God, it was like the last day on earth, when everything is destroyed! (Sharecropper, Karimpur, interview notes 2009)

> Because of the gas field we live under the threat of fire. Like an earthquake, everything moves and there's a roaring sound. When the fire goes up we have to go to a safe place; we fear that the fire will engulf us. The flame is so bright that it illuminates everything even though it's night. If you dropped a piece of sewing on the ground you could find it. We run around madly. Last year Harun's wife was so scared that she fled the house, leaving her children behind. People leave their valuables. Everyone is scared for their life! Whenever Chevron ups the fire our relatives call us to see if we've survived and they live 15 miles away! Some villagers fled by rickshaw.
>
> They do this when we go to bed at night. They don't let us know they're going to up the fire. If we had known before, we would have been prepared. (Labourer, Kakura, interview notes, 2009)

In an early focus group discussion with men in Kakura (in 2008) we heard the following statements:

> We are always scared about the fire – when it comes it will spread over the whole village and kill everyone.

And:

> We have gained nothing from the gas field, apart from the threat of setting our village on fire.

Whether or not the flaring is 'safe' is beside the point,[3] for such an analysis is based upon the technical knowledge of those operating the plant, which Chevron has not shared with the local population. Within the analysis of people living in the villages close to the plant, the flames are dangerous and terrifying. How can they be seen as benign, when they rear up from this site of global capitalism which, rather than offering inclusion and connection, has excluded them from its profits and operations, not to say its epistemological orders? Within the localised knowledge of people in Kakura and Karimpur, the flames are, I suggest, a terrifying reminder of their powerlessness and dispossession.

'BEFORE THE GAS FIELD': ENVIRONMENTAL TALES OF RUPTURE AND LOSS

A similar reading can be made of the narratives of environmental change that we heard in Chapter 3. As with the flaring, these narratives are based upon empirical observation: blow-outs can and do occur at gas fields in Sylhet; there have been observable changes to the environment. Yet as Stuart Kirsch (2006) has noted among the Yonggom of Papua New Guinea, indigenous analyses of mining's devastating effects are based on holistic understandings of the interconnectedness of people and their physical environments rather than narrow 'scientific' evidence.

In the first account the trope of 'before' and 'after' is used to organise the speaker's observations of environmental changes which, in his analysis, affect his ability to survive. The analysis is pointedly political: things were promised but not provided. The account ends with a dramatic pronouncement on the risks the speaker faces, were farming to no longer sustain him: 'otherwise we will die'.

Because of the gas field us farmers are badly affected. Before the gas field the yields were very good. Now we have to deal with scarcity of water; without water the yields are poor ... it's hard to graze cattle or goats because there's less grazing land. It's difficult to bring cattle from one side of the road to the other because they're so high. Before the gas field we used to get straw, which we used as fuel. Now there's nothing here and we have to buy fuel. We had fish and the land was fertile; now a whole month will go by and we don't eat fish. Where are the fish? There is no water in the river. If we plant *aman*, then waterlogging is a big problem. When the road was built they promised culverts but the pipes are too narrow and the water can't pass through. We want deep tube wells in the area; it will provide water to our land. We can survive by farming. Otherwise we will die. (Interview notes, 2008)

In the next account, given by a young woman in Kakura, the fertility of the soil is directly linked to the extraction of gas, which 'has been channelled outside'. This has left 'the ground empty'. The imagery is vivid, the analysis acute: the wealth of the fields has been pumped away, the once fertile and sustaining land left empty and denuded. How different from the description of Chevron's community relations officer, who, as we heard in Chapter 5, told us: 'When we first came here there was nothing.'

Paddy doesn't grow like it used to; the fertility of the soil has decreased. A farmer used to get 10 *maunds* of paddy from 1 *kiare* of land, but now he only gets 4. People think the soil fertility has decreased due to use of machinery. They think our hidden wealth [the gas] has been channelled outside – the riches underground have been brought to the surface, leaving the ground empty. It is this which has affected the fertility of the soil. (Interview notes, 2008)

The next narrator draws upon similar imagery: the gas is being extracted from the land, leaving an emptiness that will lead to death:

The gas field has killed us. We've lost land ... Trees are being destroyed by the gas. In my *bari* garden, the beans plants are all dying ... Because the gas is being extracted from the land there's nothing left underneath. The whole village will be drowned; we'll turn into a river. (Small landowner, Karimpur, interview notes 2009)

In his moving account of the altered landscapes created by the Ok Tedi copper and gold mine in Papua New Guinea, Kirsch describes how, as they face their emptied out and transformed landscape, the Yonggom experience acute rupture, not only of their livelihoods, but also of their history and identity: As he writes: 'What is the meaning of these empty places? Given the relationship between place and memory, the destruction of these landscapes also threatens history. These are not just empty places, but also scenes of loss' (2006: 190).

That the altered environment disrupts memories and symbolic forms of connection as well as actual livelihoods is powerfully evoked by Samsun Khan's descriptions of looking out from his house onto a transformed landscape: no longer the vista of family fields he has seen since childhood, but the gas field, which has caused a 'fire to burn in my heart'. For Samsun Khan, the plant's technological connection to the gas supply has led to his disconnection from his village. Fighting with Chevron, finding new enemies in the post-gas field politics of the area, he is exiled to Sylhet Town, rarely returning to his role as landowner and local patron.

A similar sense of disconnection from the landscape and his memories of the *desh* as beautiful and peaceful was evoked by one of the British men we got to know over the course of the research. In a discussion about the environmental effects of the gas field, which is situated only a few hundred feet from his *bari*, Tufael told of his shock and sense of dislocation on returning to find what had happened in the fields next door. As he put it, describing the smell and noise: 'It's like living on top of an industrial site' (Interview notes, 2009).

COMPLAINTS AND THEIR DENIAL

As Fatema and I approach along the North Pad road, a man is waiting for us outside his small *bari*, situated next to the road. This is Karim Miah, and he has things to show. Leading us eagerly into his house, he and his wife point to the kitchen wall, which is divided by a gaping crack. At the back of the property, in the area normally used for washing up, a tube well and maybe a vegetable plot, the land has subsided, slipping down the steep embankment that has been built for the road. His house was physically moved by Chevron, Karim Miah says, since the road ran straight through it. The new house they built for him is obviously damaged, but Chevron's people no longer visit him, despite his frequent requests. When they wanted his land they were available, but now the road is built, no-one comes near to hear their complaints.

We heard similar comments from a wide range of people, who felt that, in contrast to the days when the site was being constructed and the land acquisition process was still under way, they no longer had any line of communication with Chevron, despite the company's claims of 'partnership' with the community. Indeed, Chevron has no formal grievance procedures in Duniyapur, yet this is an accepted practice within international guidelines for social impact assessments, for example as laid out by the International Association for Impact Assessment.[4] The reason, I was told by Chevron officials, was that there would be too many complaints to deal with, the situation would be impossible to manage.

That no-one likes to be on the receiving end of complaining is noted by James Wilce in his ethnography of lamentation and 'troubles-telling' in Bangladesh. If complaints can feel like a 'weapon hurled' (2003: 18), Wilce argues, they are also the recourse of the weak, subconscious forms of resistance, accruing to somatised symptoms rather than outright attacks on the system (2003: 19). In contrast to the largely female complainants studied by Wilce, in Duniyapur the (largely male) complainants are directly explicit and oppositional, breaking into angry shouts and accusations rather than mumbled grumbling. Yet even if such complaints are heard they are unlikely to acted upon by those in power. Instead, statements such as the following, made by a labourer in Kakura, are dismissed by the elite as 'talking too much' (*anek kotha bole!*), a local put-down, implying that the speaker is somehow out of control, being too bossy or gabbling nonsensically.

> How are we supposed to survive? We don't get any work. We used to do manual work before the gas field, now we don't get any form of work. We're not offered employment by the gas field ... it's privileged outsiders who get work there rather than local village people! (Fieldnotes, 2008)

Don't go to Kakura, I was told by friends in Nadampur. The people are too demanding and talk too much. To have to hear all their complaints might cause me suffering (*anek kastor*).

If claims and complaints are to be denied, particular forms of knowledge are brought into play by those who seek to undermine them. As I have argued throughout the book, the epistemological orders that support different types of claim are not equal, but arranged hierarchically, with scientific or quantitative knowledge valued more highly by those in power than the localised, relational knowledge of the poor. Once again, we are returned to the contestation of knowledge and information, with the 'truth' almost impossible to verify, since the epistemologies through which that truth is to be established are so different, and the actual content of Chevron's impact assessments and contracts hidden from public view. The research on which this book is based, for example, was dismissed by Chevron executives as 'hearsay', for it has been largely of a qualitative rather than a quantitative nature. That *hearing* what people *say* might actually be a valid exercise did not seem to have been considered by them.[5] When told of ongoing poverty in Duniyapur those in charge of the community engagement programme expressed surprise. How could this be, they asked, when so many NGOs had been funded to provide the people with so many benefits and programmes? Posed as a technical problem leading to a technical solution (income generation projects, micro-credit, etc.) rather than a political problem (inequality, lack of rights and justice) needing political solutions, the gulf in ways of knowing and forms of analysis seemed during this conversation to be insurmountable.[6]

CONNECTION AND DISCONNECTION IN DUNIYAPUR

Throughout this book I have argued that one way in which to understand and analyse the entitlement systems which structure people's access to resources in Duniyapur is via the metaphor of connection. In a short while I shall suggest that this metaphor can help us think about the various forms and meanings of 'development' that surround the gas field. First, though, a quick review of the evidence.

In the first part of the book, we saw how the legacy of colonialism in the newly formed Bangladesh has involved a weak state which, since its earliest years, has been based on patronage and governed via the politics of factionalism and vendetta. What is spoken of as corruption at the level of the state is mirrored in a system of entitlement within Duniyapur which relies heavily upon social connections to gain access to resources and social protection: nasty patronage or nice social capital, according to context and one's interpretation. In Duniyapur these connections are vital for securing access to land, as well as to foreign sources of capital via overseas migration. Networks of patronage are transnational as well as local: the poor are often supported by relatives and neighbours in the UK.

In Chapters 3 and 4, we saw how in their everyday struggles for credit and resources, the poor are largely reliant upon social connections for their survival. Dwindling opportunities in agriculture, partly due to the loss of land to the gas field, but also resulting from wider processes of land fragmentation, overpopulation and the disinvestment in land-based livelihoods of wealthy and often absent *Londoni* owners, mean that these struggles appear, in the accounts of the poorest, to be ever more desperate. For many, the gas field was initially seen as an opportunity to become formally connected to global capitalism, leading to a version of development that may be unfashionable in the global arena but remains desired by people who don't have it: a working infrastructure, regular, salaried employment and the provision of health and education by the state, or, failing that, the corporation. This vision, of industrialisation and regular employment in the formal sector has not, however, to come to fruition. The gas field employs only small numbers of unskilled staff and does not offer training to provide those skills for local people. Moreover, those labourers who do find work at the gas field are hired by labour contractors, who tend to use informal networks and terms of employment. This ensures an 'easy flow of labour' for Chevron.

In Chapter 5 we saw how the CSR programmes offered by Chevron to villages surrounding the gas field involve connection and disconnection in radically different ways. By promoting development projects which aim at sustainability, or the ultimate disconnection by the donor, the company presents itself as right thinking and ethically motivated ('The Chevron Way'). This allows it to connect to fashionable global moralities of empowerment and helping-people-to-help-themselves, thus adding to its global reputation. Ultimately, of course, the connection that Chevron desires is to the gas, increasing its profits and share of the market. Its use of discourses of neoliberal development in its community engagement programmes thus enables it to make claims to the moral high ground as well as promises to 'community leaders' while connecting materially to the gas. Meanwhile, the buzzwords/fuzzwords (Cornwall and Eade, 2010) of sustainability and self-help, and their attendant ideologies, allow the company to eschew direct connections to the landless and land poor who live around the gas field, either as patron or as a quasi-state. These discourses, plus labour regimes in which local labour is only hired on a casual basis by contractors, supports the 'corporate ethic of detachment' (Cross, 2011), which allows corporations such as Chevron to pull out with relative ease when gas supplies run out, or Bangladeshi politics become too fraught: evidence, if any were needed, of the deterritorialising tendencies of contemporary global capitalism. In the final, paradoxical twist to the tale of CSR, in order for the company to make its moral claims it has to present itself as socially connected to local communities via statements of 'partnership'.

Chapter 5 also illustrated how the discourse of CSR utilises distinct narrative forms and types of knowledge. Following other anthropologists of development such as David Mosse, Tanya Murray-Li and Dinah Rajak, I described how Chevron's community engagement programme narrates success, editing out dissension seamlessly in its promotional literature. Relying upon quantitative data such as surveys and consultancy reports, the programmes involve unquestioned assumptions about the nature of community, local leaders and the solutions to poverty (training and micro-credit).

In Chapter 6 we encountered a quite different sort of knowledge: that of local and national protesters, who opposed the construction of the gas field and the presence of multinationals in Bangladesh. Drawing not on neoliberal moralities of individual empowerment and sustainability, but Marxist-influenced critiques of imperialist exploitation, these narratives systematically undermine the neoliberal claims of Chevron to be contributing to the development of Bangladesh, while making nationalist claims for the sovereignty of Bangladesh, its rights over resources and its place in the global order. Similar analyses are made by people in Duniyapur, though these are based upon localised knowledge and a critique of personal, rather than global relationships and hierarchies. For both local protesters and nationalist activists, however, the struggle is about far more than simply whether or not Chevron should be offered contracts by the government to extract natural gas; it is about wider questions concerning the future of Bangladesh and its role in global capitalism. As Suzana Sawyer has noted in Ecuador:

> Social conflict over things like land and petroleum was about more than the materiality of their use. Struggles over the control of land and oil operations in Ecuador were as much about configuring the nation under neoliberalism – rupturing the silences around social injustice, provoking a space of accountability, reimagining narratives of national belonging – as they were about the material use and extraction of rain forest resources. (2004: 16)

In this chapter we have turned from narratives which directly challenge Chevron and the elite leaders who have complied with the company, to tales of rupture and disconnection, organised around stories of the flaring that occasionally takes place at the gas field as well as of environmental change. While the violent rupture of a blow-out leads to the ultimate disconnection, the narratives show that some people are being subjected to a less dramatic but arguably no less violent form of rupture, from their agricultural and fishing-based livelihoods, which are being slowly eroded by a more directly profit-oriented, money-based economy, land shortage and, despite Chevron's attempts to provide 'alternative livelihoods', the lack of long-term, viable employment prospects. Yet while the stories of connection via 'partnership with the community' made by Chevron have a global audience, the stories of loss and rupture told by the poorest people in Duniyapur remain largely unheard.

DISCORDANT DEVELOPMENTS

If people need connections to survive, then poverty might be understood as a state of *disconnection*, and impoverishment as the process whereby this happens: one's connections to people and the resources they control becoming increasingly tenuous, and one's grip upon entitlements ever more fragile. In this instance, claims to connection are likely to become more desperate. As I have attempted to show, this process is under way for the landless and land poor of Kakura and Karimpur who are faced with the slow diminishment of patron–client relations as the wealthy landowners who once supported them have moved away from the area and the local economy is increasingly tipped against their interests. Small wonder that to their patrons they have become 'very demanding'.

The ultimate disaster is one that remains untold, at least within the pages of this book: there is a crisis, one's husband dies, or the house is destroyed in a flood; the crops fail and the debts can never be repaid. Sometimes it is a violent dispute that leads to the rupturing of the links, the threat of violence or its actuality. Whatever the causes, life in the *desh* is no longer tenable: one must leave, grab a few possessions and go somewhere else. If one is lucky, it will be another village or region, where there may be some work or opportunities and people one knows: the colonies and huts on the periphery of Nadampur are filled with people who say they came for the work, or because they could no longer survive back in the *desh*, be this 20 or 200 miles away (Gardner and Ahmed, 2009). For those less lucky – usually women – there is no destination, just a ghostly drifting from village to village, maybe with a child on one's hip, in search of itinerant work or alms. It is these women who turn up in the yard of Shuli's *bari* on a daily basis. With their wail of *Ya Allah*! they wait on the step until someone appears from inside the building to offer a small handful of grains or a *ruti* (flat bread) with a little salt or chilli. These people are the disconnected: those with no tethering in a village or town, no social connections and only the most weak of claims, their migrations the opposite of those of the *Londonis* and their relatives, whose movement from the *desh* has led to new and formal connections *bidesh*.[7]

The formalised and secure connections that *Londonis* have with Britain, where they have citizenship and work within a regulated and formal economy reminds us that there are different ways of being connected. Indeed, I suggest that there are two forms of connection in Duniyapur and its transnational spaces. The first type is formal, based on legal ownership, contracts and rights. The second is informal, based on social relationships and moral claims. In reality these types of connection are not easily separable: formal connections (e.g. the contract that Chevron has with the government of Bangladesh) are reinforced by morally based claims (via the practice of community engagement, for example). People also operate within both systems: they own land or sell their labour in formalised arrangements, but their livelihoods also depend in part upon informal social links. Yet, however blurry the distinction, what the story of Duniyapur shows is that the more wealth and power one has, the more likely one is to possess formal connections, rights and entitlements. The poorer one is, in contrast, the more one relies upon informal connections and the more risky one's entitlements are.

What is 'development'? Much ink has been spilt within anthropology in analysing it as a discourse, steeped in neo-colonial assumptions and operating as a form of governance. Yet while these perspectives reveal the power play involved in projects and programmes of improvement, they focus more on the institutions and discourses of the developers than the socio-political relations of poverty which, while structured in part by global relations, are played out and experienced within local domains. To understand development as discourse is helpful, but one also has to understand the relationships of poverty and inequality that exist above and beyond the discursive practices of the developers, however the two may be intertwined. And for anthropology to be engaged it cannot always be politically neutral or remain silent on questions of progressive change. This is why in writing this book, I have been unable to avoid the question: *how might things be better?*

One way of answering this question is to think about progressive change in ways other than economic development. Sen, for example, argues persuasively that 'development' is freedom. This formulation includes freedom from poverty, as well as the forms of political and personal freedom enjoyed by the majority of the population of the Northern hemisphere (Sen, 1999). While the de-linking of the concept of development from economics is to be applauded, I wonder if 'freedom' does not chime too deeply with neoliberal and Western-centric ideologies of individualism and independence for

Duniyapur, where, above all, it is connection and the interdependence of people that matters. Another alternative is via the term 'inclusion', or 'inclusive citizenship'. Naila Kabeer defines this as referring 'both to people's ability to claim their legally recognised rights on an equal basis as well as to the extent to which the law deals with them in a way that guarantees their equality' (2002: 1).

While *inclusion* refers to membership of a given group or activity (the state, for example), *connection* refers to a relationship, whether this be to the state, the corporation or one's patron. The metaphor of formal connection may therefore help us think about progressive change, not only at the level of the nation state but also in terms of everyday lives. For example, formal connections to employers involve contracts and a range of provisions, such as sick leave, days off and regular payment. Similarly, if people are formally connected via their citizenship to democratically elected governments which are accountable for their actions; getting things done, for example receiving compensation, or access to seeds or fertilisers, does not involve 'knowing the right people' or indeed the payment of bribes. And since the government is democratically elected, it can be held accountable when it fails to provide health care or medicine to its population. More generally, the local or national economy is connected to global capital via trade and other forms of exchange that are balanced, with profits being shared fairly between places.

This is the world – of inclusion and formal, secure connection – that many people conjured up when they first heard of the gas field. It is the world that the *Londonis* inhabit, and for a brief period it seemed that some of these formalised connections might come to the *desh*. There would be a hospital, schools, a fertiliser factory and power plant; people would find employment. Most symbolic of all, the area would be connected to the gas supply: modernisation would finally arrive. What we have seen, however, is that this world and its promised freedoms never came. There was no formal connection to be had: not to the gas supply, nor to the gas field. Those who found a connection to Chevron did it through the old methods: contracts were given to the elite and their benefits spread to their relatives.

What was offered instead of the formalised connections and inclusions that people so desperately wanted was another version of 'development', which allows Chevron to have a material connection to the gas supply while remaining unconnected to the local population. In this version of 'development' the poor are 'helped to help themselves' via savings schemes that rely upon their informal connections to both those who control the programmes ('the local leaders' and NGO workers) as well as to other members of their savings groups. To be a member of one of these groups one has to be recommended by the VDO. Those excluded from the programmes complain that the process whereby beneficiaries are chosen is unfair and lacks transparency. Meanwhile Chevron does not employ people directly but through labour contractors, who, as we have seen, draw upon social connections and patronage to ensure an 'easy flow of labour'. Clearly, while Chevron officials claim that their aim is to 'empower people', they are not assisting them in making the formal connections that they need in order to enjoy the security, entitlements or rights within modern, democratic states that constitute Sen's vision of 'development as freedom', and might also be thought of as enabling true 'empowerment'.

NEW STORIES, NEW CONNECTIONS

Sitting over coffee in the air-conditioned offices of Chevron in Gulshan, Dhaka, I am trying to explain to a small group of executives why it is that despite their Alternative Livelihood Programmes, poverty persists in Duniyapur. As they listen politely to my explanations of land shortages, mechanisation and monetarisation, one of the executives comments that these processes are part and parcel of industrialisation. Since the nineteenth century, as pre-capitalist livelihoods have given way to capitalism, peasants and their animals have lost their access to the commons and their traditional ways of making a living have been swept aside. Bangladesh desperately needs its energy supplies, he goes on; economic growth will eventually bring real changes and benefits to the country.

Perhaps he is right. It is certainly true that in many ways the story of Duniyapur is an old one. Within stories of global 'friction' (Tsing, 2005), the connections and disconnections involved seem to lead to marginalisation and exclusion as much as to freedom and prosperity. Mining, Free or Special Economic Zones, factories and power plants: all involve the loss of land. While some people find jobs, others lose their livelihoods, experiencing what Harvey has termed the 'switching crises' of moving from one form of production to another as profound rupture. 'We can no longer graze our cattle,' the farmers say; or 'There is no land left to sharecrop', and one can hear the echoes of similar stories refracted across space and time, whether told by starving peasants in nineteenth-century England or dispossessed shifting cultivators in Melanesia in 2011.

How might the story change, to one which involves inclusion and connection rather than disconnection and rupture for the rural poor? While industrialisation, the loss of land and agrarian livelihoods are probably inevitable, as my account of Duniyapur and its gas field indicates, changing the story's ending to one which involves more hope for those caught up in the maelstrom of change is largely a question of rights: to make claims, assert grievances and be heard. People's ability to influence government is vital too: remember the story of Tata's ultimate failure to dispossess farmers in West Bengal. In Duniyapur, however, all too often there are no legal channels for claims, and grievances are dismissed or ignored, especially when the claimants are very poor. As Naila Kabeer argues, projects of inclusive citizenship face huge challenges in many parts of the postcolonial world where kinship remains a central organising institution and the state remains weak. Not only are notions of citizenship fragmented and partial; people who depend upon patronage for their basic needs are unlikely to claim their rights, since the risks to the hierarchical relationships on which they depend are too great (Kabeer, 2002). Ultimately, the changing of the story therefore involves political struggle, wherein: 'The stirrings of a willingness to contest their devalued status on the part of subordinate groups marks the beginning of their journey from subject to citizen' (2002: 13).

In Duniyapur these stirrings are already well advanced. As we have seen, many people are happy to denounce the 'local leaders' who they claim sold them down the river, even if these men are also local patrons or even members of the same lineage. They are also quick to make claims against government officials and Chevron based on a concept of rights, modern government and accountability. Rather than people being too cowed or subordinate, the problem is that the structures in which to make their claims do not exist. If they are threatened with police brutality as they protest against forcible land acquisitions, so be it. If their house has a crack down the middle due to the drilling and the community liaison officer doesn't choose to help: tough. If the contractor takes a cut of his labourers' wages, only a fool would make a fuss, especially if she wants to stay in work.

If what is needed are structures whereby rights and claims count, these will never develop within a system of informal connections or patronage but via processes of inclusive citizenship and accountable government. Crucially, at least to my tale of multinationals and CSR, some of these structures can be delivered by corporations working in places such as Duniyapur. This means formalised employment, where possible, with contracts and the ethical standards of employment that companies such as Chevron give to their employees in their own countries. More centrally, if global corporations are to bring benefits to the places where they operate, they have to be accountable, via formal grievance procedures and, centrally, through revealing the details of their contracts with the government. Once this is done, the rumours and conspiracy theories that animate opposition and activism will disappear, like shadows under a ray of light. Finally, multinationals can help support governments working towards transparency and support anti-corruption drives; it is initiatives such as these that DFID promotes as the highest level of CSR.

It is not simply that transparency will lead to the end of the politics of rumour. More importantly, it will mean that, armed with this information, the population can pressurise the government to ensure that multinationals pay high taxes, which help fund state-provided health and education services, and so on. As citizens with formalised rights, people in places where land is lost or the environment affected, can make legal claims for redress. If companies such as Chevron are to be truly 'socially responsible', they should be taking direct action to support these processes, for example by influencing governments to sign up to initiatives such as the Extractive Industries Transparency Initiative. It is this, perhaps, that is the biggest lesson that Duniyapur and its stories can teach us: without transparency and accountability, CSR programmes are like gossamer in the wind: insubstantial and weightless, unable to offer any real form of connection.

Appendix: The Chevron Way

Taken from the Chevron website:
www.chevron.com/about/chevronway/

The Chevron Way explains who we are, what we do, what we believe and what we plan to accomplish. It establishes a common understanding not only for those of us who work here, but for all who interact with us.

Vision

At the heart of The Chevron Way is our vision ... to be *the* global energy company most admired for its people, partnership and performance.

Our vision means we:

- safely provide energy products vital to sustainable economic progress and human development throughout the world;
- are people and an organization with superior capabilities and commitment;
- are the partner of choice;
- earn the admiration of all our stakeholders – investors, customers, host governments, local communities and our employees – not only for the goals we achieve but how we achieve them;
- deliver world-class performance.

Values

Our company's foundation is built on our values, which distinguish us and guide our actions. We conduct our business in a socially responsible and ethical manner. We respect the law, support universal human rights, protect the environment and benefit the communities where we work.

Integrity

We are honest with others and ourselves. We meet the highest ethical standards in all business dealings. We do what we say we will do. We accept responsibility and hold ourselves accountable for our work and our actions.

Trust

We trust, respect and support each other, and we strive to earn the trust of our colleagues and partners.

Partnership

We have an unwavering commitment to being a good partner focused on building productive, collaborative, trusting and beneficial relationships with governments, other companies, our customers, our communities and each other.

Diversity

We learn from and respect the cultures in which we work. We value and demonstrate respect for the uniqueness of individuals and the varied perspectives and talents they provide. We have an inclusive work environment and actively embrace a diversity of people, ideas, talents and experiences.

Ingenuity

We seek new opportunities and out-of-the-ordinary solutions. We use our creativity to find unexpected and practical ways to solve problems. Our experience, technology, and perseverance enable us to overcome challenges and deliver value.

Protecting People and the Environment

We place the highest priority on the health and safety of our workforce and protection of our assets and the environment. We aim to be admired for world-class performance through disciplined application of our Operational Excellence Management System.

High Performance

We are committed to excellence in everything we do, and we strive to continually improve. We are passionate about achieving results that exceed expectations – our own and those of others. We drive for results with energy and a sense of urgency.

Notes

1 DISCORDANT DEVELOPMENTS: AN INTRODUCTION

1. See www.asianews.it/news-en/Six-dead,-100-reportedly-wounded-in-Bangladesh-electricity-protest-5196.html (accessed 5 December 2010).
2. Similar observations have been made by Welker (2010), in her work on mining company CSR in Indonesia.
3. An excellent example of work which does exactly this, though focusing upon mining platinum rather than oil extraction is Dinah Rajak's (2011) ethnography of the Anglo-American mining corporation in South Africa; see also Smith and Helfgott (2010) and Ballard (2003).
4. See: http://londonminingnetwork.org/2009/07/worldwide-protests-against-vedanta/; see also Patel and Das (2008).
5. The research was funded by the ESRC/DFID Joint Programme (Third Call). I am very grateful for their support.
6. To preserve anonymity, I have scrambled the names and identities of all our informants in Bibiyana.
7. See for example Moody (2007); see also the annual report, *The True Cost of Chevron* (http://truecostofchevron.com/).
8. Though see Mosse (2005) for a description of how highly unsatisfactory PRA can be for researchers.
9. While there is nothing inherently wrong with household surveys they only capture one aspect of reality, and, if misused, can lead to terrible muddles. Ask someone in Kakura, for example, what their job is (as would be the procedure for many of the surveys carried out in rural Bangladesh) and they will almost certainly tell you that they are unemployed. What they won't tell you is that they have varied and complex sources of income, which change over the year.
10. See: www.asianews.it/news-en/Six-dead,-100-reportedly-wounded-in-Bangladesh-electricity-protest-5196.html (accessed 14 October 2010).
11. See: www.accessmylibrary.com/coms2/summary_0286-18709714_ITM (accessed 7 October 2011).
12. See: www.asianews.it/news-en/Six-dead,-100-reportedly-wounded-in-Bangladesh-electricity-protest-5196.html.
13. See Neilson (2010) for a detailed analysis of the Singur resistance movement.
14. See: www.adb.org/Documents/News/BRM/brm-201002.asp.
15. See: www.energybangla.com/index.php?mod=article&cat=SomethingtoSay&article=1839 (accessed 15 October 2010).
16. It should be noted that at the time of writing Asia Energy is still lobbying the government for a contract to continue with its plans: www.minesandcommunities.org/article.php?a=9866 (accessed 15 October 2010).
17. See: www.bbc.co.uk/news/10603687 (accessed 9 November 2010).
18. See: http://current.com/green/76365342_bangladesh-on-the-brink.htm (accessed 9 November 2010).

19. See: CIA Factbook, at https://www.cia.gov/library/publications/the-world-factbook/geos/bg.html (accessed 9 November 2010).
20. Ibid.
21. Ibid.
22. On the resource curse, see in particular, Collier (2007), M. Ross (1999, 2003), Robinson et al. (2006), Auty (1993).
23. For a summary of the anthropology of mining, see Ballard (2003).
24. As Robinson et al. put it: 'for every Venezuala or Nigeria there is a Norway or Botswana' (2006: 451).
25. See: http://eiti.org/supporters/companies (accessed 11 December 2010).
26. Transparency International gave Bangladesh a score of 2.4 in 2010, compared to 1.1 for Somalia, the bottom ranking country, and 9.3 for Denmark, New Zealand and Singapore.
27. See: www.deccanchronicle.com/business/bangladesh-discovers-gas-field-huge-reserves-466 (accessed 11 November 2010).
28. See: www.chevron.com/Documents/Pdf/ChevronWayEnglish.pdf. Compare this document to the anti-Chevron campaign, the True Cost of Chevron, at: http://truecostofchevron.com/report.html (accessed 12 November 2010).
29. See, for example, DFID's Issues Paper, 'DFID and CSR' at: http://webarchive.nationalarchives.gov.uk/+/www.dfid.gov.uk/pubs/files/corporate-social-resp.pdf (accessed 12 November 2010).
30. See: www.pacificfreepress.com/news/1/6893-bp-crime-against-nature-and-humanity-in-pictures.html (accessed 23 November 2010).
31. See Moody (2007), also the Mines and Communities website: www.minesandcommunities.org/ (accessed 12 November 2010).
32. See: http://chevrontoxico.com/news-and-multimedia/2009/0916-the-chevron-way.html (accessed 12 November 2010).
33. For more examples, see Moody (2007); for ethnographic exploration of indigenous analysis of the loss and devastation caused by mining at Ok Tedi, PNG see Kirsch (2006).
34. See: www.unglobalcompact.org/ (accessed 19 November 2010). The ten principles of the Global Compact are:

   1. Businesses should support and respect the protection of internationally proclaimed human rights.
   2. Businesses should make sure they are not complicit in human rights abuses.
   3. Businesses should uphold the freedom of association and the effective recognition of the right to collective bargaining.
   4. Businesses should uphold the elimination of all forms of forced and compulsory labour.
   5. Businesses should uphold the effective abolition of child labour.
   6. Businesses should uphold the elimination of discrimination in respect to employment and occupation.
   7. Businesses should support a precautionary approach to environmental challenges.
   8. Businesses should undertake initiatives to promote greater environmental responsibility.
   9. Businesses should encourage the development and diffusion of environmentally friendly technologies.
   10. Businesses should work against corruption in all its forms, including extortion and bribery.

35. See: www.riotinto.com/documents/Media-Speeches/RPW_CSR_-_Chatham_ House_161001.pdf (accessed 19 November 2010).

36. See: www.ethicalconsumer.org/CommentAnalysis/CorporateWatch/primark. aspx (accessed 27 November 2010).

37. For anthropological analyses of the fair trade movement and the audit cultures involved, see Dolan (2007), De Neve (2009), Luetchford (2008) and Cross (2011).

38. See, for example, Boyle (2009) in *Resurgence Magazine*: www.resurgence.org/ magazine/article2711-living-without-oil.html (accessed 26 November 2010).

39. See: http://truecostofchevron.com/media/ (accessed 26 November 2010).

40. See: www.chevron.com/weagree/?statement=community (accessed 28 November 2010).

41. See: www.chevron-weagree.com/ (accessed 28 November 2010); with thanks to Benji Zeitlyn for sending me these links.

42. See: www.bbc.co.uk/news/world-latin-america-12460333 (accessed 28 November 2010).

43. At the Freeport mine in West Papua, for example, the company's 'one percent trust fund offer' was flatly rejected by the Tribal Council, who declared that they would never succumb to bribery and/or accept the land settlement that the company had proposed (Kennedy and Abrash, 2002: 63).

44. See: www.economist.com/node/10491077?story_id=10491077 (accessed 28 November 2010).

45. See, for example, DFID's Issues Paper, 'DFID and CSR' at: http://webarchive. nationalarchives.gov.uk/+/www.dfid.gov.uk/pubs/files/corporate-social-resp.pdf (accessed 12 November 2010).

46. The World Bank makes a similar case for the role of business in development, though in the following statement, the suggestion is that 'global challenges' create a 'business case for action' rather than a moral case, as implied by DFID's approach: 'The private sector is a crucial partner in development – a source of knowledge, skills and resources. Above all, enterprises create economic opportunities to lift people out of poverty. At the same time, global challenges – be it epidemics, such as HIVAIDS, global warming or corruption – are increasingly impacting private sector operations and creating a business case for action.' See: http://web.worldbank.org/WBSITE/EXTERNAL/WBI/ WBIPROGRAMS/CGCSRLP/0,,menuPK:460901~pagePK:64156143~piPK: 64154155~theSitePK:460861,00.html (accessed 6 December 2010).

47. 'DFID and corporate responsibility: an issues paper', http://webarchive. nationalarchives.gov.uk/+/www.dfid.gov.uk/pubs/files/corporate-social-resp. pdf (accessed 8 December 2010).

48. See: http://eiti.org/ (accessed 8 December 2010).

49. Personal communication, Joseph Williams, of the NGO Publish What You Pay (2011).

50. See: www.guardian.co.uk/business/2011/feb/20/george-osborne-oil-mining-africa (accessed 07/10/11).

51. See: www.riotinto.com/documents/Media-Speeches/RPW_CSR_-_Chatham_ House_161001.pdf (accessed 19 November 2010). My thanks to Andrea Cornwall, who passed this quotation to me.

52. In recent research conducted for SIDA (Swedish International Development Cooperation Agency) in Bangladesh, rural informants spoke of 'hello power':

the use of mobile phones to gain access to people and institutions that would otherwise be inaccessible to them (personal communication, David Lewis).

53. Figures released by the International Monetary Fund (IMF) for 2010 rank Bangladesh 155th out of 182 countries, with a GDP of US $1,565 per capita (as opposed to Quatar, at the top of the scale with US $88,232 or the UK which ranks 20th with $35,053. See: http://en.wikipedia.org/wiki/List_of_countries_by_GDP_(PPP)_per_capita (accessed 3 February 2011).

54. For a critique of Putnam's positive stance on social capital see Putzel (1997).

55. See Charsley (2005) for discussion of marriage migration between Britain and Pakistan; see also Shaw and Charsley (2006).

56. One of the many complaints we repeatedly heard in the villages surrounding the gas field was that Chevron's staff were rarely seen around the place.

57. Whether or not Sylheti is a separate language is fiercely contested (see Zeitlyn, 2010).

58. See: http://theyesmen.org/blog/activists-derail-massive-chevron-ad-campaign-spark-media-vaudeville (accessed 4 February 2011).

2   HISTORIES OF CONNECTION: COLONIALISM, MIGRATION AND MULTINATIONALS

1. See: http://yourdemocracy.newstatesman.com/parliament/ban-on-imports-child-labour/HAN12742860 (accessed 7 October 2011).

2. See: http://news.bbc.co.uk/1/hi/world/south_asia/3598980.stm (accessed 7 October 2011).

3. See Gardner (2002b) on transnational burial.

4. In 2009 Bangladesh received a ranking of 2.4, compared to 9.4 for the highest ranking country (Norway) and 1.1. for the lowest (Somalia). Overall the country was ranked 139th out of 180 (see: www.transparency.org/policy_research/surveys_indices/cpi/2009/cpi_2009_table) (accessed 7 July 2010).

5. For excellent accounts of the history of modern Bangladesh, see Lewis (2011) and van Schendel (2005).

6. See for example: 'Energy resources and security: what Bangladesh government needs to do.' S.M. Shaheedullah and Anu Muhammed, New Age, 17 February 2009 (accessed at: http://banglapraxis.wordpress.com/2009/02/17/energy-resources-and-security-what-bangladesh-government-needs-to-do; accessed 17 August 2010).

7. See: www.finlays.net/about-finlays/history (accessed 17 August 2010).

8. 'I was so rushed that I had not time to go into details,' said Cyril Radcliffe, architect of the Partition (cited in Van Schendel, 2005: 39).

9. See, for example, the Bangla2000 website: www.bangla2000.com/bangladesh/war.shtm (accessed 30 June 2010).

10. The spectre of the 1974 famine continues to stalk Bangladesh. During our fieldwork in 2008 there was talk in the Bangladeshi media of a 'silent famine' that was gathering in strength as a result of the price hike in basic foodstuffs.

11. See, for example, 'Ignoring executions and torture: impunity for Bangladesh's security forces', Human Rights Watch: www.hrw.org/en/reports/2009/05/18/ignoring-executions-and-torture-0 (accessed 28 March 2011). In 2010, a scandal broke in the UK concerning the British police's training of the Rapid Action Battalion, which was accused of being a 'death squad'; see: www.thefirstpost.

co.uk/73132,news-comment,news-politics,bangladesh-death-squad-trained-by-british-cops (accessed 28 March 2011).

12. See for example, http://news.bbc.co.uk/1/hi/world/south_asia/5400784.stm (accessed 28 March 2011).

13. See: www.guardian.co.uk/world/gallery/2010/jun/30/bangladesh-protest#/?picture=364397793&index=3 (accessed 28 March 2011).

14. Between 1990 and 2001, the GDP increased by 60 percent (Toufique and Turton, 2002).

15. While the average remittances per person in South Asia were US $33, in Bangladesh they were US $41, an indication of the importance of migration for the country (UN, 2009). The real figures are probably much higher: a large proportion of the transfer of remittances is informal.

16. *Monga* experienced in the north-west, is a seasonal shortfall of food production, in which the poorest often migrate to other areas to find work (Chowdhury et al., 2009).

17. See: www.unicef.org/infobycountry/bangladesh_bangladesh_statistics.html#79 (accessed 28 March 2011).

18. A remark attributed to Henry Kissinger in 1971. See: www.unicef.org/infobycountry/bangladesh_bangladesh_statistics.html#79 (accessed 28 March 2011).

19. See: www.bdwebnews.com/national/power-water-hungry-people-mount-protest-road-block-at-mohakhali-uno-engr-in-barisal-assaulted/ (accessed 12 July 2010).

20. See: 'Power hungry people set ablaze PDB office', United News of Bangladesh, www.highbeam.com/doc/1G1-152036423.html (accessed 12 July 2010).

21. In 1993 the government divided its territory into twenty-three blocks, which were put out to tender to foreign companies. During the first round, eight blocks were awarded to four companies.

22. These companies operate fields at Kailashtila, Rashidpur, Beani Bazaar, Salda and Fenchuganj.

23. See: www.reuters.com/article/idUSSGE6500HF20100601 (accessed 28 March 2011).

24. See: http://gurumia.com/2010/02/07/reserve-of-bibiyana-doubles/ (accessed 8 July 2010).

25. See: www.minesandcommunities.org/article.php?a=9866 (accessed 12 July 2010).

26. For example, a blow-out at Magurchhara in 1997 while Occidental was drilling for gas caused considerable ecological damage to the forested area where the drilling was taking place, and cost the country an estimated 9 *crore taka* (i.e. 9 million *taka*). See: www.corpwatch.org/article.php?id=13727 (accessed 12 July 2010).

27. The Bangladesh government has banned women from certain categories of labour migration. They therefore officially only make up 1 percent of this figure (Siddiqui, 2003).

28. As mentioned above, until 1947 Sylhet was part of Assam rather than Bengal and had a different system of land administration.

29. Interestingly, the main steamer stations on the Kusiara River are prime *Londoni* areas today: Enatganj, Sherpur, Moulvi Bazaar, Baliganj and Fenchugan (Gardner, 1995: 41).

30. Choudhury (1993: 68) estimates that the number of Bengali men in East London in 1939 was between 150 and 200.
31. Some of which were bogus.
32. Choudhury (1993: 133) recounts how the process cost £1 and took two weeks.
33. For a more detailed discussion of immigration legislation, see Clarke (1992).
34. See: www.statistics.gov.uk (accessed 9 October 2011).
35. See ONS, 'Labour market', www.statistics.gov.uk/CCI/nugget.asp?ID=1089& Pos=2&ColRank=2&Rank=768 (accessed 6 March 2008).
36. See: http://operationblackvote.wordpress.com/2010/06/24/labour-force-survey-black-unemployment-up/ (accessed 7 July 2010).
37. While in the 1970s and 1980s it was mostly wives who travelled to the UK to join their husbands, today almost as many men apply for settlement visas to join their British-based wives. Foreign Office figures show that in 2005, 1,530 settlement visas were granted to Bangladeshi grooms (with 330 refused), in contrast to 2,133 issued to brides (with 590 refused). These figures have remained relatively stable since 2001. A 2004 report from the Home Office cites a rise of 14 percent in husbands admitted from the Indian subcontinent since 2003, compared to a rise of 12 percent in wives (see *Control of Immigration: Statistics. United Kingdom, 2004*; www.homeoffice.gov.uk/rds/pdfs05/hosb1405.pdf, accessed 2 May 2008).
38. 'Ashrafisation' – that is, taking on the ritual styles of higher-status groups. See Vreede-De Stuers (1968) and Osella and Osella (2000) for discussion of these processes in Kerala.
39. At the time of writing (6 July 2010).
40. I have been shown correspondence between Andrew Fawthrop, the CEO of Chevron in 2007, and transnational residents of Dighalbak in which their objections were raised.
41. Field notes, p. 48.
42. Field notes, p. 47.
43. According to the accounts of local people, connection to the gas supply was promised in the early negotiations with Unocal.

3 MATERIAL CONNECTIONS: RESOURCES AND LIVELIHOODS IN DUNIYAPUR

1. All the names in this and other chapters have been changed to preserve the anonymity of our informants.
2. The research team were shown copies of letters written by Samsun Khan to the Chevron Bangladesh CEO in which he pleaded with Chevron to drop this case. We did not see any correspondence from Chevron.
3. See Hulme (2004) for a detailed exploration of how one household in Mymensingh juggles services provided by state and private agencies.
4. Unicef defines the poverty line as a household with an income of less than US $1.25 a day; see: www.unicef.org/infobycountry/bangladesh_bangladesh_statistics.html#79 (accessed 28 March 2011).
5. As the situation was known within Bangladesh.
6. Since so many business people and government officials were put in gaol.
7. This work was funded by DFID Development Research Centre into Migration, Poverty and Globalisation, at the University of Sussex (www.migrationdrc.org/index.html).

8. The term 'colony' is used locally, and may have spread from India, where low-cost, slum-style 'colonies' were built for scheduled castes after independence (personal communication: F. Osella).

9. 1 *kiare* = 0.3 of an acre.

10. Smaller parcels of land were lost along the routes of the roads and pipelines. Overall, firm data on landholdings and land compensation was difficult to come by, and these figures are based on estimates given to us by informants.

11. See also Parry (1999) for description of a similar shift away from agriculture in India.

12. The Alternative Livelihoods Project run by FIVDB and financed by Chevron includes credit for fish farming (see Chapter 5).

13. Funded by Chevron.

14. Data from the 1980s fieldwork in Nadampur shows that women were often paid in *chaal* (husked rice) whereas men were more likely to be paid in *taka*, or with a mixture of unhusked rice and Bangladehsi *taka*.

15. Each of these districts is several hundred kilometres away.

16. Our research did not involve a scientific survey of environmental changes. This account is therefore based wholly on what I observed plus what local people told us.

17. This will be discussed in more detail in Chapter 5.

18. Chevron built culverts under the roads but unfortunately we found that these were blocked with weeds.

19. For example, the expenditure of at least 80 percent of the daily income on food (Breman, 2007: 341).

20. See for example, the World Bank web page, 'Choosing and estimating a poverty line': http://web.worldbank.org/WBSITE/EXTERNAL/TOPICS/EXTPOVERTY/EXTPA/0,,contentMDK:20242879~menuPK:435055~page PK:148956~piPK:216618~theSitePK:430367~isCURL:Y~isCURL:Y,00.html (accessed 12 November 2009).

21. I am particularly indebted to Habib Raham for his account of the history of Kakura.

22. Chevron has financed slab latrines for nearly all the households surrounding the gas plant; they have also distributed smoke-free *chulas*.

23. Twenty-seven households were tracked in total.

24. In Bangladesh the main rice crop is the *aman* crop, which is harvested in November/December and planted in the spring, being naturally irrigated during the summer rains. *Boro* rice involves a second harvest, involving high-yield varieties and mechanised irrigation systems.

25. I shall return to this comment in Chapter 6. The availability of work from Chevron is discussed later in this chapter.

26. Bengali measurement of weight: 1 *maund* = approximately 40 kg.

27. Friends in Village Development Bangladesh, the NGO contracted by Chevron to carry out the Alternative Livelihoods Programme (see Chapter 5).

28. This comment points to differences in the land quality, due to the roads that link the North and South Pads.

29. 'Baseline survey of UNOCAL working area, 2006', Centre for Women and Child Studies, Dhaka.

30. The community relations official at the plant told us that 500 people had originally been employed; others reduced this figure to several hundred.

31. Though see Parry (1999) for description of industrial work in the steel plants of Bhilai.

4   OUR OWN POOR: SOCIAL CONNECTIONS, 'HELPING' AND CLAIMS TO ENTITLEMENT

1. The patron–client relations that exist within lineages is discussed in detail in Gardner (1995).
2. Wood's (2003: 9c) description of the patronage of 'lineages and feudal legacies' in South Asia is deeply resonant of Duniyapur.
3. According to Islam, one-third of the meat should go to the household, one-third to relatives and friends and one-third to the poor.
4. *Zakah* is payable at a rate of 2.5 percent of most types of wealth; see: www.muslimhands.org/en/gb/zakah/ (accessed 4 December 2009).
5. See, for example, www.Islamicaid.org.uk: 'For £45 we offer Qurbani on your behalf.'
6. Women usually give up their share of their inheritance to their brothers in the expectation that, should they divorce, their brothers will provide economic support and shelter.
7. See also Hulme (2004), for a case study approach to understanding poverty and coping strategies in Bangladesh.
8. Roads are on higher land/embankments.
9. See Pattenden (2010) for summary of debates concerning micro-credit in South Asia.
10. In contrast, the loans offered by the FIVDB programme tend to be taken up by middle income households, who use them to start up small businesses (see Chapter 5).
11. Rahsheed's research in Comilla shows that *dalal* are often relatives or neighbours, meaning that there is far less risk involved for those acquiring papers and plane tickets from them (Rahsheed, 2008).
12. This section is based in part on my paper, 'Keeping connected: security, place and capital in a "Londoni" village in Sylhet' (Gardner, 2008).
13. According to national census data, over 60 percent of people of Bangladeshi and Pakistani origin were living in low-income households in 2001; see: www.statistics.gov.uk/cci/nugget.asp?id=269 (accessed 2 May 2008).
14. A more risky and unusual route is to go illegally to the UK with an agent who supplies forged papers.
15. See Jordan Smith for similar observations in Nigeria (2007). Jordan Smith's work is discussed in more detail in Chapter 6.
16. As described in the Introduction (Chapter 1), the modern kitchen that the family had built at the other end of the house, with its increasingly dusty gas cooker and stainless steel sink, has never been used.
17. For recent work that discusses the silencing of pain, testimony and story telling, see F. Ross (2003), Donnan and Simpson (2007) and West (2003).

5   CLAIMS OF PARTNERSHIP AND ETHICAL CONNECTION: CHEVRON'S PROGRAMME OF 'COMMUNITY ENGAGEMENT'

1. See: www.chevron.com/globalissues/corporateresponsibility/2007/documents/Chevron_CR_report_050208.pdf (accessed 2008).
2. See Gardner (2008) for discussion of the relationship between status and work in Sylhet.

3. For discussion of similar development 'buzzwords and fuzzwords' see Cornwall and Eade (2010).
4. See: www.chevron.com/countries/bangladesh/inthecommunity/ (accessed 23 February 2010).
5. See: www.oxfam.org.uk/oxfam_in_action/what_we_do/index.html (accessed 23 February 2010).
6. See: www.chevron.com/countries/bangladesh/inthecommunity/ (accessed 23 February 2010).
7. Interview with Steve Wilson and Naser Ahmed of Chevron Bangladesh (3 December 2008).
8. See Zalik (2004) for discussion of Shell's 'partnership development' and security agenda in Nigeria.
9. The project goal was : 'to assist the Bibiyana Gas Field affected households and disadvantaged people to enhance their productive potential, improving their asset base and make sustainable use of them to overcome poverty through alternative livelihood' (Alternative Livelihood Programme for Vulnerable Families of Bibiyana, *Annual Report*, 2006–2007).
10. Ibid.
11. Personal communication, N. Ahmed, March 2010.
12. According to Chevron's *Bangladesh Fact Sheet* (2008), since 1998 the company has spent the paltry sum of $2 million on community development in Bangladesh.
13. According to literature produced by Chevron, they distributed 1,300 sanitary latrines among poorer households living near the field in the first year of operations, plus another 1,400 by March 2007 (Chevron, 2008).
14. I never saw these stoves being used; they were unsuitable for the *lakri* (firewood) used for cooking, I was told when I asked about a disused Chevron *chula* I noticed in someone's yard.
15. Production costs were 800 *taka*.
16. Personal communication from FIVDB field officer.
17. Scooter rickshaw, run on natural gas.
18. See Zalik (2004) on the creation of 'partnerships' by Shell in Nigeria.
19. As we saw in Chapter 3, many people access credit via a range of sources, including local moneylenders, NGOs, and the 'help' of wealthier neighbours or relatives. The terms of NGO loans are often too difficult to meet: high interest payments, paid at very regular intervals, and coercive NGO officials, for whom repayment is a sign of 'success', were all mentioned to us by informants. The ALP programme was viewed relatively favourably: it had more flexible terms of repayment than, say, the Grameen Bank, which also operates locally.
20. For a summary of recent debates concerning micro-credit in South Asia, see Pattenden (2010: 488–91) and Rosenberg (2010).
21. Perhaps 'empowerment' has become one of those 'fuzzwords' that impart feelings of warmth and hope while having little relationship to political projects of empowerment epitomised by Paulo Freire's work in the 1970s, or feminism in the 1980s (cf. Batliwala, 2010: available at: www.oxfam.org.uk/resources/downloads/bk-deconstructing-development-buzzwords-010910-en.pdf; accessed 3 October 2011).
22. This observation is reflected in our data.
23. Chevron's literature reports that 40 women were trained, but our research revealed that the programme has had mixed results. Many of the women

receiving the original training were unmarried; by the time they had finished the training, however, they had married and moved elsewhere. Other women complained that embroidery work was highly labour intensive, and not sufficiently well paid to make it worth their while. One women, for example, told us that for two to three days work on a piece, she only received 25 *taka*.

24. See Eyben (2004) for discussion of representations of gender and development in DFID brochures.

25. The Chevron *Bangladesh Newsletter* of July 2008 contains nine such photographs, in 24 pages.

26. Chevron *Bangladesh Newsletter*, Issue 2, July 2008.

27. Ferguson does not discuss the CSR programmes of transnational mining companies in Africa, though these certainly exist; on Chevron's community programmes in Nigeria and Angola, see, for example: www.chevron.com/countries/nigeria/inthecommunity/ and http://careers.chevron.com/global_operations/country_operations/angola/ (accessed 23 February, 2010).

6   RUMOUR AND ACTIVISM: POLITICS BREAKS OUT

1. This report was not commissioned by Chevron but was an effort to use the research for poverty reduction, as required by my funders, the ESRC/DFID.

2. For more discussion of the anthropology of rumour, see Kirsch (2002), Masquelier (2000), White (1997, 2000) and Turner (2004).

3. The Country of Origin Report 2009 states that 440,684 people were arrested by the caretaker government in 2007 under various charges (Home Office, 2009).

4. See: www.guardian.co.uk/world/2011/apr/05/muhammad-yunus-loses-batttle-grameen-bank (accessed 6 April 2011).

5. As Reyes and Begum point out in their report: 'Bangladesh is so politicised that it is practically impossible for a large investor like Unocal to be perceived as neutral' (2005: 6).

6. Unocal was merged with Chevron in 2005. For the purposes of this account I shall refer to the company as Unocal.

7. In 2010 news broke on WikiLeaks of the training of Bangladesh's 'death squad' by the British police: www.guardian.co.uk/world/2011/jan/26/bangladesh-death-squad-killings-britain?INTCMP=SRCH (accessed 6 April 2011).

8. Beyond this story, I have no evidence that the arrest took place.

9. The relationship between governments and oil/mining companies is highly complex and varies according to context. In Nigeria, for example, WikiLeaks has revealed documents that show that Shell inserted staff into all of the major ministries. See: www.guardian.co.uk/business/2010/dec/08/wikileaks-cables-shell-nigeria-spying, accessed 5April 2011.

10. Clearly, 'the people' could never be characterised as 'Goliath', for ultimately few of the demands of the Demand Realisation Committee were met.

11. Interview notes, September 2009; see also www.cetri.be/spip.php?article1355 (accessed 5 April 2011).

12. See interview with Anu Muhammed at: http://bangladeshwatchdog.blogspot.com/2009/09/oil-gas-and-mineral-resources-of-our.html (accessed 16 August 2010).

13. See: http://farakkacommittee.com/grand_rally.html (accessed 16 August 2010).

14. See: www.facebook.com/topic.php?uid=64091569136&topic=9117 (accessed 16 August 2010).
15. See interview with Anu Muhammed: http://bangladeshwatchdog.blogspot.com/2009/09/oil-gas-and-mineral-resources-of-our.html (accessed 16 August 2010).
16. Interview with Nur Mohammad, 20 September 2009.
17. Personal communication, Habib Rahman, 2011.
18. For detailed discussion and analysis of events at Phulbari, see Nuremowla (forthcoming). For postings concerning Phulbari and links to other sites since 2004, see the website of the lobbying organisation, Mines and Communities: www.minesandcommunities.org//list.php?r=73 (accessed 17 August 2010).
19. See: www.facebook.com/topic.php?uid=64091569136&topic=9117 (accessed 17 August 2010).
20. In 2009, the National Committee's demands to the government can be summarised as follows:

    1. Proprietorship of all mineral resources lies with the people; existing production share contracts made with multinationals do not benefit the national economy, only the multinationals.
    2. Compensation for losses from Magurcchara and Tengratila to be paid to the government by Chevron and Niko, and judicial action against corrupt officials involved in Chevron's over-expoitation of gas reserves at Bibiyana and damage done to the Lawachhara Forest during seismic surveys.
    3. Maritime boundaries and resources to be properly demarcated.
    4. Open pit mining should be banned and Asia Energy driven from the country.
    5. National capacity for the extraction of resources should be developed.
    6. Electricity supply should be 'unshackled from the current vicious policies, agreements and institutional provisions' with multinationals, which mean that electricity is sold back to the government at unreasonably high rates.
    7. Trial of ministers, bureaucrats, etc. involved in contracts that benefit multinationals at the cost of Bangladesh (Shaheedullah and Muhammed, 2009).

21. See: www.news.org.bd/?p=12978 (accessed 18 August 2010).
22. See interview with Anu Muhammed at: http://bangladeshwatchdog.blogspot.com/2009/09/oil-gas-and-mineral-resources-of-our.html (accessed 16 August 2010).
23. See: www.bangladesh2day.com/newsfinance/2010/March/25/All-Chevron-operated-fields-have-larger-gas-reserves.php (accessed 18 August 2010).
24. Personal communication from Joseph Williams of Publish What You Pay.
25. See interview with Anu Muhammed at: http://bangladeshwatchdog.blogspot.com/2009/09/oil-gas-and-mineral-resources-of-our.html (accessed 16 August 2010).
26. See discussion at: http://rumiahmed.wordpress.com/2009/12/19/corruption-allegations-surface-against-sajeeb-wazed-joy/ (accessed 18 August 2010).

7   BLOW-OUT! STORIES OF DISCONNECTION AND LOSS

1. A video of a blow-out at a gas field in Bangladesh is available on YouTube, and can be accessed at: www.youtube.com/watch?v=aaNlXf7rlnE (accessed 7 April 2011).

2. For discussion of 'giving voice' through stories in contexts of violence, see F. Ross (2003) and West (2003).
3. Flaring is neither safe nor benign but a major cause of global warming and pollution. See: http://en.wikipedia.org/wiki/Gas_flare (accessed 6 April 2011).
4. See: info@iaia.org
5. With thanks to James Fairhead for this insight.
6. The systematic undermining of oppositional accounts can be more confrontational. As the film *Crude* shows, lawyers putting the case against Chevron in their claim for compensation in Ecuador found that not only was their evidence continually disputed, but also their research methods, including the laboratories where samples of (it was alleged) oil-polluted soil had been analysed. See: www.crudethemovie.com/ (accessed 8 April 2011).
7. I recount the story of a woman in this position in my book *Songs at the River's Edge* (Gardner, 1991).

References

Abrar, C. ed. 2000 *On the Margin: Refugees, Migration and Minorities*. Dhaka: RMMRU.

Adams, C. 1987 *Across Seven Seas and Thirteen Rivers: Life Stories of Sylheti Pioneers in Britain*. London: Tower Hamlets Arts Project.

Afsar, R. 2000 *Rural Urban Migration in Bangladesh: Causes, Consequences, Challenges*. Dhaka: Dhaka University Press.

Appadurai, A. 1990 'Disjuncture and difference in the global cultural economy', *Public Culture* 2(2): 1–24.

Arrighi, G. 2006 'Spatial and other "fixes" of historical capitalism', in C. Chase-Dunn and S.J. Babones (eds) *Global Social Change: Historical and Comparative Perspectives*. Baltimore, MD: Johns Hopkins University Press, pp. 201–13.

Auty, R. 1993 *Sustaining Development in Mineral Economies: The Resource Curse Thesis*. London: Routledge.

Ballard, 2003 'Resource wars: the anthropology of mining', *Annual Review of Anthropology* 32: 287–313.

Bannon L. and Collier P. 2003 'Natural reosurces and conflict: what we can do', in I. Bannon and P. Collier (eds) *Natural Resources and Violent Conflict: Options and Actions*. Washington, DC: World Bank.

Batliwala, S. 2010 'Taking the power out of empowerment: an experiential account', in A. Cornwall and D. Eade (eds) *Development Discourse: Buzzwords and Fuzzwords*, London: Practical Action Publishing, pp. 111–21.

Behal, R.P. 1985 'Forms of labour protest in Assam Valley Tea Plantations, 1900–1930', *Economic and Political Weekly* 20(4): 19–26.

Blowfield, M. and Frynas, J.G. 2005 'Setting new agendas: critical perspectives on CSR in the developing world', *International Affairs* 81(3): 499–513.

Bourdieu, P. (1983). 'Forms of capital', in J.C. Richards (ed.) *Handbook of Theory and Research for the Sociology of Education*. New York: Greenwood Press.

BRAC 2008 *The State of Governance in Bangladesh: Confrontation, Competition, Accountability*. Dhaka: Institute of Governance Studies, BRAC University.

Breman, J. 1996 *Footloose Labour: Working in India's Informal Economy* Cambridge: Cambridge University Press.

Breman, J. 2007 *The Poverty Regime in Village India: Half a Century of Work and Rural Life at the Bottom of the Economy in Southern Gujarat*. Oxford: Oxford University Press.

Burton, T. 2002 'When corporations want to cuddle', in G. Evans, J. Goodman and N. Lansbury (eds) *Moving Mountains: Communities Confront Mining and Globalisation*. London: Zed Press, pp. 109–25.

Charsley, K. 2005 'Unhappy husbands: masculinity and migration in transnational Pakistani marriages', *Journal of the Royal Anthropological Institute* 11(1): 85–106.

Chase-Dunn, C. and Babones, S. (eds) 2006 *Global Social Change: Historical and Comparative Perspectives*. Baltimore, MD: Johns Hopkins University Press.

Chatterjee, J. 1995 *Bengal Divided: Hindu Communalism and Partition 1932–1947.* Cambridge: Cambridge University Press.

Chevron, 2007 *Corporate Social Responsibility Report.* Available at: http://www.chevron.com/globalissues/corporateresponsibility/2007/ (accessed 15 October 2011).

Chevron 2008 *Bibiyana Gas Field First Anniversary Report.* Dhaka: Chevron.

Choudhury, Y. 1993 *The Routes and Tales of the Bangladeshi Settlers.* Birmingham: Sylhet Social History Group.

Chowdhury, S., Mobarak, A. and Bryan, G. 2009 *Migrating Away from a Seasonal Famine: A Randomized Intervention in Bangladesh.* Human Development Research Paper 2009/41. Available at: http://mpra.ub.uni-muenchen.de/19224/1/MPRA_paper_19224.pdf (accessed 13 October 2011).

Christian Aid 2004 *Behind the Mask: The Real Face of CSR.* Available at: http://www.st-andrews.ac.uk/~csearweb/aptopractice/Behind-the-mask.pdf (accessed 8 December 2010).

Clarke, J. 1992 'National Exclusions', in A. Cambridge and S. Feuchtwang (eds) *Where you Belong.* Aldershot: Avebury, pp. 14–31.

Clifford, J. and Marcus, G. (eds) *Writing Culture: The Politics and Poetics of Ethnography.* Berkeley: University of California Press.

Colley, P. 2002 'The political economy of mining', in G. Evans, J. Goodman and N. Lansbury (eds) *Moving Mountains: Communities Confront Mining and Globalisation.* London: Zed Books, pp. 19–37.

Collier, P. 2007 *The Bottom Billion: Why the Poorest Countries are Failing and What Can Be Done about It.* Oxford: Oxford University Press.

Comaroff, J. and Comaroff, J.L. 2000 'Millennium capitalism: first thoughts on a second coming', *Public Cultures* 12(2): 291–343.

Cornwall, C. and Eade, D. (eds) 2010 *Deconstructing Development Discourse: Buzzwords and Fuzzwords.* London: Practical Action Publishing.

Cornwall, A. and Pratt, G. 1999 *Pathways to Participation: Reflections on PRA.* London: IDTG Publishing.

Cross, J. 2011 'Detachment as corporate ethic: materialising CSR in the diamond supply chain', *Focaal – Journal of Global and Historical Anthropology* 60: 34–46.

De Neve, G. 2009 'Power, inequality and corporate social responsibility: the politics of ethical compliance in the South Indian garment industry', *Economic and Political Weekly* 44(22): 63–71.

Department for International Development (DFID) undated *DFID and Corporate Social Responsibility: An Issues Paper.* Available at: http://webarchive.nationalarchives.gov.uk/+/http://www.dfid.gov.uk/pubs/files/corporate-social-resp.pdf (accessed 9 October 2011).

Devine, J., Camfield, L., Gough, I. 2008 'Autonomy, dependency or both? Perspectives from Bangladesh', *Journal of Happiness Studies* 9(1): 105–38.

Doane, D. 2005 'The myth of CSR: the problem with assuming that companies can do well whilst also "doing good" is that markets don't really work in that way', *Stanford Social Innovation Review* fall: 23–9.

Dolan, C. 2007 'Market affections: moral encounters with Kenyan Fairtrade flowers', *Ethnos* 72(2): 239–61.

Donnan, H. and Simpson, K. 2007 'Silence and violence among Northern Ireland border Protestants', *Ethnos* 72(1): 5–28.

Donziger, S. 2009 'Chevron-Toxico: the campaign for justice in Ecuador', available at: http://chevrontoxico.com/news-and-multimedia/2009/0916-the-chevron-way. html (accessed 8 December 2010).

Douglas, M. 1990 'No free gifts', Foreword to M. Mauss, *The Gift: The Form and Reason for Exchange in Archaic Societies*. London: Routledge (reprinted Routledge Classics, 2002), pp. ix–xxiii.

Evans, G., Goodman, J. and Lansbury, N. 2002 *Moving Mountains: Communities Confront Mining and Globalisation*. London: Zed Press.

Eyben, R. 2004 'Battles over booklets: gender myths in the British aid programme', *IDS Bulletin* 35(4): 73–81.

Ferguson, J. 1990 *The Anti-Politics Machine: 'Development', Depoliticisation, and Bureaucratic Power in Lesotho*. Cambridge: Cambridge University Press.

Ferguson, J. 1999 *Expectations of Modernity: Myths and Meanings of Urban Life on the Zambian Copperbelt*. Berkeley: University of California Press.

Ferguson, J. 2005 'Seeing it like an oil company: space, security and global capital in neo-liberal Africa', *American Anthropologist* 107(3): 377–82.

Foucault, M. 1972 *The Archaeology of Knowledge*. London: Tavistock Publications.

Fryer, P. 1984 *Staying Power: The History of Black People in Britain*. London: Pluto Press.

Gardner, K. 1991 *Songs at the River's Edge: Stories from a Bangladeshi Village*. London: Virago (reprinted by Pluto Press, 1996).

Gardner, K. 1993a '*Desh–Bidesh*: Sylheti images of home and away', *Man* 28(9): 1–15.

Gardner, K. 1993b 'Mullahs, miracles and migration: travel and transformation in rural Bangladesh', *Contributions to Indian Sociology* NS 27(2): 213–35.

Gardner, K. 1995 *Global Migrants, Local Lives: Migration and Transformation in Rural Bangladesh*. Oxford: Oxford University Press.

Gardner, K. 1997 'Mixed messages: contested "development" and the Plantation Rehabilitation Project', in R. Grillo and R.L. Stirrat (eds) *Discourses of Development: Anthropological Perspectives*. Oxford: Berg, pp. 133–57.

Gardner, K. 2002a *Age, Narrative and Migration: Life History and the Life Course amongst Bengali Elders in London*. Oxford: Berg.

Gardner, K. 2002b 'Death of a migrant: transnational death ritual and gender among British Sylhetis', *Global Networks* 2(3): 191–205.

Gardner, K. 2006 'The transnational work of kinship and caring: Bengali British marriages in historical perspective', Special Edition, A. Shaw and K. Charlesly (eds) *Global Networks* 6(4): 373–89.

Gardner, K. 2008 'Keeping connected: security, place and social capital in a Londoni village in Sylhet', *Journal of the Royal Anthropological Institute* NS 14: 447–95.

Gardner, K. and Ahmed, Z. 2009 'Degrees of separation: informal social protection, relatedness and migration in Biswanath, Bangladesh', *Journal of Development Studies* 45(1): 124–49.

Gardner, K. and Lewis, D. 1996 *Anthropology, Development and the Post-Modern Challenge*. London: Pluto Press.

Gardner, K. and Lewis, D. 2000 'Dominant paradigms overturned or "business as usual"? Development discourse and the White Paper on International Development', *Critique of Anthropology* 20(1): 15–29.

Gardner, K. and Mand, K. 2012 'My away is here: place, empowerment and mobility among British Bengali children', in K. Gardner and K. Mand (eds) *Through Children's Eyes: Transnational Migration Revisited* Special Issue, *Journal of Ethnic and Migration Studies*.

Glynn, S. 2002 'Bengali Muslims: the new East End radicals?', *Ethnic and Racial Studies* 25(6): 969–88.

Grillo, R. and Stirrat, R.L. (eds) 1997 *Discourses of Development: Anthropological Perspectives*. Oxford: Berg.

Grima, B. 1991 'The role of suffering in women's performances in Paxto', in A. Appadurai, F.J. Korom and M. Mills (eds) *Gender, Genre and Power in South Asian Expressive Traditions*. Philadelphia: University of Pennsylvania Press, pp. 78–101.

Gronemeyer, M. 1999 'Helping', in W. Sachs (ed.) *Thec*. London: Zed Books, pp. 53–70.

Guterson, H. 1997 'Studying up revisited', *Political and Legal Anthropology* 20(1): 114–19.

Harvey, D. 2003 *The New Imperialism*. Oxford: Oxford University Press.

Havini, M. and Johns, V. 2002 'Mining, self determination and Bougainville', in G. Evans, J. Goodman and N. Lansbury (eds) *Moving Mountains: Communities Confront Mining and Globalisation*. London: Zed Press, pp. 125–47.

Home Office, UK Government 2008 *Country of Origin Report: Bangladesh*. London: Home Office Publications.

Home Office, UK Government 2009 *Country of Origin Report: Bangladesh*. London: Home Office Publications.

Huda, S. 2006 'Dowry in Bangladesh: compromising women's rights', *South Asia Research* 26(3): 249–268.

Huda, K., Rahman, S. and Guirguis, C. 2008 'Social capital and what it represents: the experience of the ultra poor in Bangladesh', *Journal of Power* 1(3): 295–315.

Hulme, D. 2004 'Thinking "small" and the understanding of poverty: Maymana and Mofizul's story', *Journal of Human Development* 5(2): 161–77.

Human Rights Watch 2009 'Ignoring executions and torture: impunity for Bangladesh's security forces', available at: http://www.hrw.org/en/reports/2009/05/18/ignoring-executions-and-torture-0 (accessed 28 March 2011).

Hussain, E. 2006 *The Islamist*. London: Penguin.

Islam, H.E. 1987 *Overseas Migration from Bangladesh: A Micro-Study* Chittagong: Chittagong Rural Economics Programme, Chittagong University.

Jahangir, B.K. 1982 *Rural Society: Power Structure and Class Practice*. Dhaka: Dhaka University Press.

Jansen, E. 1987 *Rural Bangladesh: Competition Over Scarce Resources*. Dhaka: Dhaka University Press.

Jenkins, R. 2005 'Globalisation, CSR and poverty', *International Affairs* 81(3): 525–40.

Jordan Smith, D. 2007 *A Culture of Corruption: Everyday Deception and Popular Discontent in Nigeria*. Princeton, NJ: Princeton University Press.

Kabeer, N. 2002 'Citizenship, affiliation and exclusion: perspectives from the South', *IDS Bulletin* 33(2): 1–15.

Kapelus, P. 2002 'Mining, CSR and "the community": the case of Rio Tinto, Richards Bay Minerals and the Mbonambi', *Journal of Business Ethics* 39: 275–96.

Kennedy, D. and Abrash, A. 2002 'Repressive mining in West Papua', in G. Evans, J. Goodman and N. Lansbury (eds) *Moving Mountains: Communities Confront Mining and Globalisation*. London: Zed Press, pp. 59–75.

Khan, I. and Seeley, J. 2005 *Making a Living: The Livelihoods of the Poor in Bangladesh*. Dhaka: Dhaka University Press.

Khan, M. 2009 'Chevron's seismic survey, USAID's Nishorgo project and Bangladesh's Lawachara National Park: a critical review', available at: http://wrap.warwick. ac.uk/1852/ (accessed 6 October 2011).

Kirsch, S. 2002 'Rumour and other narratives of political violence in West Papua', *Critique of Anthropology* 22: 53–79.

Kirsch, S. 2006 *Reverse Anthropology: Indigenous Analysis of Social and Environmental Relations in New Guinea*. Stanford, CA: Stanford University Press.

Kirsch, S. 2010a 'Sustainability and the BP oil spill' (Guest Editorial), *Dialectical Anthropology* 34(3): 295–300.

Kirsch, S. 2010b 'Sustainable mining', *Dialectical Anthropology* 34(3): 87–93.

Klein, N. 2002 *No Logo: No Space, No Choice, No Jobs*. London: Picador.

Korten, D. 2002 'Predatory corporations', in G. Evans, J. Goodman and N. Lansbury (eds) *Moving Mountains: Communities Confront Mining and Globalisation*. London: Zed Press, pp. 1–19.

Leach, M. 1991 'Engendered environments: understanding natural resource management in the West African Forest Zone', *IDS Bulletin* 22(4): 17–24.

Lewis, D. 2011 *Bangladesh: Politics, Economy and Civil Society*. Cambridge: Cambridge University Press.

Lewis, D. and Hossain, A. 2008 'A tale of three villages: power, difference and locality in rural Bangladesh', *Journal of South Asian Development* 3(1): 30–51.

Li, Tania Murray 1996 'Images of community: discourse and strategy in property relations', *Development and Change* 27: 501–27.

Li, Tania Murray 2007 *The Will to Improve: Governmentality, Development and the Practice of Politics*. Durham, NC: Duke University Press.

Luetchford, P. 2008. *Fair Trade and a Global Commodity: Coffee in Costa Rica*. London: Pluto Press.

Mahmood, R.A. 1991 *Employment of Bangladeshis Abroad and Uses of Their Remittances*. Dhaka: Bangladesh Institute of Development Studies.

Marcus, G. and Fisher, M. 1986 *Anthropology as Cultural Critique*. Chicago: University of Chicago Press.

Masquelier, A. 2000 'Of head hunters and cannibals: migrancy, labor and consumption in the Mawri imagination', *Cultural Anthropology* 15(1): 84–126.

Mattingly, C. 1998 *Healing Dramas and Clinical Plots: The Narrative Structure of Experience*. Cambridge: Cambridge University Press.

Metcalf, B. and Metcalf, T. 2002 *A Concise History of India*. Cambridge: Cambridge University Press.

Moody, R. 2007 *Rocks and Hard Places: The Globalisation of Mining*. London: Zed Press.

Mosse, D. 2005 *Cultivating Development: An Ethnography of Aid Policy and Practice*. London: Pluto Press.

Mumby, D.K. (ed.) 1993 *Narrative and Social Control: Critical Perspectives* Newbury Park, CA: Sage.

Myerhoff, B. 1992 *Remembered Lives: The Work of Ritual, Story Telling and Growing Older*. Ann Arbor: University of Michegan Press.

Nader, L. 1974 'Up the anthropologist – perspectives gained from studying up', in D. Hymes (ed.) *Reinventing Anthropology*. New York: Vintage Books, pp. 284–311.

Neilson, K.B. 2010 'Contesting Indian development? Industrialisation, land acquisition and protest in West Bengal', *Forum for Development Studies* 37(2): 145–70.

Nuremowla, S. 2011 Resistance, rootedness and mining protest in Phulbari. Unpublished doctoral thesis, submitted to University of Sussex, September.

Office for National Statistics 2002 'Minority ethnic groups in the UK'.

Ong, A. 2006 *Neoliberalism as Exception: Mutations in Citizenship and Sovereignty.* Durham, NC: Duke University Press.

Osella, F. and Osella, C. 2000 *Social Mobility in Kerala: Modernity and Identity in Conflict.* London: Pluto Press.

Parry, J. 1986 'The gift, the Indian gift and "the Indian gift"', *Man* 21(3): 453–73.

Parry, J. 1999 'Lords of labour: working and shirking in Bhilai', *Contributions to Indian Sociology* 33(1–2): 108–140.

Parry, J. 2001 'The "crisis of corruption" and the "idea of India": a worm's eye view', in I. Pardo (ed.) *Morals of Legitimacy: Between Agency and the System.* New Directions in Anthropology. Oxford: Berghahn Books, pp. 27–55.

Patel, F. and Das, S. 2008 'Orissa's highland clearances: the reality gap in R and R', *Social Change* 38(4): 576–608.

Pattenden, J. 2010 'A neo-liberalism of civil society? Self-help groups and the labouring class poor in rural South India', *Journal of Peasant Studies* 37(3): 485–512.

Peach, C. (ed.) (1996) *Ethnicity in the 1991 Census: The Ethnic Minority Populations of Britain*, vol. 2. London: HMSO.

Peel, M. 2009 *A Swamp Full of Dollars.* London: I.B. Tauris.

Purvez, M.S.A. 2004 *Making Use of Mediating Resources: Social Network of the Extreme Poor in Bangladesh*, Livelihoods of the Extreme Poor Study (LEP). Dhaka: Impact Monitoring and Evaluation Cell, Proshika.

Putnam, R.D. (2000) *Bowling Alone: The Collapse and Revival of American Community.* New York: Simon and Schuster.

Putzel, J. 1997 'Accounting for the "dark side" of social capital: reading Robert Putnam on democracy', *Journal of International Development* 9(7): 939–49.

Rahman, M.H. and Manprasert, S. 2006 'Landlessness and its impact on economic development: a case study on Bangladesh', *Journal of Social Sciences* 2: 54–60.

Rahsheed, R.S. 2008 'Overseas labour migration from rural Bangladesh: livelihoods, capital and risk in two villages in Comilla', unpublished thesis, University of Sussex.

Rajak, D. 2007 'In good company: an ethnography of corporate social responsibility', unpublished doctoral thesis, University of Sussex.

Rajak, D. 2009 'I am the conscience of the company: responsibility and the gift in a transnational mining corporation', in K. Browne and L. Milgram (eds) *Economics and Morality*, Society for Economic Anthropology Monographs. Lanham, MD: AltaMira Press, pp. 211–33.

Rajak, D. 2011 *In Good Company: An Anatomy of Corporate Social Responsibility.* Stanford, CA: Stanford University Press.

Reyes, D. and Begum, S. 2005 *Corporate Engagement Project Field Report*, CDA Collaborative Learning Projects, available at: http://cdainc.com/publications/cep/fieldvisits/cepVisit19Bangladesh.pdf (accessed 16 July 2010).

Riaz, A. 2004 *God Willing: The Politics of Islamism in Bangladesh.* Lanham, MD: Rowman and Littlefield.

Robbins, J. 2004 *Becoming Sinners: Christiantity and Moral Torment in a Papua New Guinea Society.* Berkeley: University of California Press.

Robins, N. 2006 *The Corporation that Changed the World: How the East India Company Shaped the Modern Multinational.* London: Pluto Press.

Robinson, J., Torvick, R. and Verdier, T. 2006 'The political foundations of the resource curse', *Journal of Development Economics* 79(2): 447–68.

Rogaly, B. and Coppard, D. 2003 'They used to eat, now they go to earn: the changing meanings of seasonal migration from Puruliya District in West Bengal, India', *Journal of Agrarian Change* 3(3): 395–433.

Rosenberg, R. 2010 *Does microcredit really help poor people?* Focus Note 59. Washington, DC: CGap.

Ross, F. 2003 'On having voice and being heard: some after-effects of testifying before the South African Truth and Reconciliation Commission', *Anthropological Theory* 3: 325–41.

Ross, M. 1999 'The political economy of the resource curse', *World Politics* 51(2): 297–322.

Ross, M. 2003 'The natural resource curse: how wealth can make you poor', in L. Bannon and P. Collier (eds) *Natural Resources and Violent Conflict: Options and Actions*. Washington, DC: World Bank, pp. 17–42.

Sachs, W. (ed.) 1999 *The Development Dictionary: A Guide to Knowledge as Power*. London: Zed Books.

Samaddar, R. 1999 *The Marginal Nation: Transborder Migration from Bangladesh to West Bengal*. Dhaka: Dhaka University Press.

Sawyer, S. 2004 *Crude Chronicles: Indigenous Politics, Multinational Oil and Neoliberalism in Ecuador*. Durham, NC: Duke University Press.

Scarry, E. 1985 *The Body in Pain: The Making and Unmaking of the World*. New York: Oxford University Press.

Scott, J. 1985 *Weapons of the Weak: Everyday Forms of Peasant Resistance*. New Haven, CT: Yale University Press.

Scott, J. 1998 *Seeing Like a State: How Certain Schemes to Improve the Human Condition have Failed*. New Haven, CT: Yale University Press.

Sen, A. 1982 *Poverty and Famines: An Essay on Entitlement and Deprivation*. Oxford: Oxford University Press.

Sen, A. 1999 *Development as Freedom*. Oxford: Oxford University Press.

Shaheedullah, S.M. and Muhammad, A. 2009 'Energy resources and security: what Bangladesh government needs to do', *New Age* 17 February, available at: http://banglapraxis.wordpress.com/2009/02/17/energy-resources-and-security-what-bangladesh-government-needs-to-do (accessed 6 October 2011).

Shaw, A. and Charsley, K. (eds) 2006 *Transnational Marriage* Special Issue of *Global Networks* 6(4).

Siddiqui, T. 2003 'Migration as a livelihood strategy of the poor: the Bangladesh case', Refugee and Migratory Movements Research Unit University of Dhaka.

Siddiqui, T. 2005 *International Labour from Bangladesh: A Decent Work Perspective*. International Labour Organization Working Paper 26; Geneva, available at: http://www.ilo.org/wcmsp5/groups/public/---dgreports/---integration/documents/publication/wcms_079174.pdf (accessed 6 October 2011).

Smith, J. and Helfgott, F. 2010 'Flexibility or exploitation? Corporate social responsibility and the perils of universalization', *Anthropology Today* 26(3): 20–3.

Stirrat, J. and Henkel, H. 1997 'The development gift: the problem of reciprocity in the NGO world', *Annals of the American Academy of Political and Social Science* 554: 66–80.

Tagore, R. 2001 'Earth', in *I Won't Let You Go*, trans. K.K. Dyson. Newcastle on Tyne: Bloodaxe Books.

Toufique, K. and Turton, C. 2002 *Hands not Land: How Livelihoods are Changing in Rural Bangladesh*. Dhaka: Institute of Development Studies.

Tsing, A.L. 2005 *Friction: An Ethnography of Global Connection*. Princeton, NJ: Princeton University Press.

Turner, S. 2004 'Under the gaze of the "Big Nations": refugees, rumours and the international community in Tanzania', *African Affairs* 103: 227–47.

Ul-Hoque, A. 2011 'Generation terrorised: Muslim youth, being British and not so British', unpublished doctoral thesis, School of Oriental and African Studies, University of London.

United Nations 2009 *Human Development Report: Bangladesh*. New York: United Nations.

United Nations 2010 *Human Development Report: Bangladesh*. New York: United Nations.

U.S. Department of State 2008 Human rights report 2008: Bangladesh, http://www.state.gov/g/drl/rls/hrrpt/2008/sca/119132.htm (accessed 16 October 2011).

van Schendel, W. 1981 *Peasant Mobility: The Odds of Life in Rural Bangladesh*. Assen: Van Gorcum.

van Schendel, W. 2005 *The Bengal Borderland: Beyond Nation and State in South Asia*. London: Anthem South Asian Studies.

van Schendel, W. 2009 *A History of Bangladesh*. Cambridge: Cambridge University Press.

Vertovec, S. 2010 *Transnationalism*. London: Routledge.

Vreede-de Stuers, C. 1968 *Parda: A Study of Muslim Women's Life in North India*. Assen: Van Gorcum.

Weber-Fahr, M. 2002 *Treasure or Trouble? Mining in Developing Countries*. Washington, DC: World Bank Group and International Finance Corporation.

Welker, M. 2009 '"Corporate security begins in the community": mining, the CSR industry and environmental advocacy in Indonesia', *Cultural Anthropology* 24(1): 142–79.

West, H. 2003 'Voices twice silenced: betrayal and mourning at colonialism's end in Mozambique', *Anthropological Theory* 3(3): 343–65.

West, H. and Sanders, T. 2003 'Power revealed and concealed in the new world order', in H. West and T. Sanders (eds) *Transparency and Conspiracy: Ethnographies of Suspicion in the New World Order*. Durham, NC: Duke University Press, pp. 1–38.

White, L. 1997 'The traffic in heads: bodies, borders and the articulation of regional histories', *Journal of South African Studies* 23(2): 325–38.

White, L. 2000 *Speaking with Vampires: Rumor and History in Colonial Africa*. Berkeley: University of California Press.

Wilce, J. 2003 *Eloquence in Trouble: The Politics and Poetics of Complaint in Rural Bangladesh*. Oxford: Oxford University Press.

Wood, G. 2003 'Staying poor, staying secure: the "Faustian bargain"', *World Development* 31(3): 455–71.

Wood, G. 2005 'Poverty, capabilities and perverse social capital: an antidote to Sen and Putnam', in I. Khan and J. Seeley (eds) *Making a Living: The Livelihoods of the Poor in Bangladesh*. Dhaka: Dhaka University Press.

Zalik, A. 2004 'The Niger delta: "petro violence" and "partnership development"', *Review of African Political Economy* 31(101): 401–24.

Zeityln, B. 2010 'Growing up glocal', unpublished thesis, University of Sussex.

Index

Compiled by Sue Carlton

and family reunification 80–2
from India to West Pakistan 63
illegal 44, 76, 152, 154
impact on villages of migrants 82–5,
  86
and remittances 76, 99
to Middle East 84–5, 152, 153
to UK 62, 99–101, 104, 116, 162
Mirpur, Dhaka 13
mobile phones 72
Mohammad, Nur 10, 202, 213, 214,
  217
morality 47–9
  and consumerism 29–31
  and CSR 27, 28, 31, 165
  and entitlement 96, 138, 139, 158
  moral panics 29
Mosse, David 164, 169, 176, 178,
  235
Moulavi Bazaar 73, 87
Muhammed, Anu 10, 202–3, 211,
  214–15, 216, 217, 218–19,
  220–1
Muir, John 62
Mujibur Rahman, Sheikh 64, 65, 66
multinational companies 3–4, 5, 24
  anti-multinational activism 11, 59,
    60, 168, 212, 213–15
  different languages 49–50
  and Special Economic Zones 16,
    240
  see also transnational extractive
    corporations
Muslim-Hindu relations 117

Nadampur 4, 8–9, 77, 82–3, 87, 114,
  118, 146–7
  agricultural work 106–7
  and environmental change 109
  landownership 100, 101, 104
  and migration 84, 85, 140, 152
naming 6, 87, 91
narratives 5–6
  alternative 192–3
  and claim-making 49, 50, 51
  differential value of 52–3
  of environmental change 110
  of project success 192
  and rumours of corruption 193–5

National Committee to Protect Oil,
  Gas, Mineral Resources, Power
  and Ports (NCPOGMPP) 10, 50,
  212, 213, 214, 216, 217
  countering propaganda 218–19
nationalism 65, 66, 98, 217
  and activism 48, 49, 50, 55, 191,
    210, 213, 236
  used by Chevron 182, 183, 236
natural gas see gas and coal reserves;
  gas fields
natural resource abundance
  and corruption 20–1
  and economic prosperity 18–21
  and violent conflict 21–3
  see also resource curse
natural resource trap 19
neoliberalism 5, 7, 11, 16, 75, 170,
  177, 186–7, 192
  and consumerism 30
  and corporate responsibility 5, 28,
    32, 34, 50, 165
  and development 39, 174–5, 211,
    222, 235
  and ethics/morality 40, 50, 165,
    168, 183, 187, 236
  and ideal of self-help 54, 167, 183
  and risk 227
nepotism 48, 69, 155–6
Newmont mining development, Batu
  Hijau 33
Niger Delta 25
Nigeria 19, 20, 194
  corruption 20, 48, 205–6
Nike 28
Niko 89, 213, 220
North Pad 1, 4, 6, 87, 175, 198
nuclear power 16

Occidental 1, 49, 73, 87, 88, 95, 213,
  220
Oil and Gas Journal 73
Ok Tedi mine, Papua New Guinea 51,
  231
Ong, A. 169, 177
open cast mine, Phulbari 13, 33, 74,
  214–15
Operation Clean Heart 68

Pakistan see Bengal; East Bengal; East
  Pakistan

CPSIA information can be obtained
at www.ICGtesting.com
Printed in the USA
FSHW011558141219
65088FS